SECT

NADER HASHEMI
DANNY POSTEL
(*Editors*)

Sectarianization

Mapping the New Politics
of the Middle East

OXFORD
UNIVERSITY PRESS

OXFORD
UNIVERSITY PRESS

Oxford University Press is a department of the
University of Oxford. It furthers the University's objective
of excellence in research, scholarship, and education
by publishing worldwide.

Oxford   New York

Auckland   Cape Town   Dar es Salaam   Hong Kong   Karachi
Kuala Lumpur   Madrid   Melbourne   Mexico City   Nairobi
New Delhi   Shanghai   Taipei   Toronto

With offices in

Argentina   Austria   Brazil   Chile   Czech Republic   France   Greece
Guatemala   Hungary   Italy   Japan   Poland   Portugal   Singapore
South Korea   Switzerland   Thailand   Turkey   Ukraine   Vietnam

Oxford is a registered trade mark of Oxford University Press
in the UK and certain other countries.

Published in the United States of America by
Oxford University Press
198 Madison Avenue, New York, NY 10016

Library of Congress Cataloging-in-Publication Data is available
Nader Hashemi and Danny Postel.
Sectarianization: Mapping the New Politics of the Middle East.
ISBN: 9780190664886

Printed by Bell and Bain Ltd, Glasgow

CONTENTS

CONTENTS

ACKNOWLEDGMENTS

This book is a product of the collective efforts of the faculty and staff at the Center for Middle East Studies at the University of Denver's Josef Korbel School of International Studies. We would like to begin by thanking the Global Peace and Development Charitable Trust for its generous and ongoing support of our center's activities. We are also indebted to the Dean of the Josef Korbel School, Ambassador Christopher Hill, and his staff for their support for our center's work. It is a pleasure to have them as colleagues. We are especially grateful to Janet Roll, Jane Bucher-McCoy, Jennifer Thompson, Alicia Kirkeby, Emily Hinga, Jennifer Keane, Joanne Napper, Andrew Chiacchierini, and Ann Irving.

Two people who deserve special recognition and thanks are Tiffany Wilk, our hard-working and phenomenal Administrative Assistant, and Dominic Nelson, our outstanding intern. Dominic had the unenviable task of tracking down references, making numerous trips to the library and starting the bibliography. Without his efforts, this book would have been far more difficult to assemble. Amin Mashayekhi did an excellent job in completing the bibliography on short notice and with due diligence. And Marilyn Cosson, our Work-Study student, helped with proofreading the text.

Other colleagues affiliated with the University of Denver who were supportive of this project in various ways include Tom Farer, Erica Chenoweth, Micheline Ishay, Andrea Stanton, Randall Kuhn, and Joel Day. We would also like to extend a word of thanks to Marwa Daoudy, George Irani, Steven Heydemann, and Marc Lynch.

We are deeply in debt to our editor, Jon de Peyer, for his enthusiasm for this project and the steady hand that guided it to realisation. We are

ACKNOWLEDGMENTS

enormously grateful to Mary Starkey, whose extraordinary craftsmanship in copy-editing the manuscript substantially improved the quality of the book. We also wish to thank Daisy Leitch, Hurst's Production Director, for her steady and patient hand in shepherding the book to fruition.

We would also like to thank the baristas at Keith's Coffee Bar on Downing, Stella's Coffee Haus on Pearl, La Belle Rosette on University, and the Bardo Coffee House on Broadway in Denver, not only for making the countless double cortados that fueled the editing of this book but for tolerating the frequently high-decibel exchanges this process involved.

Finally, we are enormously grateful to the contributors to this volume for their invaluable intellectual contributions and their patience over the long haul of the editorial process. We are thrilled to have worked with them on this project.

ABOUT THE CONTRIBUTORS

Madawi Al-Rasheed is Visiting Professor at the Middle East Centre at the London School of Economics (LSE). She is the author of *Contesting the Saudi State: Islamic Voices from a New Generation* (2006), *A History of Saudi Arabia* (2010), *A Most Masculine State: Gender, Politics and Religion in Saudi Arabia* (2013), and *Muted Modernists: The Struggle over Divine Politics in Saudi Arabia* (2015), editor of *Kingdom Without Borders: Saudi Arabia's Political, Religious and Media Frontiers* (2008), and co-editor of *Dying for Faith: Religiously Motivated Violence in the Contemporary World* (2009).

Adam Gaiser is Associate Professor of Religion at Florida State University. He is the author of *Muslims, Scholars, Soldiers: The Origin and Elaboration of the Ibāḍī Imamate Traditions* (2010) and *Shurat Legends, Ibāḍī Identities: Martyrdom, Asceticism and the Making of an Early Islamic Community* (2016). He is currently at work on a book titled *The Umma Divided: Islamic Sects and Schools.*

Fanar Haddad is Senior Research Fellow at the Middle East Institute at the National University of Singapore and the author of *Sectarianism in Iraq: Antagonistic Visions of Unity* (2011). He previously lectured in modern Middle Eastern politics at the University of Exeter and at Queen Mary, University of London, and was a Research Analyst at the Foreign and Commonwealth Office of the United Kingdom.

Ussama Makdisi is Professor of History and the Arab-American Educational Foundation Chair of Arab Studies at Rice University. He is the author of *The Culture of Sectarianism: Community, History, and Violence in 19th-Century Ottoman Lebanon* (2000), *Artillery of Heaven: American Missionaries and the Failed Conversion of the Middle East* (2009), and *Faith Misplaced: The*

Broken Promise of US–Arab Relations, 1820–2001 (2010), and co-editor of *Memory and Violence in the Middle East and North Africa* (2006).

Toby Matthiesen is Senior Research Fellow in the International Relations of the Middle East at St Antony's College, University of Oxford. Previously he was Research Fellow in Islamic and Middle Eastern Studies at Pembroke College, University of Cambridge. He is the author of *Sectarian Gulf: Bahrain, Saudi Arabia, and the Arab Spring That Wasn't* (2013) and *The Other Saudis: Shiism, Dissent and Sectarianism* (2015).

Vali Nasr is Dean of and Professor of International Relations at The Johns Hopkins University's Paul H. Nitze School of Advanced International Studies (SAIS). He is the author of *The Dispensable Nation: American Foreign Policy in Retreat* (2013), *The Shia Revival: How Conflicts within Islam Will Shape the Future* (2006), and *Islamic Leviathan: Islam and the Making of State Power* (2001). He served as special advisor to Ambassador Richard Holbrooke, US President Obama's Special Representative for Afghanistan and Pakistan.

Stacey Philbrick Yadav is Associate Professor of Political Science and Chair of Middle Eastern Studies at Hobart and William Smith Colleges, and a former research fellow at the American Institute for Yemeni Studies. She is the author of *Islamists and the State: Legitimacy and Institutions in Yemen and Lebanon* (2013). She has written for the *Middle East Journal, Studies in Ethnicity and Nationalism*, the *Washington Post* blog *The Monkey Cage*, and *Middle East Report* (MERIP).

Paulo Gabriel Hilu Pinto is Professor of Anthropology and Director of the Center for Middle East Studies at the Universidade Federal Fluminense in Brazil. He is co-editor of *Ethnographies of Islam: Ritual Performances and Everyday Practices* (2012) and *Crescent over Another Horizon: Islam in Latin America, the Caribbean, and Latino USA* (2015), and a contributor to the book *Dispatches from the Arab Spring: Understanding the New Middle East* (2013).

Eskandar Sadeghi-Boroujerdi is British Academy Postdoctoral Fellow in the Department of History at the University of Manchester. He is Associate Editor of the *British Journal of Middle Eastern Studies* and a Series Editor of *Radical Histories of the Middle East* (Oneworld Publications). He is the author of *Political Theology in Post-Revolutionary Iran: Disenchantment, Reform and the Death of Utopia* (forthcoming). He is the former Iran analyst for the Oxford Research Group.

ABOUT THE CONTRIBUTORS

Bassel F. Salloukh is Associate Professor of Political Science at the Lebanese American University (LAU) in Beirut. He is co-author of *The Politics of Sectarianism in Postwar Lebanon* (2015) and *Beyond the Arab Spring: Authoritarianism and Democratization in the Arab World* (2012) and co-editor of *Persistent Permeability? Regionalism, Localism, and Globalization in the Middle East* (2004). He is Senior Nonresident Research Fellow at the Interuniversity Consortium for Arab and Middle Eastern Studies (ICAMES) in Montréal.

Yezid Sayigh is a Senior Associate at the Carnegie Middle East Center in Beirut and a columnist for the Arabic language newspaper *al-Hayat*. Previously he was Professor of Middle East Studies at King's College London. He is the author of *Armed Struggle and the Search for State: The Palestinian National Movement, 1949–1993* (1999). His recent reports include *Crumbling States: Security Sector Reform in Libya and Yemen* (June 2015), *Missed Opportunity: The Politics of Police Reform in Egypt and Tunisia* (March 2015), and *Militaries, Civilians and the Crisis of the Arab State* (December 2014).

Timothy D. Sisk is Professor of International and Comparative Politics at the Josef Korbel School of International Studies, University of Denver. He is the author of *International Mediation in Civil Wars: Bargaining with Bullets* (2008) and *Statebuilding: Consolidating Peace after Civil War* (2013), editor of *Between Terror and Tolerance: Religious Leaders, Conflict, and Peacemaking* (2011), and co-editor of *From War to Democracy: Dilemmas of Peacebuilding* (2008), *The Dilemmas of Statebuilding: Confronting the Contradictions of Postwar Peace Operations* (2009), and *Democratisation in the 21st Century: Reviving Transitology* (2017).

Madeleine Wells is a Foreign Affairs Officer at the United States Department of State, where she focuses on the Arabian Peninsula. She holds a Ph.D. in Political Science from the George Washington University. Her work has appeared in *Foreign Policy*, the *Washington Post* blog *The Monkey Cage*, *Sada* (an online journal published by the Carnegie Endowment for International Peace), *Middle East Report* (MERIP), *The Conversation*, and the Project on Middle East Political Science (POMEPS).

About the Co-Editors

Nader Hashemi is the Director of the Center for Middle East Studies and an Associate Professor of Middle East and Islamic Politics at the

Josef Korbel School of International Studies, University of Denver. He is the author of *Islam, Secularism and Liberal Democracy: Toward a Democratic Theory for Muslim Societies* (2009).

Danny Postel is the Assistant Director of the Middle East and North African Studies Program at Northwestern University and a Research Affiliate of the Center for Middle East Studies at the Josef Korbel School of International Studies, University of Denver. He is the author of *Reading* Legitimation Crisis *in Tehran* (2006). Together they are the co-editors of *The People Reloaded: The Green Movement and the Struggle for Iran's Future* (2010) and *The Syria Dilemma* (2013).

INTRODUCTION

THE SECTARIANIZATION THESIS

Nader Hashemi and Danny Postel

Soon after the death of the Prophet Muhammad in 632 AD, a debate emerged within the early Muslim community over the question of succession. One group, who would come to be known as the Sunnis (from the term *ahl al-sunna wa-l-jama'a*, meaning the people of tradition and the consensus of opinion), argued that the next leader should be chosen from among the close companions of Muhammad. Another group, who would come to be known as the Shi'a (from the term *shi'at 'Ali*, meaning partisans of Ali), believed that the new leader must come from among the immediate family of the Prophet. This early dispute revolved around the proper function of a Muslim leader and the broader question of the moral basis of legitimate political and religious authority in Islam. Over the course of the next 1,400 years this disagreement produced the two main branches of Islam, whose overlapping yet distinct theologies and contending interpretations of history trace their origins to this seventh-century schism.[1]

Notwithstanding the historical and theological significance of this divide, the contention of this book is that it does not explain the explosion of sectarian conflicts in the Arab Islamic world today—in Iraq, Syria, Yemen, Pakistan, and beyond—or the rise of groups such as

1

ISIS. The attempt to make sense of the turmoil engulfing the Middle East today through this seventh-century prism badly distorts our understanding of this critical region of the world.

The New Orientalism: Sectarian Essentialism and Middle East Exceptionalism

This claim may sound perplexing given the prevailing conventional wisdom, which holds the exact opposite. Major world leaders, public intellectuals, policy analysts, and media commentators have sought to explain the current instability in the Middle East as a function of ancient blood feuds rooted in putatively primordial hatreds and antagonisms between Sunnis and Shi'a. These conflicts, we are told, have been brewing beneath the surface since the dawn of Islam. Authoritarian strongmen had managed to keep a lid on these enduring rivalries, but with the unraveling of their control as a result of the Arab uprisings, this perennial feature of Muslim societies—rooted in unyielding intolerance—has surfaced, producing the current chaos and turmoil afflicting the region.[2]

One of the most prominent proponents of this view has been none other than US President Barack Obama. On several occasions Obama has spoken of "ancient sectarian differences" as a means of explaining the conflict in Syria. These "ancient divisions," he asserts, propel the instability in the Arab world, which is "rooted in conflicts that date back millennia."[3]

Other prominent American politicians, both Republican and Democratic, have made similar claims. Senator Ted Cruz has suggested that "Sunnis and Shiites have been engaged in a sectarian civil war since 632 … it is the height of hubris and ignorance to make American national security contingent on the resolution of a 1,500-year-old religious conflict."[4] Mitch McConnell, the Majority Leader of the US Senate, has observed that what is taking place in the Arab world today is "a religious conflict that has been going on for a millennium and a half."[5] US Middle East Peace Envoy (and former Democratic Senator) George Mitchell has also embraced this narrative to explain the turmoil in the Arab world:

> First is a Sunni-Shi'a split, which began as a struggle for political power following the death of the Prophet Muhammad. That's going on around the world. It's a huge factor in Iraq now, in Syria and in other countries.[6]

Former Vice-Presidential candidate (and Alaska governor) Sarah Palin offered a more straightforward proposal for US Middle East policy: "Let Allah sort it out."[7]

2

Mainstream journalists and political commentators on both the left and the right have advanced similar arguments. *New York Times* columnist Thomas Friedman asserts that the "main issue [in Yemen today] is the 7th century struggle over who is the rightful heir to the Prophet Muhammad—Shiites or Sunnis."[8] Commenting on the rise and expansion of ISIS, the liberal comedian and television host Jon Stewart took to his popular *Daily Show* to observe that the last time Sunnis and Shi'a coexisted was in 950 AD. This is "the only time it has ever happened, over 1000 years ago." The popular TV host and liberal commentator Bill Maher argued that the early modern period was a more accurate reference point for understanding contemporary conflict in the Middle East, in that Muslims were experiencing the equivalent of the Christian wars of religion. "This seems to be like the moment when the Muslims are having their 16th century," he quipped. "The Sunnis and the Shiites are going to have this out and we just have to let them have it out." The right-wing TV pundit Bill O'Reilly similarly observed that "the Sunni and Shi'a want to kill each other. They want to blow each other up. They want to torture each other. They have fun … they like this. This is what Allah tells them to do, and that's what they do."[9]

More respectable voices in the academic and policy communities have put forward variations of this thesis. According to Richard Hass, President of the Council on Foreign Relations, a key factor that explains the instability in the Middle East today is that this "is a deeply flawed part of the world that never came to terms with modernity."[10] Others, such as the historian Joshua Landis, have suggested that the Middle East is going through a "great sorting out" similar to central Europe during World War II, where national borders shifted to create more ethnically homogeneous states. In the Arab world, by contrast, after the collapse of the Ottoman Empire and the 1919 Paris Peace Conference, the new borders that emerged produced a situation where you have "all these different peoples living cheek by jowl, many of them not wanting to live together; not knowing how to live together."[11] Do these observations help us understand sectarian conflict in the Middle East today? Stating the obvious, Shadi Hamid has observed:

> There is a temporal problem with the "ancient hatreds" thesis. … If there is something constant about a culture and its predisposition to violence, then how can we explain stark variations in civil conflict over short periods of time?[12]

SECTARIANIZATION

The Sectarianization Thesis: A Social Theory of Sectarianism

This book forcefully challenges the lazy and Orientalist reliance on "sectarianism" as a catch-all explanation for the ills afflicting the Middle East today. We propose to shift the discussion of sectarianism by providing an alternative interpretation of this subject that can better explain the various conflicts in the Middle East and why they have morphed from nonsectarian or cross-sectarian (and nonviolent) uprisings/movements into sectarianized battles and civil wars. The contributors to this volume—who include political scientists, historians, anthropologists, and religious studies scholars—examine this phenomenon as it has unfolded over a definite period of time via specific mechanisms. Through multiple case studies (Iraq, Syria, Lebanon, Bahrain, Yemen, Kuwait, Saudi Arabia, Iran) and with historical and theoretical chapters exploring the nature and evolution of sectarianization, they analyze and map this process, exploring not only *how* but *why* it has happened.

* * *

In his widely read 2006 book *The Shia Revival: How Conflicts within Islam Will Shape the Future*, Vali Nasr presciently argued that the nature of politics in the Middle East had changed. The dominant concepts and categories in the study of the Middle East, such as modernity, democracy, fundamentalism, and nationalism, were no longer sufficient to explain the politics of the region, he maintained. According to Nasr, it "is rather the old feud between Shi'as and Sunnis that forges attitudes, defines prejudices, draws political boundary lines, and even decides whether and to what extent those other trends have relevance."[13]

Looking back, we can see how perceptive this observation was. Conflict between sectarian Muslim groups has intensified dramatically in recent years. But why? What explains the upsurge in sectarian conflict at this particular moment in multiple Muslim societies? How can we best understand this phenomenon?

To answer this question, we propose the term *sectarianization*: a process shaped by political actors operating within specific contexts, pursuing political goals that involve popular mobilization around particular (religious) identity markers. Class dynamics, fragile states, and geopolitical rivalries also shape the sectarianization process. The term *sectarianism* is typically devoid of such reference points. It tends to imply a static given, a trans-historical force—an enduring and immutable characteristic of the Arab Islamic world from the seventh century until today.

The theme of political authoritarianism is central to the sectarianization thesis. This form of political rule has long dominated the politics of the Middle East, and its corrosive legacy has deeply sullied the polities and societies of the region. Authoritarianism, not theology, is the critical factor that shapes the sectarianization process. Authoritarian regimes in the Middle East have deliberately manipulated sectarian identities in various ways as a strategy for deflecting demands for political change and perpetuating their power. This anti-democratic political context is essential for understanding sectarian conflict in Muslim societies today, especially in those societies that contain a mix of Sunni and Shi'a populations. To paraphrase the famous Clausewitz aphorism about war as a continuation of politics by other means, sectarian conflict in the Middle East today is the perpetuation of political rule via identity mobilization.[14]

Religious Sectarianism and Political Mobilization

To make better sense of the politics of sectarianization, the literature on ethnic political mobilization is instructive. There are functional similarities between ethnic and religious mobilization that can prove illuminating. In the social sciences, at least three schools of thought compete to explain ethno-nationalist mobilization: primordialism, instrumentalism, and constructivism.[15] These can be useful reference points in explaining the rise of religious sectarianism and political mobilization in Muslim societies, given that most mainstream forms of political Islam are in effect religious forms of nationalism: their proponents have accepted the borders of the post-colonial state and are fundamentally concerned with changing the internal politics of their home countries.[16] Muslim sectarian discourses of power and their underlying political paradigm can be seen as "ethnic" in the sense that they are concerned with the politics of group identity, where the group in question self-identifies with a particular interpretation of religion as a key marker of identity.

As the scholar of religion and conflict David Little has written, there are several other ways in which ethnicity and religion are connected. In his survey and analysis of nationalist conflicts, Little observes that there "is a widespread tendency of ethnic groups in all cultural contexts to authenticate themselves religiously that lends plausibility to the term, 'ethno-religious'." He goes on to note that in particular cases:

it is artificial to try to distinguish too sharply between religious and nonreligious ethnic attributes. In those instances where religious identity becomes ethnically salient, language, customs, even genealogy, take on strongly religious overtones.[17]

This suggests that functionally speaking, ethnicity and religion are deeply intertwined and overlapping, and often mutually reinforce each other. Aspects of the Sunni-Shi'a divide confirm this view. The way this divide is frequently framed as one between Persian Shi'a and Arab Sunnis lends credence to the salience of the social science literature on nationalism and ethnic politics in assessing religious sectarianism in Muslim societies today.

Returning to the three schools of thought on what we can now call the "ethno-religious": primordialism views ethno-religiosity as a shared sense of group identity that is organic, deeply embedded in social relations and human psychology. For primordialists, ethno-religiosity is based on a set of intangible elements rooted in biology, history, and tradition that bind the individual to a larger collectivity. Ethno-religious mobilization is tied to emotional and often irrational notions of group solidarity and support.[18] In societies where other forms of social solidarity around gender, labor, or class are weak, ethno-religious mobilization is often an integral part of political life. But one of the major criticisms leveled at primordialism is that it does not explain the link between identity and conflict. While primordialism has utility in identifying where ethno-religious ties are prevalent, it does not tell us how it can be a factor in mobilizing identity during times of upheaval. The existence of multiple identities among social actors suggests that they are often manipulated as part of a mobilization process into cause-and-effect scenarios.[19]

Instrumentalism, by contrast, suggests that ethno-religiosity is malleable and part of a political process. The idea of manipulation thus figures centrally in this school of thought. By emphasizing in-group similarities and out-group differences, as well as invoking the fear of assimilation, domination, or annihilation, ethno-religious leaders can stimulate identity mobilization.[20] For instrumentalists, ethno-religious mobilization is a tool in the service of actors who are able to advance their political and economic interests by acting as political entrepreneurs. Placed within a larger context of conflict escalation, instrumentalism allows us to make cross-comparisons between societies with similar social cleavages.

INTRODUCTION

Constructivism adopts a middle ground between primordialism and instrumentalism. Its proponents argue that ethnicity/religious identity is not fixed, but is rather a political construct based on a dense web of social relationships that form in the context of modernity.[21] Like primordialists, constructivists recognize the importance of seemingly immutable features of ethnic/religious identity, but they disagree that this inevitably leads to conflict. On the other hand, constructivists share with instrumentalists the view that elites and leadership play a critical role in the mobilization process. Disagreement emerges, however, over the degree to which these identities can be manipulated. In brief, constructivists do not believe that ethnicity/religion is inherently conflictual, but rather that conflict flows from "pathological social systems" and "political opportunity structures" that breed conflict from multiple social cleavages that lie beyond the control of the individual.[22]

With this framework as a backdrop, sectarianism in the Middle East today becomes more intelligible. Sectarian identities could not be mobilized unless differences in beliefs and historical memory compelled religious groups into collective action around particularistic identities. Therefore, two critical questions emerge: why are these conflicts intensifying now; and why in this particular region of the world? In other words, what explains the flaring of sectarian conflict at specific moments in time and in some places rather than others? Sunni-Shi'a relations, for example, were not always conflict-ridden, nor was sectarianism a strong political force in modern Muslim politics until recently. How did Syrians and Iraqis with different sectarian identities manage to coexist for centuries without mass bloodshed? How did these pluralistic mosaics come unglued so precipitously? What are the key forces driving sectarianization?

The level of intensity of sectarian conflict also varies geographically where Sunni and Shi'a populations coexist. What factors explain this variation? While the role of religious leaders and political entrepreneurs is particularly salient in answering these questions, Vali Nasr, in his contribution to this volume, suggests that we must examine the agency of state actors in identity mobilization.[23]

In the past, theories of ethnic conflict have generally treated the state as a passive actor in identity mobilization. The standard narrative held that competition from within society among contending ethnic groups would inevitably shift to the arena of the state as these sub-state actors vie for control of various state institutions as a means of enhancing their

7

power over rival groups. The intensification of these struggles would eventually lead to the weakness, collapse, or failure of the state. Drawing on research from South and Southeast Asia, Nasr has suggested, however, that "far from being passive victims of identity mobilization," states have a logic of their own and:

> can be directly instrumental in ... manipulating the protagonists and entrenching identity cleavages. Identity mobilization here is rooted in the project of power acquisition by state actors, not the behavior of societal elites or community actors. These state actors do not champion the cause of any one community but see political gain in the conflict between the competing identities.[24]

Nasr's insight helps deepen our theoretical understanding of identity mobilization, in that it pushes the conversation beyond putatively primordial differences and manipulation by religious authorities, to focus attention on state behavior and state-society relations. This brings us to the national contexts that shape sectarian differences in the Muslim world today.

National Contexts

Most Muslim-majority societies are Sunni, and between 85 and 90 per cent of the total global Muslim population is Sunni—but Iran, Iraq, Azerbaijan, and Bahrain are Shi'a majority societies, and significant Shi'a populations also live in Lebanon, Afghanistan, Kuwait, Yemen, Saudi Arabia, Pakistan, and Syria.[25] Critically, what these societies share in common is that most of their political systems are decidedly undemocratic, and various forms of authoritarianism dominate their political landscapes. These overarching facts shape the ebb and flow of political life, and influence the relationship between sects, the rise of sectarianism, and the behavior of political and religious leaders.

Authoritarian states in the Muslim world have several distinguishing features which influence sectarian relations. They suffer from multiple political, economic, environmental, and demographic crises that have steadily become worse with each passing decade. Their inability to democratically address these problems, coupled with expanding corruption, nepotism, and cronyism, has produced a crisis of legitimacy. As a result, the ruling political elites closely monitor and attempt to control civil society by limiting access to information and the freedom of association of their citizens. Joel Midgal's concept of a "weak state" best describes these regimes.[26] In his formulation, based on an innovative model of state-society relations, "weak states" suffer from limited power and capacity to exert social control. They often cannot and do not control sections of the countries (within both urban and rural areas) over which they claim sovereignty. Moreover, they confront highly complex societies made up of a "mélange of social organizations" such as ethnic and religious groups, villages, landlords, clans, and various economic interest groups which limit the state's reach into society and compromise its autonomy. "Dispersed domination" describes these states, where "neither the state (nor any other social force) manages to achieve countrywide domination."[27] While the state is too weak to dominate society, it is often strong enough to manipulate it, and to effectively respond to crises that threaten national security and regime survival.

In weak states, politics revolves around "strategies of survival."[28] State leaders and political elites are fundamentally concerned with both their staying power and staying *in* power. Thwarting rivals who might threaten them both from within society and among various state organizations is a key obsession that drives and informs political decisions. A common tactic to preserve and perpetuate political rule in a weak state is to manipulate social and political cleavages via a divide-and-rule strategy. This gives ruling elites greater room to maneuver in the short term, at the cost of social cohesion in the long term. This dominant feature of the politics of weak states also suggests why, in Vali Nasr's words, "state actors are principal agents in identity mobilization and conflict in culturally plural societies, and the manner in which politics of identity unfolds in a weak state is a product of the dialectic of state-society relations."[29]

Weak states, therefore, are more prone to sectarianism because manipulating identity cleavages is a dominant feature of their politics. As David Little has observed in his analysis of religion, nationalism and intolerance, "authoritarian states appear to draw life from ethnic or religious intolerance as a way of justifying the degree of violence required to maintain [and perpetuate] power."[30]

During the 1960s and 1970s, in several Muslim countries, political opposition to ruling regimes took the form of various socialist, communist, and left-wing political movements. In an attempt to pacify these oppositional currents, Islamic political groups were allowed greater freedom of movement and association in the hope that they would challenge the popularity of these secular opposition groups, thus deflecting criticism from the state itself (and the ruling elites who controlled it). The most dramatic case of this was Egypt, when Anwar Sadat released scores of Muslim Brotherhood members from jail and allowed exiled leaders to return home.[31] Similarly, in an attempt to enhance the capacity of the Pakistani state and solidify political control, General Muhammad Zia ul-Haq launched an Islamization program in the late 1970s which, despite its pretensions to Islamic universalism, was in essence a campaign of Sunnification of the country's social and political life, and was therefore viewed as a threat by religious minorities—especially the Shi'a community, who considered these policies detrimental to their sociopolitical interests. The severe rupture in sectarian relations in Pakistan that soon followed was significantly shaped by this development, but, as Nasr demonstrates in his chapter in this volume, it was deeply influenced by regional and international variables as well.

The Geopolitics of Sectarianism: 1979, 2003, 2011

The key regional development that shaped the rise of sectarianism was the 1979 revolution in Iran. Western-backed dictatorships in the Middle East, particularly Saudi Arabia, feared that the spread of revolutionary Islam could cross the Persian Gulf and sweep them from power in the same manner as the Pahlavi monarchy had been toppled. In response, the Saudi kingdom and other Sunni authoritarian regimes invested significant resources in undermining the power and appeal of the Iranian revolution, seeking to portray it as a distinctly Shi'a/Persian phenomenon based on a corruption of the Islamic tradition.[32] Sunni Muslims, they argued, should not be duped by this distortion of the Prophet Muhammad's message. Anti-Shi'a polemics in the Sunni world increased dramatically during this period, fueled by significant sums of Arab Gulf money. Sunni-Shi'a relations were deeply affected by this development, and Pakistan was an early battleground where this conflict played out.[33]

The key international event at this time was the Soviet occupation of Afghanistan. Western support for the Afghan Mujahedeen, backed by Saudi petrodollars, produced a Sunni militant movement that attracted radical Islamists from around the world, most notably Osama Bin Laden and Ayman al-Zawahiri. This constellation of forces eventually morphed into al-Qaeda. The ideological orientation of these Salafist-jihadi groups was decidedly anti-Shi'a, both in theory and practice, buttressed as it was by a neo-Wahhabi reading of the world.[34]

The Saudi-Iranian rivalry is critical to understanding the rise of sectarianism in Muslim societies at the end of the twentieth century. Both Tehran and Riyadh lay claim to leadership of the Islamic world, and since 1979 they have battled for hearts and minds across the Middle East, North Africa, and parts of Asia.[35] This conflict has, however, experienced ebbs and flows, and sectarian relations in the region have mirrored this pattern. The conflict was particularly acrimonious during the 1980s, when Saudi Arabia and its Gulf allies strongly backed Saddam Hussein during the Iran-Iraq war. The conflict reached its apex in 1987, when 400 Iranian pilgrims were killed in Mecca during a protest march at the annual Hajj pilgrimage. The Saudi and Kuwaiti embassies in Tehran were attacked in retaliation.[36]

Following the end of the Iran-Iraq war in 1988, and the death of Ayatollah Khomeini in 1989, tensions between Tehran and Riyadh gradually subsided and relations improved. The ascendance in Iran of more pragmatist (such as Ali Akbar Hashemi Rafsanjani) and then reformist (such as Mohammad Khatami) leaders led to a restoration of diplomatic relations. A cold peace was established that lasted for most of the 1990s.[37] But the 2003 US invasion and subsequent occupation of Iraq marked a turning point in Saudi-Iranian relations, and subsequently in sectarian relations across the region.

The toppling of Saddam Hussein dramatically affected the regional balance of power. The rise of Shi'a Islamist parties in Iraq allied with Iran set off alarm bells in the Gulf Cooperation Council (GCC) countries. The subsequent Iraqi civil war, which after 2006 had a clear sectarian dimension to it, further inflamed Sunni-Shi'a relations across the Middle East. The rise of Hezbollah in Lebanon was also a factor during this period. Its ability to expel Israel from southern Lebanon in 2000 and its perceived victory against Israel in the summer of 2006 increased the popularity and prestige of this Shi'a militant group as a revolutionary force on the Sunni "Arab street." An opinion poll at this time listed the Secretary General of Hezbollah, Hassan Nasrallah, as the most popular leader in the region, a fact that highlights both the chasm between state and society in the Arab world and explains how anti-imperialism trumped sectarian identity at the grassroots level during this period.[38]

Around this time, King Abdullah II of Jordan reflected a common concern among Sunni Arab regimes when he invoked the specter of a new "Shi'a Crescent." Linking Beirut with Tehran and running through Damascus and Baghdad, this perceived rolling thunder threatened to dominate the politics of the region in the name of a new brand of transnational Shi'a solidarity.[39]

The "Arab Spring" of 2011 marked another turning point in Saudi-Iran relations and, consequently, in Sunni-Shi'a relations more broadly. The Arab uprisings shook the foundations of Middle East authoritarianism. Both Iran and Saudi Arabia relied on sectarianism to deflect attention from popular demands for political change and to advance their influence in the region. The Saudi case is easier to diagnose and is better known. The Saudi regime blamed protests in Bahrain and in eastern Saudi Arabia on a Shi'a conspiracy allegedly orchestrated from Tehran, while the Assad regime and its Iranian backers attributed the (nonviolent) Syrian protests of 2011 to Salafist "terrorists" supported by Riyadh and hell-bent on toppling Iran's key regional ally in Damascus. The Iranian case of sectarianization is more subtle and less well known.

In February 2011 Iran's opposition Green Movement called for a demonstration in solidarity with the uprisings in Tunisia and Egypt.[40] The Iranian regime denied them official permission and attempted to suppress this initiative. As a consequence, the leaders of the Green Movement were apprehended and put under house arrest (where they remain to this day). The Green Movement's leaders were never officially charged or put on trial, but in the official narrative of the Islamic Republic they were guilty of the crime of sedition (*fitna*) for allegedly attempting to topple the regime. Regime hardliners called for their execution. Fear of the Arab Spring spreading to Iran was the regime's key purpose in blocking the Green Movement's planned demonstrations and arresting opposition leaders.[41] This is where Saudi Arabia comes into the picture.

When the Green Movement protests first rocked Iran during the summer of 2009, the Iranian regime immediately blamed Saudi Arabia as a co-conspirator of the protesters. It claimed that Saudi Arabia, in collusion with the United States and the United Kingdom, had spent a billion dollars trying to foment regime change in Tehran. Invoking grand conspiracy theories, the hardline editor of the pro-regime newspaper *Kayhan*, Hossein Shariatmadari, later wrote that "Saudi Arabia sent money for the leaders of the sedition [i.e. the Green Movement] but banking issues were an obstacle to its transfer to Iran."[42] Mirroring the House of Saud, which frequently invokes Persian/Shi'a intrigue to explain discontent within the kingdom's borders, Iran's clerical elite often blame Riyadh and Wahhabism for internal and regional problems. For example, the Islamic Republic recently claimed that the UN Special Rapporteur on the Situation of Human Rights in the Islamic Republic of Iran, Ahmed Shaheed, received a million-dollar bribe from Saudi Arabia to write reports critical of Iran, pointing to WikiLeaks documents as evidence.[43]

In the case of Syria, Iran has utilized a distinct sectarian narrative, albeit a subtle one, to mobilize support for the Assad regime, as Eskandar Sadeghi-Boroujerdi explains in his chapter in this volume. While officially Tehran claims that it is supporting the "legitimate" government in Damascus and fighting ISIS, all Syrian rebels are depicted as Salafi–jihadis who are bent on exterminating minorities should Assad be toppled. As the war in Syria has dragged on, Iran has organized a transnational Shi'a militia movement from among the poor and devout Shi'a communities of Afghanistan, Pakistan, and Iraq. These militias are recruited through an explicitly sectarian narrative that draws on classic Shi'a themes of persecution, martyrdom, and sacrifice. The imminent threat of the destruction of Shi'a shrines in Syria is invoked, and financial compensation, educational opportunities, and Iranian citizenship are offered as an incentive package.[44]

While Yemen, Iraq, and Lebanon have been battlegrounds in the Iranian-Saudi rivalry in recent years,[45] the conflict in Syria has become ground zero in the war of position between the two regional hegemons. Both countries are heavily invested in the Syrian war. The political stakes are much higher. The consequences for the regional balance of power are enormous, depending on which side prevails. This largely explains why the war continues and is now into its sixth year, while the prospects for a political settlement remain bleak.[46]

In January 2016 relations between Tehran and Riyadh plummeted further when Saudi Arabia staged a mass execution. Among those put to death was the dissident Saudi Shi'a cleric Nimr al-Nimr. Protests immediately erupted in regional countries with substantial Shi'a populations. The Saudi embassy in Tehran was torched, and relations between the two countries were severed. Several of Saudi Arabia's closest allies either broke or downgraded diplomatic relations with Iran. Sectarian tensions throughout the region were deeply affected by these developments.

One measure of heightened sectarianism were trends on social media. In the two days following the Nimr execution, 900,000 anti-Shi'a slurs and

30,000 anti-Sunni slurs were recorded across the Arabic Twittersphere.[47] This deepened the divide between the communities at a time when tensions in Saudi-Iranian relations had already been exacerbated by feuding over falling oil prices and the September 2015 Hajj stampede that killed over 400 Iranian pilgrims. Even Turkey, which has historically tried to remain above the fray by acting as a peacemaker and honest broker, was dragged into the dispute.[48] Mobilization around sectarian identities became much easier as a result of these events. This was arguably the intention of those responsible for stoking this latest round of conflict between Saudi Arabia and Iran.

* * *

This book's two sections tackle the problem of sectarianization from distinct angles. Section I aims to provide a big-picture framework, placing sectarianization in historical, theoretical, and geopolitical perspective, with chapters by some of the preeminent scholars in the field.

"The sectarian belongs not to the peculiar, but to the particular," writes the historian Ussama Makdisi in "The Problem of Sectarianism in the Middle East in an Age of Western Hegemony." Makdisi, author of the influential study *The Culture of Sectarianism*, emphasizes sectarianism's specifically *modern* horizons.[49] "It is not some medieval artifact but a product of modern forces and circumstances, and a history that, after 1798, or 1821, or 1856, and certainly after 1920, can no longer be thought of as purely Middle Eastern, or Arab or Islamic." His chapter is an attempt to chart "a research agenda that can explore the dialectic between local histories of sectarian animosities (in whatever part of the Middle East) and Western intervention" and "to recuperate a history of coexistence in the Middle East"—something we need today "more urgently than ever before," he exhorts.

The political scientist Bassel F. Salloukh skillfully maps the region-wide coordinates of the sectarianization process and their complex interplay with larger geopolitical dynamics in his chapter, "The Sectarianization of Geopolitics in the Middle East." The wave of sectarianism currently spreading across the region "like wildfire," he contends, is rooted "not in timeless pre-modern primordial cultural affinities" but rather in "the deployment, by domestic and regional actors alike … of sectarianism to defend their authoritarian orders against local rivals or as a fig-leaf for otherwise geopolitical battles." Saudi Arabia and Iran in particular "have deployed sectarian identity, narratives, and symbols to neutralize both domestic and external regime threats in what is otherwise a grand geopolitical contest." He shows how these dynamics have intensified in the aftermath of the Arab uprisings, a process with "devastating" consequences for the region.

In his chapter "The Arab Region at a Tipping Point," Yezid Sayigh attempts to make sense of the chaos engulfing the Middle East today—crystalized in the emergence of ISIS—by revisiting the legacy of the Sykes-Picot borders a century after they were drawn and asking whether the current paroxysm of sectarianism in the region should be traced, as some argue, back to the 1916 imperial agreement. "The real threat," Sayigh contends, "comes not from where the borders are located but what has been happening in recent decades *within* these borders"—a toxic mix of political repression, socioeconomic stagnation, and human underdevelopment. "Those who insist on re-framing the region's societies and politics as governed by sect and ethnicity miss this important point," he writes. "This prompts them to seek or endorse new political arrangements that, by ignoring socioeconomic realities, are equally flawed and likely to be at least as unstable."

Closing Section I, Adam Gaiser, a scholar of religion, proposes "A Narrative Identity Approach to Islamic Sectarianism." This theoretical framework "shifts the study of Islamic sectarianism away from sect identification as an inherent aspect of religious identity and toward sect identification as a dynamic and conscious process of adoption, maintenance, and manipulation of certain types of narrative identities in particular places and at particular times." Individuals "emplot themselves (or find themselves emplotted)" in specific "sect narratives." The sect narratives that appeal to, say, Iraqi Shi'a and to ISIS volunteers vary dramatically and in revealing ways. But what interests Gaiser is how the process of sectarian identification and narrative emplotting "accumulates, changes and develops—even breaks down—over time." Indeed, "sectarian actors may decide for various reasons to stop participating in their sect narratives, thus downplaying the sectarian element of their identities."

Vali Nasr's chapter, "International Politics, Domestic Imperatives, and Identity Mobilization: Sectarianism in Pakistan, 1979–1998," nicely bridges Sections I and II ("How Sectarianization Works: Case Studies") in providing both a rich theoretical discussion of the contours of sectarianism and a textured examination of how the sectarianization process played out in Pakistan in the 1980s. Although the bulk of the chapter originally appeared in 2000,[50] the analysis remains bracingly relevant to the current moment. Indeed, this tour de force laid much of the conceptual groundwork for the sectarianization thesis: it was a study of the sectarianization process before the advent of the term.

Likewise, Fanar Haddad's chapter on "Sectarian Relations Before 'Sectarianization' in pre-2003 Iraq" offers both a robust theoretical argument and an illuminating case study. Haddad, the author of the definitive book on sectarian politics in Iraq,[51] provides a useful genealogy of the term "sectarian"—a "what we talk about when we talk about sectarianism" guide, to paraphrase Raymond Carver.[52] He then paints a textured portrait of the intricacies of Sunni-Shi'a relations in Iraq before the watershed 2003 US invasion. The explosion of sectarian conflict we see in Iraq today "is not simply a product of the fact of sectarian plurality in and of itself," he argues, but rather "a product of the emergence of the modern nation-state"; it flows from "contested political dynamics to do with nation building, national identity, the (mis)management of sectarian plurality, and, ultimately, state legitimacy."

In his chapter on Syria, the anthropologist Paulo Gabriel Hilu Pinto provides an illuminating analysis of the sectarianization of a conflict that began very differently: the uprising represented a cross-section of Syrian society, and its demands were decidedly non-sectarian ("My Sect is Freedom," read one banner). Pinto shows how the Assad regime deliberately stoked sectarian tensions through a strategic use of repression—what Pinto calls a "sectarian distribution of violence"—but also how some Sunni religious leaders took the regime's bait and fueled the sectarianization of the conflict from below. He thus maps the omnidirectional "production of sectarianism" in Syria: "top-down (state generated), bottom-up (socially generated), outside-in (fueled by regional forces), and inside-out (the spread of Syria's conflict into neighboring states)."

A good deal has been written on Saudi Arabia's regional role in fueling sectarianism, but conspicuously less on the kingdom's domestic sectarian politics. Madawi Al-Rasheed, one of the leading scholarly authorities on Saudi Arabia, does just this in her chapter on "Sectarianism as Counter-Revolution: Saudi Responses to the Arab Spring."[53] She shows that immediately after the uprisings in Tunisia and Egypt began, sectarianism "became a pre-emptive counter-revolutionary strategy that the Saudi regime deployed to exaggerate religious difference and hatred and prevent the development of national non-sectarian politics." To deflect attention from the mood of revolt sweeping across the region, the Saudi regime drove a wedge between the country's majority Sunnis and its Shi'a minority, with the result that the two communities were "unable to create joint platforms for political mobilization."

Iran's role in the sectarianization of Middle East politics has been the subject of considerable analysis as well as intense debate on the world stage. The historian Eskandar Sadeghi-Boroujerdi's chapter, "Strategic Depth, Counterinsurgency, and the Logic of Sectarianization: The Islamic Republic of Iran's Security Doctrine and its Regional Implications," is among the most theoretically sophisticated and empirically nuanced treatments of this critically important theme yet to appear. He shows how Iran has contributed to the logics of sectarianization in both Iraq and Syria in distinct ways. Drawing on international relations theory, he argues that these policies are rooted "neither in supposedly primordial sectarian affinities nor in Iran's putatively exceptional, ontological compulsion to dominate the region," but are much better understood through a realpolitik lens.

In her chapter, "Sectarianization, Islamist Republicanism, and International Misrecognition in Yemen," the political scientist Stacey Philbrick Yadav, author of an important comparative study of Yemen and Lebanon,[54] provides a critical history of Yemen's tortured sectarianization process and argues that there was "nothing inevitable about the sectarian dimension of the conflict that is currently destroying the country." She shows how key "transitional" institutions that developed during and after Yemen's 2011 uprising "have been premised on forms of misrecognition that have paradoxically helped to produce the sectarianized conflict that they now aim to resolve." Tragically, the sectarian dynamic "that so many Yemenis sought to avoid—and indeed openly decried during the Arab uprisings—has been produced through war and has shaped lives and livelihoods in ways previously unimaginable."

Like the Yemeni and Syrian uprisings, Bahrain's protests began on a decidedly non-sectarian footing. Members of the small island nation's Shi'a majority as well as its Sunni minority participated in the peaceful demonstrations, chanting universal slogans demanding democratic rights.[55] So what happened? In his chapter "Sectarianization as Securitization: Identity Politics and Counter-Revolution in Bahrain," Toby Matthiesen, author of the excellent *Sectarian Gulf: Bahrain, Saudi Arabia, and the Arab Spring*

That Wasn't,[56] reviews the long history of cross-sectarian political mobilization on the island. He shows that Bahrain's ruling family "built up Sunni Islamic movements as a counter-weight to the Shi'i Islamic movements that emerged after Iran's 1979 revolution" and pursued a policy of "securitization through sectarianization" in its bloody crackdown on the 2011 protests. Sectarianization in Bahrain, he argues, is "a deliberate and long-term strategy by the regime to undermine the possibility of a broad-based coalition demanding democratic change."

"Of all the Arab states, Lebanon has had the longest and most uninterrupted experience with the sectarianization of political identities and conflicts," writes Bassel F. Salloukh in his second chapter in this volume, "The Architecture of Sectarianization in Lebanon." "But the institutionalization of sectarian identities in Lebanon's political system," he argues, "is a legacy of the country's process of state formation, not of primordial forces." He shows that the institutionalization of Lebanon's historically constructed sectarian identities "into multiple pre- and postwar power-sharing arrangements [gave] rise to the sectarianization of identity politics, communal relations, and modes of political mobilization" in the country. He suggests an "imaginative rethinking" of those arrangements given the cul-de-sac they have reached. He draws some hope from the 2015 garbage protests in Beirut as "an example of the myriad forms of resistance to the sectarian system."

Kuwait's "relatively sanguine history of sectarian relations" distinguishes the small Gulf monarchy from the "more punitive treatment of Shi'a by Saudi Arabia and Bahrain," the political scientist Madeleine Wells writes in her chapter on "Sectarianism, Authoritarianism, and Opposition in Kuwait." The sharp deterioration in regime-Shi'a relations since 2003 is "best explained by the regime's increasing authoritarianism and strategic balancing of internal oppositional forces"—specifically "the ongoing reformist demands of a vociferous tribal-Islamist-youth opposition that crystalized during the Arab Spring"—rather than by the dominant explanation of the age: "international threats from Iran." The real issue in Kuwait today, she concludes, is not sectarianism "but rather a re-entrenchment of authoritarianism."

The book's concluding chapter, "Peacebuilding in Sectarianized Conflicts: Findings and Implications for Theory and Practice" by Timothy D. Sisk, explores the prospects for de-sectarianization, or reversing the sectarianization trend gripping the Middle East. Sisk comes to this subject not as a Middle East specialist but as a comparative political scientist and one of the leading authorities on ethnic and religious violence and post-conflict peace building and state building.[57] He draws on the cases of Northern Ireland and Bosnia in search of "lessons learned" that might offer a fog light for the Middle East today. How did those societies rebuild after their cataclysms of intercommunal violence? What can those cases and others (Kashmir, Sri Lanka, Nigeria, Myanmar) teach us about the de-escalation process? Do they, and the growing body of research on social cohesion and post-conflict peacebuilding on which Sisk draws, offer insights that might apply to the de-sectarianization of Middle East politics?

Sisk's aim is both scholarly and pragmatic. His suggestions are "designed to speak to potential peace builders—typically civil society organizations and individuals within countries, but also by outsiders such as the UN, regional organizations and regional mediators, international development partners, and transnational civil society organizations seeking to build peace in a sectarianized region." With the region awash in blood, and sectarian passions reaching horrific levels, this is of urgent importance. We wanted to conclude the book on a constructive and forward-looking note. Sisk's comparative and global range, and his expertise on peace building, made him the ideal author for this chapter.

Conclusion

The key claim of this book is that sectarianism fails to explain the current disorder in the Middle East. Viewing the region through a sectarian prism clouds rather than illuminates the complex realities of the region's politics. The current instability is more accurately seen as rooted in a series of developmental crises stemming from the collapse of state authority. At the dawn of the twenty-first century a series of UN Arab Human Development Reports forecast and predicted that this region was headed for a deep crisis unless these problems were addressed.[58] The foreign policies of leading Western states toward the Arab-Islamic world have only made matters worse.

Whatever else they did or did not do, the 2011 Arab uprisings made clear that sectarianism is not the real driver of state policy in the region. The response of Sunni countries in the Middle East laid this bare. Turkey and Qatar (both Sunni) backed Muslim Brotherhood electoral victories in Tunisia and Egypt, while Saudi Arabia and the United Arab Emirates (also Sunni) opposed them and strongly backed the counter-revolutions that sought to overturn these political gains.[59] Similarly, in Libya, different Sunni regimes are backing different rebel groups that are in conflict with each other. As Gregory Gause has quipped, "if this is a sectarian fight, the Sunnis have not had their act together."[60]

Jeff Colgan has noted that in the international relations of the Middle East "the central cleavage has switched from regime type to sectarian identity" over the last half-century:

> The sectarian nature of today's rivalries in the Middle East contrasts sharply with the last time Egypt and Saudi Arabia intervened in a Yemeni civil war. In the 1960s, Egyptian President Gamal Abdel Nasser led a pan-Arab nationalist movement that threatened the legitimacy of monarchies like Saudi Arabia. Egypt, along with Iraq and other Arab republics, supported North Yemen. Saudi Arabia and other monarchies, including [Shi'i] Iran (which was a monarchy at the time), helped the royalists in South Yemen. Just like today, Yemen's battle was part of the larger political contest in the Middle East.[61]

The same also applies to the politics of Shi'a-majority countries. The April/May 2016 Iraqi political crisis that was triggered when Prime Minister Haider al-Abadi attempted to appoint a new technocratic cabinet has nothing to do with sectarianism. All the key protagonists are Shi'a Muslims, and the issues at the heart of this dispute revolve around government incompetence, corruption, and mutual distrust within and among Shi'a political parties.[62]

While it is true that religious identities are more salient in the politics of the Middle East today than they were in previous periods, it is also true that these identities have been politicized by state actors in pursuit of political gain. Authoritarianism is the key context for understanding this problem. In other words, there is a symbiotic relationship between social pressure from below—demands for greater inclusion, rights, recognition, and representation—and the refusal by the state from above to share or relinquish power. This produces a crisis of legitimacy that ruling elites must carefully manage to retain power. The result of this political dynamic is sectarianization.

Notwithstanding the rhetoric we hear from Sunni monarchies or from presidents-for-life in various Arab republics, most ruling elites are not politically wedded to a specific sectarian identity, even if their social support base is. It is not theological doctrines or loyalty to the collective

interests of a religious sect that drive the politics of the region. The core
allegiance for ruling elites is to their political thrones and their various
clients, whether Sunni or Shi'a, who can help sustain their power. In
other words, it is about power, not piety.

Sectarianism "is not an inherent historical quality of the Arab masses,"
as Madawi Al-Rasheed observes in her chapter in this volume. There are
"sectarian entrepreneurs and religious scholars who continue to flourish
in the present" by manipulating these identities in the interest of ruling
regimes, often at their request. Sectarianism, in other words, "is a modern political phenomenon that is nourished by persistent dictators whose
rule depends on invoking these old religious identities that become
lethally politicized."[63] In short, sectarianism does not explain the current
turmoil in the Middle East—the toxic brew of authoritarianism, kleptoc-
racy, developmental stagnation, and state repression is far more salient.

* * *

Sisk concludes his chapter on something of a cautionary note. He cor-
rectly observes that a recurring theme in this volume is the danger of
sectarianization taking root and becoming entrenched. As the book's
contributors demonstrate, the sectarianization process involves the
manipulation of passions and the "cultivation of hatred" (in Peter Gay's
apt phrase);[64] it is driven by the machinations of dictators and tyrants
and fueled by the bad faith of preachers and demagogues. It is, in this
sense—and contrary to the essentialists and Orientalists who view it as a
manifestation of the way "those people" simply *are*—deeply artificial.
And yet, as Eskandar Sadeghi-Boroujerdi notes in his chapter, there is a:

> very real danger of generating path dependencies whereby deficits of security
> are transfigured into totalizing sectarian animosities, perceptions of enmity
> displace relations of amity and become increasingly difficult to challenge and
> overturn.

Despite its constructed character, sectarianization has the ominous
potential to become a self-fulfilling prophecy. Putting the sectarian genie
back in the bottle is unlikely to be easy. Chapter upon chapter, case study
upon case study in this volume makes this point, and Sisk is absolutely right
to underscore this theme. We are under no illusion that unmasking sectarianization's artificiality and showing how it is produced, as this book does,
will pull the rug out from underneath the sectarianization process.

That will require years, perhaps decades, of cultural work and political organizing on the ground in the region. An obvious precondition for this is the end of war and lasting political stability. The aim of this intellectual intervention is nonetheless to redefine the terms of debate and reframe the discussion of this critical issue. And although it is principally a contribution to the scholarly literature, it has direct policy implications. We thus hope not merely to map, but also to help transform, the politics of the Middle East.

1

THE PROBLEM OF SECTARIANISM IN THE MIDDLE EAST IN AN AGE OF WESTERN HEGEMONY[1]

Ussama Makdisi

Today, more urgently than ever before, we need to recuperate a history of coexistence in the Middle East. Every carefully choreographed act of ISIS cruelty that we hear so much about presents more than an obscene vision of alleged piety. It also lashes out against a rich history of plural-ism that ISIS and its fellow-travelers appear intent upon obscuring, effac-ing, and denying. From the outset let me say two things. First, I do not accept romantic notions of age-old coexistence. Second, still less do I accept or believe in ahistorical notions of a deep, or medieval oriental religiosity that allegedly haunts the Middle East. Such notions are the essence of vapid scholarship and journalism. The geopolitical context of today is not the same as that before the US invasion of Iraq in 2003, or that of a hundred years ago, let alone that of a millennium ago.

The great Sigmund Freud wrote in *Civilization and its Discontents* about what he called the "narcissism of minor differences" that, *in any society*, could turn into something far more dangerous, namely group hatred.

Freud's point was that every society carries within it the possibility of turning on its constituent parts. "Civilized society," he wrote, "is perpetually threatened with disintegration."[2] The modern Arab world is no exception. Yet mainstream Western journalism about the Arab world routinely informs us that Sunnis and Shi'a are today replaying an original schism from Islam 1,300 years ago. Take the BBC correspondent Jeremy Bowen, who informs us solemnly that the "weight of a millennium and a half of sectarian rivalry is crushing hopes of a better future." Bowen describes Saddam Hussein as "the Sunni strongman who fought Shia Iran."[3] But what does this phrase "the Sunni strongman" actually mean? Saddam Hussein, after all, was also Tiqriti, Ba'athi, Iraqi, and Arab. He collaborated at different points with the USA, the Soviet Union, the Shah's Iran, and Saudi Arabia. Saddam Hussein also killed Sunni Kurds and Arabs and communists and anyone else who threatened his rule. He invaded Sunni Kuwait—all inconvenient facts that complicate Bowen's absurdly one-dimensional and highly misleading sectarian narrative.

Think indeed of how Western journalism such as Bowen's and many books in English about the Middle East routinely identify individuals from the region as being either "Sunni" or "Shi'i" or "Christian," although these individuals almost never openly identify themselves as such, whereas this same journalism refuses (understandably) to begin every description of Barack Obama as the "black" Obama or of Hillary Clinton as the "white" Clinton.

I do not, of course, deny the salience of sectarian affiliations in the Middle East. But far too often, it seems to me, we allow a word—"Sunni" or "Shi'i"—to take the place of a coherent, historically grounded argument, as if being Sunni or Shi'a is self-evident, as if it precludes other forms of identification, and as if it were a singular identity. The reality is that, like the words "fanaticism" or "barbarism" or "terrorism," analytically speaking, there is no such thing as a transhistorical sectarianism. There are, instead, specific, and admittedly sometimes horrifying, sectarian episodes that come about for a number of interrelated ideological, political, economic, and cultural reasons. I do not, in other words, see sectarianism as a stable, obvious, ever-present, singular social reality that floats above history. For this very reason, I do not see my task in this brief essay to try and explain each and every sectarian event, for there is no such thing as an endlessly repeating story of sectarianism.

Rather, my main point is to begin to think about how and why the idea of sectarianism, and the sectarian, has come to haunt the modern imaginary of the Arab world in much the same way that the idea of racism has haunted the modern imaginary of the USA. This is not because sectarianism itself is age-old or free-floating—I have already indicated that analytically speaking there is no such thing—but that, much like racism in the contemporary USA, sectarianism is a diagnosis that makes most sense when thought about in relation to its ideological antithesis. To identify and condemn racism in America, in other words, one presumably must uphold an idea of equality and emancipation. To identify and condemn sectarianism in the Arab world, one presumably has to uphold an idea of unity and equality between (and among) Muslims and non-Muslims.

Where, then, to begin the story of modern sectarianism in the Middle East? As I have been grappling with what I see as the pervasive medie-valization of the Middle East in both America and the Arab world (think of how the otherwise radically different Bernard Lewis and the Syrian poet Adonis both juxtapose an allegedly medieval Arab world with an allegedly normative modern secular West), I am returned once again to the importance of the nineteenth century as a point of departure for any meaningful discussion of contemporary sectarian problems in the region. I say this for at least two reasons. First, because the breakdown in the nineteenth century of a longstanding Ottoman imperial system that had ruled for centuries over a vast multi-religious, multi-ethnic, and multi-linguistic landscape opened the ideological and political space for new political imaginaries, horizons and vocabularies—some of which were more inclusive and some far less so. The Ottomans conquered Constantinople in 1453. They also conquered Damascus, Jerusalem, Mecca, and Cairo in 1516 and 1517, and ruled these areas until the fall of the empire as a result of World War I. And yet, intercommunal vio-lence between Muslim and Christian Ottomans occurred primarily in the nineteenth century, that between Arabs and Jews occurred mainly in the twentieth century, and that between Sunnis and Shi'a is unfolding before our eyes in the twenty-first century.

The second, and frankly more important, reason why I begin in the nineteenth century is that I think that the advent of the problem of sec-tarianism should be thought of as an expression of a global nineteenth century that introduced notions such as nationalism and citizenship and political equality irrespective of religious affiliation to many parts of the world. My point is that many states struggled in the nineteenth century with new ideas of secular citizenship and equality, and struggled to reconcile these new notions of equality with longstanding convictions about religious and/or racial difference. To put this point in simple, even crude, terms: at the same time as the USA struggled with slavery and black emancipation, and Europe with the emancipation of Jews, the Ottoman Empire was confronted with the question of the place of non-Muslims in what had long been a Muslim empire.

The DNA of Modern Sectarianism

To the extent that we can speak about the DNA of modern sectarianism, it surely lies in the fact that the Ottoman Empire had for centuries existed as what sociologist Karen Barkey describes as an "empire of difference."[4] That is to say, the precept of the House of Osman was to encourage, regulate, and maintain a dizzying patchwork of highly different and highly differentiated ethnic, linguistic, and religious communities that coexisted and conflicted across the empire. The so-called *millet* system reinforced the emphasis on religion in a profoundly unequal political and social order. At the top of this "empire of difference" sat the "shadow of God on earth," the Sultan, whose rule was legitimized by his supposed upholding of Islam, his defense of the realm against infidels, and his stamping out of heresy within it.

What mattered for our story is that Ottoman Muslim supremacy was deeply imbued within the ideological, political, and legal terrain of the empire. The Sultan was also theoretically committed to maintaining order among, and the tranquility of all, his disempowered and disenfranchised imperial subjects, including Christian and Jewish *dhimmi*s. The point that needs to be made about this Ottoman system is not that it was "tolerant" or "intolerant"—toleration in this empire, as in all empires, was but one of several imperial strategies that included coercion. Rather, the point that needs to be made is that the empire witnessed centuries of coexistence in which different Muslim and Christian and Jewish communities, and the ecclesiastical leaderships of different communities, accepted the fact that they were bound to live side by side—to literally coexist—for the foreseeable future.

The Rise of a Modern Sectarian Politics

What, then, is the difference between this pre-nineteenth-century form of Ottoman rule and what I would describe as a nineteenth-century politics of modern sectarianism? Three overlapping, interconnected, factors. The first is the rise of ethno-religious nationalism, particularly in the Balkans, that fundamentally challenged Ottoman Muslim supremacy militarily, geographically, politically, and ideologically. The second, related, factor is the rise of sustained Western imperialism, imperial rivalries, and so-called imperial humanitarianism, which, in turn, precipitated a third factor, an Ottoman reformation that changed the logic and definition of empire: from being an empire of difference, the Ottoman state sought to become, paradoxically, an empire of citizens. The implications of this attempted transformation were enormous.

For the first time in the history of any Muslim state, in 1839 the Ottomans implicitly accepted a revolutionary political equality of Muslim and non-Muslim subjects. They declared this equality more explicitly in 1856, and, finally, announced it constitutionally in 1876. The *jizya*, or poll tax on non-Muslims, was abolished in 1855. A concept of secular Ottoman citizenship was introduced in 1869. The Ottoman purpose in this massive ideological and legal reordering of the empire or *Tanzimat* was clear: it was to stave off further European intervention and to consolidate imperial power.

But within the empire, this sudden emphasis on non-discrimination as opposed to discrimination was predictably controversial. In several quarters the formal emancipation of non-Muslims was met with unease and dismay—and in some instances with sectarian violence against Christians. In Aleppo in 1850, an anti-conscription protest degenerated into a massacre of Christians in the city. Several churches were burned and hundreds of Christian homes were ransacked. In Damascus a decade later, in July 1860, a mob turned on the Christians of the city. The unprecedented massacres of Christians in Aleppo and Damascus coincided with a civil war in neighboring Mount Lebanon between Maronite Christians and Druzes—a war which also ended in 1860 in the utter defeat and massacre of Maronite Christians in several towns.

The Layers of Sectarianism

Just like today, the Western press at the time insisted that the "civilized" world was witnessing a spectacle of age-old Muslim oriental "fanaticism" and sectarianism in the ostensibly uncivilized parts of the world. But descriptions of an inherent fanaticism hardly explain why Damascus was the scene of a massacre in 1860, as opposed to say 1800 or 1900. The sectarian episodes of Aleppo and Damascus involved Muslims and Christians (obviously), but they were not about Islam or Christianity as such; they had nothing to do with the origins of Islam, or with the Qur'an, just as today's sectarian battles have almost nothing to do with an original Shi'a–Sunni schism. Instead, these events pointed to a very specific nineteenth-century moment that witnessed three things happening simultaneously. The first was the sudden, top-down disestablishment of a system of symbolic and legal Muslim supremacy without any cultural preparation on the part of Ottoman Muslim elites whose empire was under enormous European military, political, and economic pressure. The second was the reality of Western imperialism that claimed to protect Christians in the Orient, who were themselves increasingly associated with Europe. The third was the agency of some local Christians and Muslims who adopted a more strident perspective on their new-found rights in a rapidly changing imperial landscape.

That *some* Muslim inhabitants in cities such as Damascus felt that they as Muslims were entitled to a privileged relationship to the state, which had long justified itself as a Muslim state, is not at all surprising. This dismay at reform is by no means a peculiar "Muslim" problem with equality or modernity. Consider how, in a far more structurally oppressive context, many white Americans fought bitterly against civil rights for African Americans. Equality, in other words, is not simply a virtue or a right; it is often felt to be an acute and painful concession. This feeling of resentment was compounded, of course, by the rise of Western imperialism in the Ottoman Empire—so that it became impossible to separate the emancipation of Christians from Western imperialism. The more the Ottomans tried to secularize, the more the European powers—Britain and France and Russia primarily—intervened as "Christian Powers" with a duty to protect what they saw as the oppressed Christians of the empire.

Sectarian Institutions and the Question of Sovereignty

These European interventions made it clear that as far as "civilized" Europe was concerned the reformation of the Ottoman Empire had to be based on at least two points: the first was that there had to be a sectarian political framework to resolve what were taken to be endemic sectarian hatreds. The second was that Muslim rule had to be disestablished for a modern regime of toleration to be established in the East. In other words, European powers refused to believe that a secular Ottomanism was a viable project in the sense that a secular Americanism, a secular Englishness, or a secular Frenchness was. They believed that any reformed Ottoman empire needed constant European supervision. The British consul in Erzerum in Anatolia in 1856, James Brant, admitted frankly that a reformed Turkey had to be maintained as an independent country because of the balance of power within Europe. He noted as well that her "positive independence will have to be placed in abeyance until she has learned to administer her own government on an enlightened and equitable system."[5]

The upshot was that, following the massacres of 1860, the Ottomans and European powers hammered out a series of political compromises that institutionalized sectarian political structures across the empire as a sign of an Ottoman commitment to non-discrimination. Sectarian quota systems were thus put in place in Mount Lebanon, and suggested for Bosnia and Crete. Such sectarian forms of political representation were manifestly not democratic—the inhabitants of Mount Lebanon, for example, were never consulted in the creation of the sectarian system put in place after 1861. They also entrenched and reified the communal and naturalized the idea that sectarian representation was the only viable key to resolving the problem of religious pluralism. Yet, I think it is crucially important to understand these sectarian arrangements as political arrangements that maintained religious diversity in the context of a severely compromised Ottoman sovereignty. Recall the alternatives of the time: either the discriminatory imperial state or the exclusionary Christian ethno-nationalisms that came to the fore in the nineteenth-century Balkans. Ethno-religious nationalism indicated a fundamentally different form of modern political order than that suggested by sectarian arrangements, one that was far more homogeneous but also far more exclusionary.

The point is that sectarian experiments were stopgap measures that failed to resolve the far greater problem of the spread of European Balkan nationalism and European imperialism, which increasingly stripped the empire of ever more territory, resources, and population. In regions such as Greece, the political imagination of the new Greek nation explicitly excluded Muslims. This was also the case in Serbia, Crete, and Bulgaria between 1876 and 1913. Great numbers of Muslims were forced out of Europe and the Caucasus in the 1860s and 1870s. The treaty of Berlin of July 1878 stripped away 4.5 million, mostly Christian, subjects from the empire, which also ceded 8 per cent of its most fertile territory. This was soon followed by the British occupation of Egypt in 1882, the Italian invasion of Libya in 1911, and finally the cataclysmic Balkan wars of 1912–1913. These assaults rendered the notion of a viable multi-religious citizenship obsolete in the eyes of Ottoman Turkish rulers. The Muslim share of total population went from 60 per cent before 1878 to 74 per cent by 1907.[6]

In the aftermath of these catastrophic wars, Ottoman Turkish leaders became increasingly determined to create a modern and militarized nation-state that they presumed would be essentially Muslim in order to be viable. It should come as no surprise that it was this era that witnessed the emergence of the Armenian question that led eventually to a genocide. As the Ottoman state lost more and more territory in the Balkans, it was determined to rid itself of what it now considered an untrustworthy Christian minority in Anatolia that had become a proxy for its Russian enemy, and thus had no place in what it saw as a necessarily overwhelmingly Muslim Turkish state. An empire of multi-religious subjects was well on its way to becoming a state of its Muslim citizens.

The Ecumenical Nahda

The irony here is that the Arab Levant—the Mashriq, or the region that today encompasses, roughly speaking, Lebanon, Syria, Israel, the Palestinian territories, and, depending on how broad we want to be, Egypt and Iraq—that had witnessed episodes of sectarian violence in the mid-century was largely spared the tribulations of ethno-religious nationalism, border-making, nation-state formation and ethnic cleansing in the final decades of the empire.

There was, in other words, a great *divergence* in the late Ottoman Empire, a point that I think historians have simply not emphasized enough. The same late Ottoman state that directed genocidal violence toward the Armenians left Arab Christians, Muslims, and Jews to define new forms of coexistence on the basis of equality of male citizens (15–20 per cent of total population of Greater Syria in 1914, i.e. total of 4.5 million; 10 per cent Egypt). There was no militant Arab nationalism to speak of, nor were there any major Arab Christian separatist movements. Western imperialism in the Levant was quite different from Russian and Austro-Hungarian empire-making in the Balkans. There was in the Levant, moreover, a common Arabic language. Many Arab Christians such as Butrus al-Bustani and, as Lital Levy has noted, some Jews such as Esther Moyal played important roles in the so-called *nahda* or renaissance of Arabic thought that blossomed in the second half of the nineteenth century.[7]

I do not mean to romanticize what I am calling an ecumenical *nahda*, for there were also far less ecumenical strains of thought, and indeed some significant paradoxes, silences, and taboos—especially in the realm of gender and personal status laws—at the heart of this *nahda* discourse, which I explore elsewhere.[8] Nevertheless, I don't think we have appreciated how quickly in the decades after 1860 the equality of Muslim and non-Muslim male citizens in Syria, Palestine, and Egypt became relatively uncontroversial. The ideas of outright secularism or the liberation of women were, in fact, far more controversial than political equality between male citizens in the empire, which is precisely why I emphasize here the idea of a self-consciously civilized modern *ecumenical subjectivity* that encompassed both Muslims and non-Muslims. This subjectivity allowed for different and, in several instances, ultimately incompatible understandings of the place of "refined" religion in the fostering of a new multi-religious, not anti-religious, public sphere. This sphere was legally predicated on the equality of all male subjects irrespective of religious affiliation. This same subjectivity gave rise to modern abjurations of "religious fanaticism" and, in the twentieth century, to an imagination of "sectarianism" as the antithesis of a rational modern way of life in the Arab world, and ultimately to nationalism and an idea of national unity. Perhaps equally important for us to consider, this *nahda* expression of modern pluralism occurred at precisely the same time as the Anglo-Saxon US and British empires vehemently rejected the idea of racial equality—indeed, at the same moment as the system of Jim Crow racial segregation of "separate but equal" was being established across the US South.

The Colonial Impact

The enormous and undeniable role of Western powers—particularly Great Britain and France—afterWorld War I was key to the creation of a fundamentally new sectarian terrain in the post-Ottoman Middle East. The problem is not simply that the British and the French created artificial states—all states are, after all, constructed—but the manner in which they coercively created these states along new and quite deliberately sectarian lines in the name of safeguarding religious freedom. France created a Maronite-dominated *Grand Liban* that developed the region's most explicit, yet ambivalent, sectarian form of governance. France further partitioned Syria following the establishment of its Mandate into Alawite, Druze, and Arab states based on religion and ethnicity.

Western imperialism was not monolithic, nor were its sectarian effects. The paradox of Western colonial rule was this: to deconstruct an Ottoman whole into various sectarian parts at the same time as it tried to build up viable polities in a manner that safeguarded imperial hegemony. As much as Western imperialism invented the category of the so-called moderate Arab, it also gave these Arabs, and many others besides, an opportunity to share in the elaboration of colonial rule. The creation of the Hashemite Iraqi state is one example of this. Citing the case of newly established Shi'a courts in Lebanon during the French Mandate, Max Weiss has underscored the degree to which the local agency of Shi'a clerics and intellectuals during and after the Mandate was crucial to a new legal and political sectarianization of Shi'a identity that occurred in the decades after World War I.[9] Western colonial rule, nevertheless, also systematically fanned the fears and dependency of what were for the first time, as Benjamin White has noted, described as "minorities"—Armenians in Syria and Assyrians in Iraq—across the region.[10] At the same time, perversely, they created entirely new "Islamic" institutions to prove their "respect" for the region's Arab Muslim majority: the British in Palestine created the Supreme Muslim Council; the French elevated the mufti of Beirut into a representative of all of Lebanon's Sunni Muslims. Both France and Britain further elaborated Ottoman-era sectarian personal status laws.[11]

Many Arab nationalist historians have insisted—with good reason—over decades that foreign intervention in the internal affairs of their nations has played a major role in the unfolding of events in the modern Middle East. For example, the Egyptian Samir Murqus has recently condemned what he insists is a cynical Western exploitation of Arab Christians to advance their imperialism in the region.[12] His book was published with the endorsement of the Muslim Brotherhood-affiliated judge and intellectual Tariq Bishri. Scholars and political figures such as Murqus and Bishri are right to point to European imperialism, beginning with Napoleon's invasion of Egypt in 1798, continuing with the Anglo-French partition of the defeated Ottoman Empire in 1920, and culminating with the *pax Americana* in the current Middle East. There is a brute reality of Western involvement that simply cannot be denied, nor should it for a moment be obscured or obfuscated as secondary to the "self-inflicted" wounds that allegedly really matter, as Fouad Ajami tendentiously put it.[13]

But to reduce sectarianism to a question of colonial "divide and rule" is to ignore the powerful legacies of the nineteenth century that pre-dated direct European colonial rule. This century bequeathed to colonial powers material (not raw material, because the nineteenth century had already reworked these significantly) to exploit. Reforms to a discriminatory Ottoman imperial tradition as well as aggressive European imperialism provided Arabic-speaking subjects new opportunities and imposed new limitations on their ability to adapt to and reshape a late colonial age.

* * *

Not surprisingly, one of the great counterpoints to a politically diffuse ecumenical Arabic *nahda* that had flourished under a diminished Ottoman sovereignty was the advent of British-backed political Zionism in Palestine, which sought to transform the multi-religious land of Palestine into an exclusively Jewish state. The exclusive ethno-religious nationalism of Zionism germinated not in Ottoman soil but in that of a highly racialized Europe.

It is surely significant, after all, that the terms "Arab" and "Jew" became antonyms in this period. It is significant that the first major inter-communal Arab–Jewish riots in Palestine occurred during the Mandate period. My point is that new Jewish and Arab questions were created in the Middle East where neither had previously existed. The *Nakba* of 1948, during which Palestinian Muslims and Christians were expelled en masse from their homes and lands, destroyed the *nahda* ethos in Palestine. The resulting Arab–Israeli conflict, moreover, severely compromised the *nahda* elsewhere by accelerating a xenophobic nationalism across the region, and putting enormous strain and pressure on Jewish communities elsewhere, most notably, as Orit Bashkin has described in her most recent book, in Baghdad itself.[14] The eviction of hundreds of thousands of

Muslim and Christian Palestinian Arabs ironically sealed the fate of Jewish communities in the Arab world. The loss of a multi-religious Palestine was a terrible blow that was compounded by the decline of Jewish life in the Arab world. The bifurcation of the idea of being Arab and being Jewish still haunts the Arab world.

There is no "end" to the story of sectarianism in the modern Middle East, though as I have tried to suggest here, there was a nineteenth-century beginning. The ascendancy of Zionism in Palestine was predicated on the defeat of secular Arabism. The historic defeats of 1948 and 1967, and the descent into authoritarian political culture in Egypt, Syria and Iraq, the Islamic revolution in Iran, the rise of oil-rich Saudi Arabia and the extraordinary US role in the region since the middle of the twentieth century, have radically and powerfully reshaped the post-1948 modern Middle East.

What we need, and what I hope this chapter begins to chart, is a research agenda that can explore the dialectic between local histories of sectarian animosities (in whatever part of the Middle East) and Western intervention. What we also need is more humility in our observations of the Middle East. The sectarian belongs not to the peculiar, but to the particular. It is not some medieval artifact but a product of modern forces and circumstances, and a history that, after 1798, or 1821, or 1856, and certainly after 1920, can no longer be thought of as purely Middle Eastern, or Arab or Islamic.

THE SECTARIANIZATION
OF GEOPOLITICS IN THE MIDDLE EAST

Bassel F. Salloukh

Introduction

Whether among policy gurus or media pundits, the "ancient hatreds" theme has emerged as the preferred explanation for current domestic and regional political dynamics in the Middle East.[1] Even Barack Obama, in his last State of the Union address, in 2016, invoked history to explain the current regional turmoil, suggesting that "the Middle East is going through a transformation that will play out for a generation, rooted in conflicts that date back millennia."[2] More ominously, many peoples in the region have embraced this primordial sectarian narrative, explaining contemporary regional conflicts and domestic tensions by trampolining back to the seventh century when schisms first appeared among the leaders of the Muslim community over the succession of the Prophet Muhammad. Yet this kind of "reading history backwards"[3] is nothing but a tragic expression of what Edward Said long diagnosed as an Orientalist outlook, but also the pitfalls of "the modern Orient" par-

SECTARIANIZATION

taking "in its own Orientalizing,"[4] uncritically and unconsciously inter-
nalizing Orientalism's subjugating ahistorical discourse.

Little wonder, then, that when Saudi Arabia executed the Shiʻa cleric
Shaykh Nimr al-Nimr on January 2, 2016, the reverberations of this act
assumed strictly sectarian overtones. Pro-Saudi pundits and audiences
labeled him a Shiʻa terrorist worthy of the gruesome punishment meted
out against him, while Iran and her regional allies opportunistically
appropriated his oppositional legacy, eulogizing him as yet another Shiʻa
victim of Riyadh's discriminatory policies. The reality of the situation is
much more complex, however. As Toby Matthiesen contends, "Nimr's
relationship with Iran was always more complicated than both Iranians
and Saudi leaders claimed, and he had far more in common with the
revolutionaries of the Arab Spring than with the [Salafi] jihadis executed
alongside him or the clerics who rule in Tehran."[5] Moreover, the timing
of Nimr's execution has nothing to do with sectarianism. As Marc Lynch
suggests, it was rather driven by secular political considerations preoc-
cupying decision-makers in Riyadh. These include the domestic and
regional fallout from Saudi Arabia's geopolitical confrontation with Iran
in multiple theaters, the perceived implications of the US–Iranian
nuclear deal and Tehran's concomitant reintegration into the global
economic system for its strategic relation with Washington, and, finally,
the Saudi kingdom's perennial quest to assume leadership over "a recon-
stituted 'Sunni' regional order."[6]

To be sure, then, sectarianism explains very little in a region shaped by
authoritarian regimes, incorporated lopsidedly into the capitalist world
system, and penetrated by all kinds of external actors with neo-imperial
interests.[7] Instead, I argue in this chapter that the current wave of sectarianism engulfing the region is driven primarily by regime policies
deployed to balance against often overlapping domestic *and* external
security threats.[8] More precisely, the recent spread of sectarianism like
wildfire in the Middle East is rooted in how Saudi Arabia and Iran have
deployed sectarian identity, narratives, and symbols to neutralize both
domestic and external regime threats in what is otherwise a grand geopolitical contest. Already nascent before the December 2010 explosion
of popular protest in the domestic politics of a number of weak Arab
states, this geopolitical contest deepened dramatically after the uprisings
began. They simply enabled it to spread to new arenas, namely the hitherto Hobbesian state of Syria, and altered their rules of engagement, as
in Yemen, where Saudi airpower and Gulf Cooperation Council (GCC)

36

ground troops were deployed to contain and reverse the military advances of the Houthi rebels.

The consequences of the sectarianization of this geopolitical contest are devastating. Whether in the historically weak states such as Yemen and Libya, or in the more robust ones such as Syria and Iraq, state institutions collapsed and societies fractured along newly securitized vertical cleavages. The concomitant regional explosion and reinvention of sectarian, tribal, or ethnic identities is thus not rooted in timeless, pre-modern primordial cultural affinities. It is rather the consequence of the erosion of the post-uprising states' coercive, institutional, and ideological power in a number of countries with plural societies, and the deployment, by domestic and regional actors alike, of sectarianism to defend their authoritarian orders against local rivals or as a fig-leaf for otherwise geopolitical battles.[9]

The Sectarianization of Geopolitics before the Arab Uprisings

Since its formation on the ashes of the Ottoman Empire, the Arab state system has been shaped by the overlap between domestic, transnational, and geopolitical factors.[10] This overlap assumed a number of forms, however. Whether in the salience of immaterial ideational threats in the making of Middle East international relations, domestic actors aligning with regional powers to balance against their domestic opponents, or the "omnibalancing" choices facing regime leaders, the interplay between the domestic and regional levels served the local agendas of both domestic actors and the geopolitical and state-building objectives of many states in the Arab world.[11] The 1990–1991 invasion and subsequent liberation of Kuwait exposed but also unleashed a set of overlapping domestic and trans-regional challenges that collectively underscored the challenges facing authoritarian regimes, the changing permeability of the regional system, and the explosion of transnational non-state actors.[12] The 9/11 terrorist attacks and the explosion of al-Qaeda in the Arab world magnified the role of transnational actors in a new regional system in flux.

The Battle for Iraq

The 2003 US invasion and occupation of Iraq created a new regional landscape, however, unleashing dynamics that ultimately restored the primacy of the overlapping domestic and geopolitical battles of the 1950s and 1960s. Henceforth, the region became a theater for a grand Saudi-Iranian geopolitical confrontation fought out not through classical realist state-to-state military battles, but rather through proxy domestic and transnational actors and in the domestic politics of a number of weak Arab states. As Gregory Gause has carefully noted, for both Riyadh and Tehran, the two main protagonists in this geopolitical confrontation, but also Qatar and Turkey, the objective "is not to defeat their regional rivals militarily on the battlefield. It is to promote the fortunes of their own clients in these weak state domestic struggles and thus build up regional influence."[13]

Yet lest we deny them agency, domestic actors also possess their own calculations and interests. They invite and align with regional actors in a bid to balance the political influence of their domestic opponents and advance their own local political interests.

Sabotaging post-Saddam Iraq was henceforth an objective not just of Washington's regional enemies—Iran, Syria, and Hezbollah—but also of its allies—especially Saudi Arabia and Jordan.[14] Baghdad's Arab neighbors feared that a stable and democratic Iraq would allow Washington to pursue its post-9/11 "Freedom Agenda" aggressively.[15] Consequently, they resisted US attempts to stabilize and democratize Iraq, opening their borders to Salafi-jihadi fighters en route to Iraq.[16]

Washington's growing troubles in Iraq, and Iran's ability to assume a dominant role in post-Saddam Iraq, altered the geostrategic balance of power in the region, tipping it in Tehran's favor. Riyadh reasoned that if Iran's growing regional influence was left unchecked, then it would one day be forced to confront Tehran in the Persian Gulf, the kingdom's own strategic backyard.[17] It considered Hezbollah and Hamas proxy instruments in this contest, lacking any agency of their own, merely serving Tehran's geopolitical objective to penetrate and vivisect the Arab world.[18] With US encouragement and support, Riyadh took the lead in balancing and reversing Tehran's growing regional influence, rallying to its side the "moderate" Arab states consisting of Egypt, Jordan, the Palestinian Authority (PA), Tunisia, Morocco, Yemen, Bahrain, and the United Arab Emirates (UAE), and supported implicitly by Israel. Tehran, on the other hand, sought to defend its newfound geopolitical position and expand its regional reach, in alliance with Syria, Hezbollah, Hamas, and Islamic Jihad, its junior partners in the "Axis of Resistance," backed by Russia on the international stage. While often described in sectarian terms, most famously by Jordan's King Abdullah, as a contest between allied Sunni states against an emerging "Shi'a Crescent" stretching from Iran to Israel's borders,[19] this was in fact a very realist balance-of-power contest between two states over regional supremacy.[20] Riyadh deployed sectarianism as an instrument of *Realpolitik* to rally support within the GCC countries and across the Arab world to its foreign policy vis-à-vis Iran.[21]

The Saudis at first assumed a passive policy toward US-occupied Iraq. This stance turned more proactive with the approach of the US troop withdrawal from Iraq in December 2011. Saudi strategy in Iraq henceforth consisted of preventing or sabotaging a complete Iranian takeover of the country. To this end, Riyadh marshaled an array of military and non-military assets in the Saudi repertoire. This included diplomatic support to pro-Saudi Sunni as well Shi'a politicians, material support to the Sunni tribal Sahwa (Awakening) groups in their war against al-Qaeda, and intelligence penetration of Salafi-jihadi groups operating in Iraq.[22] Riyadh was unable to prevent Iran's geopolitical victory in Iraq, however. The Saudis consequently opted to destabilize Iraq, a strategy that wrought havoc in the country, turning the contest over post-Saddam Iraq into a sectarian war. Iran, for its part, used its political skills and the paramilitary experience of the Revolutionary Guard's Quds Force to deny Washington a stable Iraq; Syria opened its borders to Salafi-jihadi fighters destined for Iraq; and Hezbollah operatives in Iran and Iraq trained Shi'a Iraqi groups in guerrilla warfare against US troops.[23]

The sectarianization of the geopolitical battle over Iraq, coupled with the post-2006 sectarianization of Iraqi politics, gradually transformed the country into another site for overlapping domestic and geopolitical battles.[24] As Toby Dodge argues persuasively, the emergence of sectarianism as the primary mode of political mobilization in post-Saddam Iraq is the result of "the deliberate development or reinvention of sectarian identities by a ruling elite that judges this the best method for rallying an alienated electorate."[25] Former prime minister Nuri al-Maliki's vengeful sectarian clientelist politics between 2006 and 2014 go a long way in explaining the alienation of Iraq's Sunni community and, consequently, the ability of ISIS to capture large swathes of what is the Sunni heartland in Iraq and maintain a continuous supply of recruits into its ranks.[26]

The consequences for Iraqi nationalism and territorial unity were disastrous, however. Centrifugal pressures are on the rise at the expense of unitary nationalist sentiments, exacerbating ethno-sectarian suspicions, mistrust, and misapprehension between Sunnis and Shi'a, and between Baghdad and Irbil.[27] For the Kurds in the north, a combination of hypermobilization in defense of the ethnic motherland plus the protection offered by the international political economy of oil, the support of regional (Israel) and international (US) allies, and good geopolitical fortunes granted them a state in all but name. As a result, Baghdad and everything south of it has become a bastion for a posse of pro-Iranian Shi'a political parties and militias, while the wasteland northwest of Baghdad is a zone of contestation among Sunni tribes, ISIS, and disgruntled former Ba'athi apparatchiks.

Lebanon

Lebanon became part of the geopolitical scramble for the region immediately following the fall of Baghdad. Emboldened by its swift victory in Iraq, Washington demanded Syrian cooperation in the "War on Terror" and the stabilization of post-Saddam Iraq; it also requested an end to Syrian interference in Lebanese affairs, the demobilization and disarmament of Hezbollah and the dismantling of its rocket arsenal in south Lebanon, and the deployment of the Lebanese Armed Forces (LAF) over all Lebanese territory, including the southern borders with Israel. Syria's refusal to comply with these US demands elicited UN Security Council Resolution 1559 of September 2, 2004. The resolution declared its support "for a free and fair electoral process in Lebanon's upcoming presidential election conducted according to Lebanese constitutional rules and devised without foreign interference or influence."

It also called on "all remaining foreign forces to withdraw from Lebanon," and mandated the "disbanding and disarmament of all Lebanese and non-Lebanese militias"—read Hezbollah and pro-Syrian Palestinian groups—in the country. Henceforth UNSCR 1559 became a tool against Damascus in the grander geopolitical contest.

As discussed in my other chapter in this volume, "The Architecture of Sectarianization in Lebanon," the assassination of Lebanon's former prime minister Rafiq al-Hariri and the subsequent withdrawal of Syrian troops from Lebanon unleashed an overlapping domestic, regional, and international contest over post-Syria Lebanon: on one side was the USA, France, the "moderate" Arab states, and their Lebanese allies in the

March 14 coalition led by the Sunni-dominated Future Movement; on the opposing side stood Iran, Syria, and their Lebanese allies led by Hezbollah. The former group sought to reposition Lebanon away from the Syrian–Iranian geopolitical camp, while the latter resisted these efforts. On its own Lebanon carried little weight, however. It was, rather, an open battlefield for the Saudi-Iranian geopolitical contest, in which each side sought, as Gause puts it, "to promote the fortunes of their own clients in these weak state domestic struggles and thus build up regional influence." Moreover, threatening to snatch Lebanon away from Syria's orbit was one way to force Damascus to cooperate in Iraq. Similarly, besieging Hezbollah in Lebanon would undermine Iran's geopolitical reach and Syria's regional influence. Consequently, from February 2005 until the promulgation of the Qatari-negotiated May 21, 2008 Doha Accord, the choreography of Lebanese politics closely followed the geopolitical script written by regional and international actors. Riyadh and Washington raised the sectarian ante and drowned Hezbollah in a sectarian quagmire to contain the party's efforts to assume control over post-Syria Lebanon, but also to tarnish its appeal as a trans-Islamic and pan-Arab liberation movement.

The Syrian Crucible

Syria was also at the heart of Saudi Arabia's strategy to contain Iran's growing regional influence. Like Washington, Riyadh viewed Damascus as the umbilical land cord linking Tehran to Hezbollah and Hamas, and the bridge allowing Iran to project its political power in the region and its material capabilities along Israel's borders. Moreover, Iran's alliance with Syria provided Tehran with political cover for its growing influence and interference in what Riyadh viewed as otherwise strictly Arab affairs. Consequently, Riyadh was determined to challenge Syria's influence in every Arab nook and cranny in an attempt to punish it for its alliance with Iran and compel it to distance itself from what was developing under Bashar al-Assad into a very close but unbalanced relationship with Tehran. This was especially true in Lebanon, Syria's own security backyard and the arena from which Damascus traditionally sought to project its own regional power.[28] Riyadh was quick to accuse Damascus of being behind the Hariri assassination, and pressured it to withdraw its troops swiftly from Lebanon and desist from interfering in its neighbor's domestic politics.[29] For its part, Damascus accused Riyadh of interfering in its own security arena and domestic politics by financing Salafi groups and jihadi cells in Lebanon and Syria, and by fomenting sectarian sentiments against the Syrian and Iranian regimes in regional organizations.[30]

This Saudi–Syrian confrontation came to a temporary halt only after Qatar succeeded in negotiating the May 2008 Doha Accord, which ended Lebanon's political stalemate following Hezbollah's military takeover of Beirut, paving the way for the election of a consensus presidential candidate, army commander General Michel Suleiman, on May 25, 2008, and the formation on July 11, 2008 of a national unity government. Qatar's success in negotiating the Doha Accord underscored the dynamic regional role it assumed during this pre-uprisings period. Situating itself between the two regional camps, Doha deployed its financial and diplomatic assets to mediate multiple inter-Arab conflicts, whether between Syria and Saudi Arabia, Iran and the other Gulf states, or between competing groups in Sudan, Yemen, Lebanon, or the West Bank and Gaza Strip; it cultivated strategic ties with Washington and served as a base for the US Fifth Fleet; hosted Salafi outcasts but also used Shaykh Yusuf al-Qaradawi and the Al Jazeera satellite channel to, respectively, control the Muslim Brotherhood's ideological production and co-opt mainstream Islamist popular opinion; and, finally, it boasted open relations with Israel.[31] Qatar's unorthodox foreign policy mix of balancing, bandwagoning, co-optation, and accommodation aimed at insulating the small shaykhdom from the multiple regional threats it faced in its immediate security environment.

The Sectarianization of Geopolitics after the Arab Uprisings

The Arab uprisings substantially transformed the behavior of a number of Middle East states, and ultimately invited direct external—namely Russian—military intervention in the region's geopolitical battles. Both Qatar and Turkey abandoned their former pragmatic stances and jumped on the uprisings' bandwagon to carve out new regional roles for themselves. Qatar used its affiliations with the Muslim Brotherhood to co-opt Islamist parties that assumed power after authoritarian regime breakdown in a bid to bolster its geopolitical weight. The small shaykhdom played a proactive role in regime change in Egypt and Libya; shelved its former differences with Riyadh, and openly endorsed regime change in Syria, offering a bevy of Salafi-jihadi groups military and material aid; it led an Arab League campaign to ostracize Damascus and expel it from Arab organizations; threatened to apply the full weight of the UN Charter's Chapter VII against the regime; successfully engineered Hamas' exit from the Iranian-Syrian alliance; and emerged as a proxy for NATO and Washington in their efforts to contain Iran.[32] In Egypt, Al Jazeera played an instrumental role popularizing and defending the Muslim Brotherhood's position in the contest between Islamist and secular groups over the drafting of a new constitution. Doha also embraced the politically beleaguered presidency of Mohamad Morsi, supplying it with an emergency financial lifeline that amounted to some $7.5 billion in its first year in power.[33] Yet in the aftermath of General Abdel Fattah al-Sisi's Saudi-backed coup of July 3, 2013, Egypt returned to Doha some $2 billion deposited by Qatar in the central bank.[34] Thereafter relations between Egypt and Doha turned sour, and the latter turned its geopolitical attention to Syria.

Turkey

Turkey's role in the region also changed after the uprisings as Recep Tayyip Erdoğan became increasingly set on regime change in Syria, turned more authoritarian at home against both the domestic opposition and the Kurds, and his discourse assumed unabashedly sectarian overtones. Ankara's stance vis-à-vis Syria mutated from being a close ally of Bashar's regime, mediating between Damascus and Tel Aviv, shielding Assad from Riyadh's sectarian accusations at its moment of peril immediately after Hariri's assassination, and using Damascus as a bridge to establish its own geopolitical influence in the Arab world, to a potential mediator between the Syrian regime and the opposition in the early stages of the uprising, then an open critic of the regime's violent crackdown on the uprising, and finally to being Riyadh and Doha's active ally in their determination to topple the regime at any cost.

Consequently, Turkey's borders with Syria became awash with all kinds of Salafi jihadis from all over the world seeking to join what was marketed as a war against a minority Shi'a-aligned regime oppressing the Sunni majority. Turkish intelligence played an instrumental role, funneling weapons and materiel to these groups in a bid not just to topple Bashar's regime, but also to balance against growing Kurdish autonomy and military assertiveness in Syria's northeast.

Indeed, as Dexter Filkins argues, ISIS "would never have metastasized as virulently as it has without Turkey's assistance."[35] Turkey's involvement in Syria, and its failure to topple the regime in Damascus, generated much domestic pushback, however. Sectarian and ethnic sentiments are on the rise in the country, a new wave of state-orchestrated violence has led to a military insurgency in the Kurdish regions, and ISIS ultimately turned its suicide attacks against Turkish cities.[36] Moreover, Erdoğan's instrumental use of Muslim Brotherhood-affiliated political parties across the Middle East to promote Turkey as the leader of a revived Sunni regional camp clashed with Riyadh's own leadership aspirations. Alternatively, efforts to reach an accommodation with Riyadh after the failure of Erdoğan's Syrian policy are bound to alienate Iran, an erstwhile ally, at a time when Ankara is increasingly dependent on the latter for natural gas imports given the nosedive Russian–Turkish relations have taken after Turkey shot down a Russian military plane in November 2015.[37] Outmaneuvered by Riyadh on the Sunni front and unable to advance its political agenda in Syria, Turkey responded by intervening in Iraq in December 2015, stationing troops near Mosul in an effort to carve out for itself a sphere of influence in northern Iraq.[38] If anything, Erdoğan's policies have taken Turkey from a foreign policy aimed at "zero problems" to a geopolitical quagmire.

Saudi Arabia

Most startling, however, is the growing assertiveness of Saudi Arabia's role in the region as it abandoned its tradition of quiet petrodollar diplomacy and proxy geopolitical battles for a newfound political bluntness and direct military intervention, with dire implications for sectarian sentiments in the region. Saudi Arabia's original stance vis-à-vis the uprisings was shaped by its very realist domestic and geopolitical objectives: to insulate the kingdom from the democratic winds of the Arab Spring, protect the survival of monarchical regimes, and undermine Iran's power in the region. It thus used its military forces, financial largess, and political clout to contain the effects of the uprisings on the Arabian Peninsula, but especially in Bahrain, Yemen, and Oman. Riyadh also extended financial assistance to support the monarchies of Morocco and Jordan against mounting domestic calls for reform in a bid to obviate any change among sister monarchical regimes.

Saudi Arabia was vocal in its opposition to the Morsi government in Egypt, labeling the Muslim Brotherhood a terrorist organization. Riyadh played an instrumental role in orchestrating Sisi's coup, and supported the new regime both politically and financially. King Abdullah minced no words praising Sisi's seizure of power, and shielded the new regime from both Washington and Doha, declaring on August 16, 2013 that "the people and government of the Kingdom of Saudi Arabia stood and still stand today with our brothers in Egypt against terrorism, extremism and sedition, and against whoever is trying to interfere in Egypt's internal affairs."[39]

Alongside the UAE and Kuwait, with whom it shares a deep antipathy toward the Muslim Brotherhood, Saudi Arabia raised some $12 billion in emergency funds for the Sisi regime, and pledged to compensate Egypt for any loss of American or European aid as a result of the military coup.[40] Sisi's regime spent some $20 billion of aid money from its Gulf allies without much impact on the government's balance sheets.[41] Riyadh's open support for the Sisi regime showed how far it was willing to go to contain and reverse the political consequences of the popular uprisings; its indirect support for anti-Islamist factions vying for power in Libya, namely via Egypt and the UAE, exposed the extent to which it considers the Muslim Brotherhood to be a threat to the survival of its own non-participatory and total-obedience model of governance.

Riyadh's use of sectarianism as an instrument of regional policy became more pronounced after the popular uprisings. It manipulated Sunni-Shi'a divisions and sentiments to shore up support for its regional allies and isolate Iran and its respective Arab allies and proxies.[42] Riyadh justified its military intervention in Bahrain's uprising by characterizing the latter as the work of Iran's Shi'a agents in the Gulf. Ignoring their genuine demands for socioeconomic and political reforms, it clamped down harshly on opposition in the kingdom's Eastern Province, labeling the demonstrators Iranian—read Shi'a *rawafidh*—agents.[43] Riyadh supported sectarian opposition against Iraq's pro-Iranian al-Maliki government and against the Hezbollah-allied government of Najib Mikati in Lebanon, and accused Tehran of meddling in the kingdom's security backyard by supporting and arming Houthi rebels in northern Yemen. But nowhere were Riyadh's sectarian tactics more evident than in Syria, whose alliance with Iran it was determined to end.[44]

The Multi-Level Struggle for Syria

The overlapping domestic, regional, and international "struggle for Syria"[45] is yet another chapter in the grand geopolitical contest underway between Saudi Arabia and Iran and their respective allies. Here again sectarianism was deployed as a fig-leaf for what were actually geopolitical battles. The metamorphosis of the popular uprising in Syria from a peaceful demand for reforms under the existing authoritarian regime to a largely regime-induced civil war with strong sectarian reverberations created a new theater for this geopolitical contest. From a country with a defensive-realist regime preoccupied with the nimble footwork of the region's geopolitical battles, Syria was transformed overnight into a battleground for at least three overlapping contests: a domestic, regime-opposition battle that manifested itself in class, regional, and sectarian undertones; a regional confrontation mainly between Saudi Arabia, Turkey, and Qatar, on one hand, and Tehran and its regional proxies, but especially Hezbollah, on the other; and, finally, an international confrontation between a USA determined to contain and reverse Iran's regional influence and an ascendant Russia bent on insulating itself from the threat of radical transnational Islamist groups, protecting its Syrian bridgehead in the Arab world, and demonstrating its newfound international reach and stature. This sectarianized geopolitical contest created a political, economic, and societal wasteland in Syria. The securitization, by both domestic and external actors, of vertical cleavages that have long coexisted with other class, ideological, or regional divisions ruptured the country along sectarian, religious, and ethnic lines.

Riyadh's near obsession with regime change in Syria is shaped in part by the idiosyncratic predilections of Saudi decision-makers.[46] They have never forgiven Damascus for Hariri's assassination. Nor have they forgotten Bashar's presumptuous words after the 2006 war with Israel, labeling Hezbollah's detractors as "half-men." Idiosyncrasies aside, however, Riyadh's use of the popular uprising to push for regime change in Syria was driven primarily by realist geopolitical calculations. It consequently free-rode on the democratic aspirations of the Syrian people to undermine Iran's regional influence. Riyadh sought to achieve this by toppling the regime of Iran's principal ally in the Arab world, replace it with one beholden to the kingdom, and, furthermore, use regime change in Syria to tip the sectarian balance of power in post-Saddam Iraq in Iran's favor. In turn, regime change in Syria would deny Iran access to the territory

of an allied state bordering Israel, substantially curtail its ability to transfer weapons and military supplies to Hezbollah, and deny the latter its
Damascus sanctuary used to procure military supplies and transport
party cadres en route for training in Iran.

As not only the producer but a major exporter of the Wahhabi worldview, Saudi Arabia funded and supported local Sunni Salafi rebel groups
fighting in Syria to achieve its geopolitical objectives.[47] Thus on September
29, 2013 it gathered some forty-three rebel brigades into a new fighting
force called Jaysh al-Islam (Army of Islam), led by Zahran Alloush, then
secretary-general of the Syrian Islamic Liberation Front.[48] Jaysh al-Islam
became Riyadh's primary boots on the ground in the battle to topple the
regime in Damascus. Similarly, Turkey and Qatar used local Sunni Salafi
rebel groups to advance their own geopolitical interests in Syria, namely
Harakat Ahrar al-Sham al-Islamiyya (Islamic Movement of the Free Men
of the Levant), which was founded in late 2011 as an umbrella organization for a number of Salafi rebel groups fighting in Syria. Court testimony
suggests that the Turkish intelligence service (MIT) helped funnel military
supplies to Ahrar al-Sham-held territory in late 2013 and early 2014
under the guise of humanitarian aid.[49] This "Islamization of rebel
forces,"[50] coupled with Riyadh's determination to lead an anti-regime
Sunni coalition of regional states consisting of Turkey and Qatar alongside the kingdom, sidelined the non-violent local opposition and contributed to the transformation of Syria's peaceful national uprising into a
sectarian military confrontation.

Iran

For its part, Tehran has invested substantial political, material, and symbolic capital in support of its beleaguered Syrian ally.[51] It shielded the
regime politically at a time when the Arab League, led first by Qatar and
then by Saudi Arabia, orchestrated a diplomatic campaign to ostracize
Damascus and lobbied Washington to undertake a military strike aimed
at crippling the regime after it was accused of using chemical weapons
against rebel forces around Damascus. Tehran managed to keep the
Syrian regime financially afloat, and supplied it with credit lines to maintain food imports. Underscoring the Iranian commitment to the survival
of the Syrian regime, General Qassem Soleimani, the commander of the
Revolutionary Guard's elite Quds Force, assumed personal control of the

Iranian military effort in Syria, coordinating the military activities of scores of Revolutionary Guard commanders and forces, Iranian proxy groups including the Lebanese Hezbollah and Iraqi Shi'a militias, and a bevy of Shi'a volunteers from Syria, Iraq, Yemen, Saudi Arabia, and even Afghanistan.[52] Tehran's use of sectarian identity and symbols to mobilize proxy Shi'a non-state actors for the battle in Syria also contributed substantially to the securitization of sectarian identities and sentiments in Syria and across the region.[53]

The wanton deaths, massive refugee waves, and colossal destruction in Syria epitomize the destructive effects of the sectarianization of regional geopolitical battles and the use of the popular Arab uprisings for otherwise geopolitical ends. As Marc Lynch argues, "Syria's war has been the greatest incubator of sectarianism" in the region.[54] Sunni-'Alawi communal massacres and religious and ethnic violence shattered the fabric of society, as sectarian animosities and modes of mobilization fill up the vacuum created in the wake of collapsing state institutions.[55] This Saudi-Iranian sectarianization of the geopolitical "struggle for Syria" was also instrumental in creating the early sanctuary and breeding grounds for the metamorphosis of al-Qaeda in Iraq (AQI) into the Salafi-jihadi killing machine ISIS has become. After all, it was its foray into Syria in defense of Sunni brothers against an "infidel" 'Alawi regime that allowed ISIS to recruit new followers from Syria, Iraq, and beyond, expand territorially, and ultimately create its cross-border caliphate.[56] The manipulation of regional identity politics by both Saudi Arabia and Iran to protect and advance their geopolitical interests, and their similar deployment by their proxies and by Salafi-jihadi groups, created the ideological and existential preconditions for the emergence and expansion of ISIS.[57]

Yemen

Saudi Arabia's military intervention in Yemen, driven largely by geopolitical considerations, is also securitizing nascent sectarian identities at the expense of far more historically relevant tribal and regional affiliations. That this transpired in a country where "sectarian differences meant almost nothing until recent years"[58] speaks volumes of the destructive power of sectarianized geopolitical battles.

Riyadh insists on perceiving the otherwise multifaceted and complex Yemeni political landscape through a strictly binary sectarian lens.[59] The

48

Houthis' historical, socioeconomic, and political grievances and wars against pro-Saudi pre- and post-uprising governments in Sanaa are brushed aside; instead, Riyadh caricatures the Houthis as nothing more than proxy agents of Tehran, possessing no local grievances of their own, created by the latter to undermine the kingdom's southern borders and advance Iran's regional influence.[60] Although Iran's support for the Houthis is, to be sure, part of the general pattern described by Gause whereby geopolitical adversaries insinuate themselves into the domestic struggles of weak states to build up their own regional influence, it would be wrong to reduce the Houthis to mere proxy agents divorced of any agency or local grievances rooted in domestic struggles over political power and resources.[61] If anything, both Saudi Arabia and Iran intervened in Yemen to protect or advance their own interests rather than to promote democracy or the wellbeing of the Yemeni people. The result is a war that has destroyed state institutions and infrastructure, the country's heritage sites, and incurred enormous human losses in a civilian population already reeling from decades of government corruption and neglect. Moreover, the use of sectarianism as an instrument of geopolitics, and the Houthis' vengeful acts as they made their way south from their mountain strongholds, devastated the country's shared national traditions and exacerbated sectarian sentiments in the Arabian Peninsula.

Conclusion

This chapter has contended that the explosion of sectarianism in the Middle East is not a consequence of immutable or timeless religious differences but is, rather, driven by the sectarianization of otherwise realist geopolitical battles and the consequent post-uprising collapse of the state's coercive, institutional, and ideological capacities in a number of countries with plural societies. Be that as it may, once securitized, sectarian identities assume a life of their own, permeating identity politics and public discourse, and feeding on state weakness, civil wars, communal fears, and powerful media platforms,[62] with devastating consequences for the territorial integrity and national unity of a number of Arab states. Consequently, and even in states far removed from the region's geopolitical contests, sectarian and ethnic sentiments are on the rise—in Morocco, Tunisia, Algeria, and as far away as Pakistan and Malaysia, courtesy of the influence of new social media, private funding campaigns, satellite channels, and the resurgence of Salafi-jihadi preaching.

The tsunami unleashed by the sectarianization of regional geopolitical contests has produced centrifugal dynamics that threaten to overhaul existing institutional territorial designs. In Lebanon, where the institutionalization of sectarian identities in the context of a centralized but weak unitary state has always constituted the raison d'être of the political system, many in the Christian, but mainly Maronite, political elite find themselves increasingly marginalized by the Sunni-Shi'a struggle over post-Syria Lebanon. Watching their political prerogatives erode steadily since the negotiation of the 1989 Ta'if Accord that brought Lebanon's fifteen-year civil war to an end, they have now raised the banner of broad political, administrative, and fiscal decentralization, a trope for a new confederal power-sharing arrangement.[63] The idea is to transfer many of the powers of the very centralized Lebanese state to elected and accountable local councils that would then assume control of the fiscal, administrative, and developmental needs of their regions. Whether it is a form of territorial or trans-territorial sectarian confederalism, a substantial cross-section of Lebanon's Christians want out of the postwar Muslim-dominated centralized state and power-sharing arrangement that relegates them to a mere appendage to the dominant Muslim political and economic elite.[64] Lebanon is no longer the Arab world's outlier state, however.

In Iraq the Kurdish state is all but a practical reality; its leaders speak openly about their determination to push for secession from Iraq once the battle against ISIS is won. Not that the Kurds are the only community in Iraq that favors broad regional autonomy. The vocabulary of *taqsim* (partition) has entered the lexicon of the South as well,[65] and it is difficult to see how the country's Sunni community will agree to join a national unity government after the battle against ISIS is won without the promise of substantial local autonomy over their own areas in a future Iraq.[66] Decentralized political orders with broad regional autonomy along tribal and ethnic lines seem to offer the only hope for future stability in Libya and Yemen as well. Even in the once hyper-centralized Syrian state there is talk of vivisecting the country along new, hitherto unthinkable, lines. In the north, Kurdish popular forces are determined to stitch together their three cantons—Afrin, Kobani, and Jazirah—into a contiguous autonomous enclave. The regime in Damascus seems to have acquiesced to this prospect, while US airstrikes, inadvertently or not, support the Kurdish military effort, to Turkey's growing chagrin. On the other hand, the strategy of both the Assad regime and Iran is to retain control of a swathe of territory running along the Zabadani–Damascus–Homs–Latakiya arc euphemistically labeled *Suriya al-mufida* (useful Syria),[67] one that comprises the country's political, economic, and demographic backbone and protects Hezbollah's military and training supply routes, and hence Tehran's geopolitical interests in the Levant. Russia's military intervention in Syria aims to help the Assad regime consolidate its control over this part of Syria, but also to use it as a launching pad to extend its authority over more territory under the cover of a negotiated political settlement with the non-Salafi-jihadi sections of the opposition.[68]

Good-Bye to All That

We should not bemoan the end of the homogenizing, authoritarian, centralized state in the crucible of instability stretching from Syria and Iraq to Yemen and Libya. Nor are other Arab states with plural societies immune from a similarly destructive fate should the same mix of domestic and geopolitical pressures overtake them. That this end has come on the ruins of popular uprisings demanding dignity, social justice, and democratic rights underscores the destructive powers of the region's authoritarian legacy, the sectarianization of its geopolitical struggles, and the realist calculations of international actors bent on protecting their strategic interests above all else. New and genuine power-sharing arrangements anchored on inclusive national governments but substantial decentralization of power to regional authorities—while eschewing the reconfiguration of territorial boundaries along explicitly sectarian, tribal, and ethnic boundaries—seem to be the only short-run policy option to restore a modicum of stability and preserve the territorial integrity of states torpedoed by domestic upheavals and sectarianized geopolitical contests. This does not mean creating sectarian or ethno-federal entities, as some neoconservatives insist, however.[69] As Lebanon and Iraq's postwar experiences suggest, the institutional architecture of any future power-sharing arrangements cannot allow for the marginalization of a sect, confessional, ethnic, or tribal group. It must, rather, be anchored on the kind of institutions that can help create, in the very long run, inter-sectarian, ethnic, tribal, and regional alliances that open up possibilities beyond narrow exclusivist affiliations and modes of political mobilization.[70] They must also empower citizens vis-à-vis accountable officials instead of herding them into sectarian, ethnic, or tribal ghettos and shackles that reify and reproduce what are otherwise modern and, in some but not all cases, recently invented forms of affiliation. After all, truly democratic and decentralized political orders may be the only antidote to the death and destruction visited upon many Arab states since the explosion of the popular uprisings. They may even be a necessary first but belated step for the possibility of a future polyphonic reimagining of the polity.[71]

The containment of the sectarian tsunami sweeping across the Middle East and beyond also entails a new regional grand bargain that reflects the current balance of power. The geopolitical sea changes occasioned by the 2003 US invasion and occupation of Iraq cannot be wished away. "The wall of containment keeping Iran out of the region has broken down—it appears, with American acquiescence," as Vali Nasr rightly contends.[72] Tehran managed successfully to project its influence across an Arab arc stretching from the Mediterranean Sea in the west to the Arabian Sea in the south, a feat that, ironically, was made possible by misguided neoconservative policies following the 9/11 terrorist attacks. Riyadh's sectarianization of geopolitical battles to roll back Tehran's penetration of this strategic Arab region has failed, however. A new grand bargain gathering the main regional and international actors, led by Saudi Arabia, Iran, Turkey, Russia, and the USA, one that demarcates clear spheres of influence for all involved, could help assuage the kingdom's fears of Iran's newfound regional power, its inevitable rapprochement with the USA following the July 14, 2015 Joint Comprehensive Plan of Action (or nuclear agreement), and its concomitant integration into the global economic system. Only then can a semblance of regional stability be restored and, consequently, can the rebuilding of states and societies shattered by sectarianized geopolitical battles commence.

3

THE ARAB REGION AT TIPPING POINT

WHY SECTARIANISM FAILS TO EXPLAIN THE TURMOIL

Yezid Sayigh

The dramatic seizure in June 2014 of the northern Iraqi city of Mosul by a coalition of Sunni Arab militias spearheaded by the Islamic State of Iraq and al-Sham (ISIS) marks what may be a fateful turning point in Iraq's history. Many have gone further, arguing that the entire system of nation-states designed in 1916, when British diplomat Mark Sykes and his French counterpart François Georges-Picot secretly planned the eventual fate of the Arab provinces of the Ottoman Empire in the aftermath of World War I, is now being erased.

This view is understandable, and has been shaped by the turmoil that has engulfed the Arab world. Libya has slipped into civil war, and faces the specter of partition, as do Iraq, Syria, and Yemen. In parallel, the declaration of ISIS's caliphate in Iraq and part of Syria is prompting jihadists in other countries to envisage copycat emirates of their own. Egypt, the largest Arab state in terms of population, is not at risk of civil war or of partition, but is on the path to social disaster. The combination of massive aid from the Gulf Cooperation Council (GCC) and high levels of domestic coercion has staved this off temporarily, but is already proving inadequate to deal with the country's fundamental economic problems and deep political malaise. If a social explosion occurs it will be massively costly, if not impossible, to contain.

The challenge to regional states is moreover increasingly framed as a struggle between the Sunni and Shi'a branches of Islam, including in several Arab countries whose populations are almost exclusively Sunni. The narrative of sectarianism as the main driver of regional and domestic politics has gained ground since the US invasion of Iraq in 2003 and the subsequent establishment of majority rule there—regarded by many Iraqi Sunnis as a formula for Shi'a domination—but the Syrian conflict since 2011 has helped make it dominant.

Both narratives of paradigmatic change are gripping, but they confuse appearances with causes. Certainly, many of the region's states are experiencing deep, structural crises, threatening societal cohesion and destabilizing internal political alignments. But framing this in terms of a sweeping challenge to the borders drawn by Sykes and Picot and of an overarching Sunni-Shi'a sectarian divide overstates the threat to existing nation-states and oversimplifies the social dynamics behind emerging political challenges, offering a poor guide to appropriate policy responses.

The Arab World's Twentieth Century

Not all Arab countries are at risk. But taken as a whole, the Arab region is at the onset of a period similar to that of the tumultuous quarter of a century after the end of World War II, in which newly independent Arab states took direct control over their populations, territory, natural resources, and government machinery and learned how to conduct foreign affairs and national defense. Now, as then, there are challenges to the legitimacy of state borders and domestic power structures, shifting regional alignments and cross-border threats, and political upheaval reflecting long-term socioeconomic transformations.

In the 1950s these dynamics led to the Arab "Cold War," which ended only after the resolution of Yemen's civil war in the mid-1960s and the disastrous 1967 war with Israel ushered in lasting reconciliation between Egypt and Saudi Arabia.[1] The role of multilateral institutions—especially the League of Arab States and the UN—in resolving disputes or managing crises was weak and ineffective then, and is now. And once again former global hegemons—Great Britain and France in the 1950s, the USA today—are in full or partial retreat, loosening constraints on local actors and altering their perceptions of threat and opportunity.[2]

But history is not repeating itself. The end of British and French empire—highlighted in the Middle East by the failed intervention in the Suez Canal in 1956—was followed by the polarizing, yet stabilizing, superpower rivalry between the USA and the Soviet Union. That is not the case now. The NATO action in Libya in 2011 was a highpoint, but the response of the USA and the European Union to events in the region since then has been feeble to the point of disinterest: the "planned" mass killing of demonstrators in Egypt in August 2013, as Human Rights Watch called it; Libya's ongoing implosion since May 2014; the massive death and destruction inflicted by Israel on Gaza's civilian population in July–August 2014; and even the advances of ISIS in Iraq since June 2014.[3]

Arab responses to geopolitical flux and transition also differ in critically important ways. Newly independent states after 1945 were inexperienced and vulnerable—most of North Africa, the Gulf littoral states, and Sudan did not even gain independence before 1951–1971—and were underdeveloped administratively and politically. But now most are overdeveloped—"fierce," as political scientist Nazih Ayubi labeled them—with massive bureaucracies and security services and decades of experience in monitoring populations and protecting borders and ruling regimes.[4]

However, "hardening" has not made most Arab states noticeably more efficient in providing basic needs and public goods and services, and certainly not more equitable in doing so. And it has not made them more tolerant of the religious, confessional, ethnic, or regional diversity of their populations, or more merciful generally. To the contrary, Arab states are probably less amenable now than in their formative years to pressures for needed political change, and less willing or able to introduce reforms allowing crucial improvements to economic performance and social equity.[5]

This sets most Arab states on a downhill path. Economic inequality and rudimentary social welfare systems in the independence period led to political unrest, and ultimately to actual or attempted regime change, in most Arab countries. But the gap between rich and poor has never been as wide or as apparent as it is now. No less seriously, the populations of Arab states then were far smaller and largely rural, allowing food subsistence at affordable cost for the vast majority. But populations now are several times larger, with greater numbers at or below the poverty line, and overwhelmingly urban, leaving them dependent on food imports and subsidies.[6]

The economic failure of a growing number of Arab states—including oil exporters such as Iraq and Libya—is particularly significant against this backdrop. It moreover explains why the most powerful ideological discourse of the independence period, Arab nationalism, has now given way to variants of Islamism that are increasingly militant and sectarian. To a large degree this reflects social changes: Arab nationalism was adopted by certain "popular classes," but remained heavily the product and domain of elites and the intelligentsia, whereas today's Salafism (and its Shi'a equivalent) is taking hold predominantly among the massive, and growing, underclass.[7]

For some, the trend reveals the power of sectarianism. But in reality it reflects the degradation and mutation of structures of political and social power and economic wealth in the decades since the Arab state system stabilized in the early 1970s. The failure to evolve in ways that were responsive to social change and democratic in economic restructuring has left most Arab states, if not all of them, struggling to meet the complex challenges of today's world. There is no external power that has the capability to provide assistance or engage in intervention of the scope and scale needed to fix their problems. Indeed, it is no longer even certain that the Arab region is important enough to generate such an interest. Barack Obama's foreign policy desire to "pivot to Asia," moving away from the complicated politics of the Middle East, confirms this development.[8] More recently, Obama has compared the region to a scene from the 2008 Batman movie *The Dark Knight*, suggesting that the Middle East is similar to Gotham city, controlled by thugs and where ISIS plays the role of the Joker who sets the city on fire. This analogy is widely interpreted as suggesting that the problems of the region cannot be fixed by outside powers, and that any deeper involvement is ill-advised; a view that is widely popular in the USA, including among key sections of the foreign policy establishment.[9]

Explaining the Chaos

In the first instance, far from being general, the challenge to existing states is very localized. The one serious challenge to the map drawn by Sykes and Picot comes from the growing autonomy of the Kurds. The deployment of the Kurdish Regional Government's army—the Peshmerga—into the strategic oil-rich city of Kirkuk in northern Iraq on June 12, 2014 fulfills a longstanding objective and takes the Kurds closer to full independence. Whether or not this is reached anytime soon, it enhances the autonomy of Syria's Kurds, although the differences in political agendas and social constituencies between the Kurdish Democratic Party of Iraq and the dominant Democratic Union Party of Syria may prevent unification of the Kurdish regions of both countries.

In the meantime, the only border that appears to have been erased so far lies between eastern Syria and western Iraq, where local Arab clans, traders and smugglers, and armed groups have moved in both directions for years. But even here, political and social dynamics in eastern Syria are not wholly interchangeable with those of western Iraq, and few fight in each other's wars, despite the emergence of a swathe of Salafist and jihadist militancy.

Clans on the Syrian side of the border, for example, align mainly with the Assad regime or with rebel groups, including al-Qaeda's affiliate Jabhat al-Nusra, whose struggle for power focuses entirely on Syria. Even when clans declare allegiance to ISIS, they do so to counter their local rivals, but their material interests and long-term political calculations still center on relations with provincial capitals and with Damascus. On the other side of the border, the insurgent Iraqi clans and other militias similarly have their sights set firmly on relations with the national capital, Baghdad.

Iraq may suffer de facto partition between Sunni and Shi'a regions as the outcome of the current fighting, but this is unlikely to be stable or lasting. Significant political parties and religious leaders in both communities still insist on coexistence and integration, while those who seek regional autonomy need to win a share of key assets—the capital and oil—and therefore will be compelled to reach mutually acceptable compromises with other communities.

And despite frequent dire predictions, the Syrian conflict is unlikely to end in formal partition, even if societal reconciliation and national reconstruction prove painfully difficult and slow. In contrast to the Sunni Arab inhabitants of Mosul, for example, who have always looked to Aleppo in Syria and southeast Turkey for their sociocultural and economic ties and may now prefer autonomy within a federal Iraqi state, their counterparts in Aleppo have never ceased to see themselves solely within the context of a unitary Syrian state.

Even ISIS, which operates as a truly cross-border movement, remains heavily focused on Iraq, where it first appeared. In Syria it has been unable to hold on to any territory west of Aleppo, or to put down genuine roots in the areas it controls in the eastern provinces of Raqqah, Deir az-Zor, and al-Hasakeh. ISIS is moreover limited geographically to the Iraqi–Syrian border. It has no presence in Lebanon and Jordan so far, and little prospect of gaining a significant local constituency in either country. This is partly due to the social and sectarian composition of Lebanon and the strength of state institutions in Jordan, but it also reflects the reaction of local populations to the specter of violence next door and to the massive influx of Iraqi and Syrian refugees over the past decade.

Second, the challenge to the existing system comes not from Sunni-Shi'a sectarianism, but from three processes that have driven it over the past two decades or more. First is the decline of state provision of critical public services such as health and education, and other forms of social welfare and safety nets amidst distorted forms of economic liberalization unaccompanied by parallel political "decompression." Second, predatory privatization in the decade prior to the start of the Arab Spring widened income disparities to levels that were unprecedented as recently as the mid-1990s, leaving 20–40 per cent of the population in many Arab countries at or below the poverty line (measured as a per capita income of $2 a day).[10]

The impact of these processes has cut across sectarian or ethnic lines in many cases. It is where they have converged with state policies that privilege certain communities or marginalize others—whether in terms of political access, social welfare, or economic opportunity—that they have generated anti-systemic counter-forces. On one hand, this explains why communities that experience worse poverty rates may not turn to militancy whereas less afflicted ones do: some southern Jordanian cities have up to four times the proportion of people in poverty than the average in the greater Amman area, for example, but are cushioned by the assurance of job security in the public sector, and so the jihadists who call for the overthrow of the governing domestic and regional order tend to come from the low-income neighborhoods of Amman-Zarqa rather than impoverished Mafraq, Ma'an, or Tafila.

On the other hand, conversely, the deliberate securitization of the Baghdad government's relations with the predominantly Sunni provinces of western Iraq under Maliki, which he employed as a means of concentrating his power and compelling his Shi'a rivals to stand behind his bid for a second and then third term in office, has revived and fueled Sunni insurgency. Similarly, longstanding government neglect of "inner-city" neighborhoods in the Lebanese cities of Tripoli and Sidon has produced Sunni militancy, just as it has in the large poverty belts around Syria's cities since 2011.

Conclusion

Sectarianism has arguably become more than a mere consequence of these processes, but its greatest potency still comes from the convergence of the above three processes. The fragility of the Levant's nation-states and porosity of their borders is being brought into sharp focus. This has generated a debate where some have suggested that the Sykes-Picot borders are no longer tenable and should be redrawn to accommodate the alleged wishes of sectarian and ethnic groups. Doing so, it is suggested, will both undo a historical injustice and enhance regional stability.[11]

This is a fundamental misreading of the roots of the turmoil in the contemporary Arab world. The real threat to the Sykes-Picot system comes not from where the borders are located but what has been happening in recent decades *within* these borders. Those who insist on re-framing the region's societies and politics as governed by sect and ethnicity miss this important point. This prompts them to seek or endorse new political arrangements that, by ignoring socioeconomic realities, are equally flawed and likely to be at least as unstable. The internal regional or communal borders of states such as Iraq, Syria, and Libya may one day be redrawn, and this might contribute to political stability. But focusing on external borders and the lines on the map as the source of the problem while ignoring the internal character and policies of post-colonial Arab states is analytically distorting, and implementing this as official policy will only perpetuate and deepen the broken politics of the Arab Islamic world.

4

A NARRATIVE IDENTITY APPROACH
TO ISLAMIC SECTARIANISM

Adam Gaiser

In this chapter I sketch a methodological approach to what contemporary academics call sects, denominations, or other kinds of intra-religious divisions among Muslims, and what Muslims of various epochs might call *firaq* (sing. *firqa*), *nihal* (sing. *nihla*), *tawa'if* (sing. *ta'ifa*) or *madhahib* (sing. *madhhab*). I open by examining and ultimately rejecting dominant social science—specifically Weberian–Troeltchian—taxonomies of sect as largely insufficient for the study of Muslim intra-religious divisions, seeking in the second part of the chapter to replace such taxonomies with what will be called a narrative identity approach. This narrative identity approach orients the study of Muslim intra-religious divisions toward questions about how Muslims acquire, maintain, and manipulate their communal affiliations, the extent to which such affiliations might overlap with other kinds of affiliations (or break down altogether), as well as the question of how local circumstances affect the "activation" of sect identification.

In attempting to answer such questions, the narrative identity approach to Islamic sectarianism treats intra-religious divisions as participatory discourses in which individuals ultimately choose to locate themselves in a plot ("emplot" themselves)—or not to do so—and which can thereby imply certain kinds of practice/behavior. Such a view shifts the study of Islamic sectarianism away from sect identification as an inherent aspect of religious identity and toward sect identification as a dynamic and conscious process of adoption, maintenance, and manipulation of certain types of narrative identities in particular places and at particular times by particular persons or groups of persons. The chapter concludes by offering some thoughts on how the narrative identity approach to Islamic sectarianism might bear on what the editors and authors of this volume have termed "sectarianization."

Taxonomies of Sect

Any discussion of intra-religious divisions among Muslims must begin, I believe, with a critical analysis of "sectarianism" as an academic field of inquiry, and end with an evaluation of the extent to which this field may or may not apply to Muslim examples of categories similar to what that field defines as "sects," "denominations," and so on. Recent academic discussions about sectarianism can be said to begin with one of the founders of modern sociology, the German theorist Max Weber (1864–1920). Weber interested himself in the study of human social behavior—its origins and development, organizations and institutions—and, as an aspect of these concerns, offered the first sociological characterization of a sect, which he contrasted with the institution of the church. Weber was interested in these institutions insofar as they provided ideal types, highlighting certain contrasting features of human social organization for the purposes of comparison.[1] Specifically, Weber was interested in refuting Marx's contention that social institutions were rooted in the economic substructure of society, aiming to show that religion could, in fact, operate as an independent variable in history.[2]

For Weber, churches had certain features—professional priesthoods, dogmas and rites, claims to universal domination—and they were compulsory organizations, meaning that the church's claims to truth went beyond individuals, compelling it to discipline those who deviated from it.[3] This last point on the mode of membership provided for Weber one of the main differences between churches and sects: people were born into churches, but they chose to be part of sects. This mode of membership, thereby, affected how a person acted in relation to the institution, as the church remained a "compulsory association for the administration of grace," while the sect offered a "voluntary association for religiously qualified persons."[4] Sects thus rejected the institutionalized grace of the church for the personal salvation offered by the sect. This meant that membership in the sect required specific actions, and unqualified members were removed from the group.[5] Weber also claimed that sects resisted hierarchies, pointing to another difference that he postulated between a sect and a church: churches are tied to the world and maintain hierarchies of individuals who dispense grace, while sects are generally apolitical and wish to be left alone.[6]

Weber's ideas were taken up and elaborated upon by his colleague and friend Ernst Troeltsch (1865–1923). As a theologian, Troeltsch hoped to relate different kinds of religious experience to various kinds of social teachings, and to thereby discover a solution to the problems facing Christians in the modern era. He thus emphasized the social behavior of churches and sects over the particular forms of social organization that they maintained.[7] Churches, he argued, tended to accommodate the state, becoming in the process associated with the ruling classes, and thus part of the social order.[8] This willingness to compromise with the world was predicated on the church's presumed ability to remain sanctified despite individual inadequacies: the sanctity of the church superseded the individual pieties of the persons that comprised it. Sects, on the other hand, aspired toward inward perfection and personal fellowship, treating the wider society sometimes with indifference and tolerance, but often with protest or open hostility. Indeed, for Troeltsch the very values of the sect existed as a remonstration of those of the wider society. He thus viewed sectarianism as something that existed among the lower classes and marginal social groups. For sect members, attainment of salvation existed in tension with secular interests and institutions. Thus, for Troeltsch, the church represented an institution of grace that was enmeshed in the wider world of politics and society, while the sect represented a smaller, voluntary group that stressed individual ethical behavior apart from the world.

Weber and Troeltsch's typologies were heavily invested in the language and history of Christianity. Not only did they draw explicitly from the history of the Catholic–Protestant splits in Europe, but both offered less a definition of church and sect than an attempt to establish these ideals as heuristic tools that would illuminate certain features of human social organization through comparison. Weber's aim in developing the typology was precisely to understand why capitalism (and the idea of secular democracy) seemed to develop only among Protestant Christians. For his part, Troeltsch hoped to find an answer to the problem of the Christian's relation to the modern world, concluding that because of its relation to society at large, the church offered the better solution.

Weber and Troeltsch's church–sect typology was itself then picked up by an American theologian, Helmut Richard Niebuhr (1894–1962), who treated churches and sects as poles on a continuum, rather than as distinct categories. Niebuhr's insight was to show how sects tended to become more church-like with time: as new generations populated the sects, and as their ways became fixed, "the original impetus to reject the norms and activities of the dominant society" gave way to acceptance.[9]

Following Niebuhr, several contemporary sociologists and scholars of religion have offered elaborations of the church–sect typology, many of whom developed it into full-fledged definitions of various church or sect-types, creating what have been called "quasi-evaluative" devices.[10] Thus, for example, Howard Becker expanded the church–sect model to include denominations and ecclesia.[11] Milton Yinger enlarged Becker's model even further, positing six types (cult, sect, established sect, class church/denomination, ecclesia, universal church) and sub-typing sects by their accepting, avoiding, or aggressive relationship to the wider society.[12] Similarly, Benton Johnson classified religious groups according to their state of tension with their social environment.[13] Rodney Stark and William Sims Bainbridge defined churches as conventional religious organizations, sects as deviant religious organizations with traditional beliefs and practices, and cults as deviant religious organizations with novel beliefs and practices.[14]

Opting for visual models, Roland Robertson and Paul Gustafson provided two-by-two tables, the cells of which offered elaborations on the church and sect types using modified Troeltschian criteria.[15] William Swatos afforded a more elaborate table with five types.[16] Bryan Wilson, arguing along classic Weberian lines that religious groups should be understood according to their soteriological function, classed several types of sects according to their "deviant" responses to the world.[17] Importantly, Wilson rejected the idea that sects must be set against a church. Rather, they may be arrayed against "secular society" as a kind of protest movement.[18]

Albert Baumgarten similarly viewed sects primarily as protest groups, emphasizing the process of boundary-creating by defining a sect as "a voluntary association of protest, which utilizes boundary marking mechanisms—the social means of differentiating between insiders and outsiders—to distinguish between its own members and those otherwise normally regarded as belonging to the same national or religious entity."[19]

As becomes clear from a brief survey of the various sociologists and religious studies scholars who developed the Weber/Troeltsch/Niebuhr church–sect (and, later, cult) typology, the notions of "sect" and "sectarianism" admit varying degrees of subtlety, and may be differentiated from other kinds of groups according to an array of diverse criteria. Broadly speaking, however, there is consensus among them that a sect is "a group that has separated to some degree from a parent body, and has boundary markers to indicate its separate identity."[20]

Lost in Translation

Given this broad consensus among this previous generation of academics, it is worth asking how applicable their conceptualizations of "sect" and "sectarianism" might be for the study of Muslim sects (*firaq*). Michael Cook has argued that Weber's notion of church–sect is, in fact, not very useful when carried over into an Islamic context: for one, Islamic sectarianism proper was first and foremost a response to religio-political developments after the death of the Prophet Muhammad, while Weber (and Troeltsch, among others) characterized sects as apolitical.[21] Secondly, membership in what might be considered a Muslim sect (notably the Shi'a, but also the Ibadiyya) is no more voluntary than that of other Muslim groups, and lastly, Shi'a possess far more hierarchical characteristics than their Sunni counterparts, making them more properly the candidates for the Weberian status of "church" than the Sunnis, upon whom Weber actually bestowed the designation.[22] Given these problems, Cook concludes that "Weber is neither so obviously right, nor so interestingly wrong, as to provide a useful starting-point for our own attempts to understand the peculiar groups we know as Islamic sects."[23]

Similarly, many of the definitions of sects and sectarianism that follow Weber turn out to be fundamentally problematic when applied to the Islamic context. One of the main issues with them revolves around their notions of church, denomination, or ecclesia as somehow set against sects and cults. While a case—however longwinded—can be made for treating Shi'a and, perhaps more appropriately, Kharijites as sects in the Weberian–Troeltschian vein, there is no good candidate for what in the early Islamic period might qualify as the church, denomination, or ecclesia from which they separated: something called "Sunnism" cannot be said to have existed before the ninth century, and the pro-'Uthman groups of the early period—mainly the Umayyads (661–750 CE)—constituted no majority; nor were they as firmly established in their rule as they might have liked to have been (as the relentless history of rebellions against them shows). Certainly, the Umayyads attempted to make themselves into the undisputed, popular, religious authorities of the early Islamic period, but such attempts failed resoundingly, as did the later 'Abbasid (750–1258 CE) efforts to do the same.[24] At best, these early groups might simply qualify as other Muslim sects: none of them meet the requirements for "churches" or parent groups.

Even Wilson's definition of sect, which helpfully leaves aside overt notions of "church," nonetheless posits sects as protest movements (and "deviant" ones at that) to be measured against the societies in which they are located. In effect, Wilson simply substitutes "society" for "church" as the normative baseline against which sects may be classed. This is not to say that what early Muslims later dubbed *firaq* (sects) were not protest movements within the midst of their societies—initially, many of them were—but simply to point out that the yardstick for measuring protest need not be a real or imagined universal such as church/denomination/ ecclesia or "society." Defining sects as "deviant" in relation to some universal, in fact, subtly replicates the historical situation of the early Christian church, revealing it to be hiding under such definitions all along.

The early Islamic situation seems, rather, to be one of several groups competing for primacy, and mutually protesting (or indeed, actively rebelling) against each other. There seems to be no center, no "parent group" or normative society from which these groups sprang and against which they defined themselves. Moreover, while many of the *firaq* (sects) were, at some point and to a certain degree, voluntary, in the heavily tribalized societies of the early Islamic period, voluntarism was quickly elided with tribal association such that sect and tribal affiliation can frequently be correlated.[25] And while most of the groups that were later described as *firaq* initially arose in protest against the Umayyads, by the 'Abbasid era one of them, the Murji'a, abandoned any vestige of revolutionary protest to be eventually absorbed into the emerging Sunni consensus. Clearly, the analytic church–sect–cult categories discussed above are not much help in characterizing early intra-religious divisions among Muslims.

Indeed, turning to the ways that early Muslims conceptualized the religious sub-groups in their midst, it is noteworthy that they tended not to use binary, tertiary, or relational terminology ("church–sect–cult" or "sect–denomination"), but rather to abstract the main groups using a singular concept. Thus, the various terms approximating the idea of "sect" in the Islamic world—*firqa/firaq*, *nihla/nihal*, *madhhab/madhahib*, and later *ta'ifa/tawa'if*—tend to evenly designate Shi'a, Kharijites, Murji'a, Mu'tazila as well as those later known under the rubric of Sunnis.[26] This is not to say that individual Muslim authors treated these groups as equally legitimate—they most certainly did not—but merely to point out that the conceptual schema underlying the Muslim imaginary of sectarianism tended to deploy one notion to describe various kinds of groups, while Christian and later "Western"/academic notions seem to replicate what is at its base a dualistic or tripartite model. Even when medieval Muslim authors designated one group as superior to the others, they tended to cite the Prophetic *hadith* that mentioned the "saving sect" (*al-firqa al-najiyya*) among the other deviant or heretical *firaq*, yet casting all of them together as *firqa*s.

Despite the serious shortcomings of church–sect typologies for the study of Muslim intra-religious divisions, there remain some elements of these theories that might be rescued: first, Weber, and, later, Wilson, approached religion in terms of its function, highlighting how religious groups such as churches and sects offered distinctive paths to salvation. They thereby distinguished sects by their soteriological responses to the world—by the ways that their answer to the question "what should we do to be saved?" implied certain kinds of relation to their social environment.[27] While I do not wish to reduce religion or sectarianism to its function alone, I do hold that the idea of salvation remains a central leitmotif for Muslim intra-religious divisions, and that soteriology might provide an important means to distinguish between them.

Second, returning in some senses to Weber's notion of the "mode of membership" in a church or sect, it is possible to see past his particular characterization (of members being born into churches, but choosing sects) toward the more interesting question of how human beings participate in religious groups and sub-groups. More recent definitions of sectarianism view it as both a practice and a discourse,[28] calling attention to how sectarian affiliation must be "activated" if it is to move from being passive or banal to being assertive or even aggressive.[29] Thus, sectarian affiliation in Iraqi society of the early 1950s and 1960s might be characterized as largely passive or banal. Iraq's dominant political discourse was one of Ba'athist socialism that downplayed, for the most part, religious and sectarian affiliations as modes of social identification. However, several factors (historical, social, and economic) gradually activated sectarian identification in Iraqi society to the point that such affiliations more and more became nodes of potential (and actual) violence. Those factors included (but are not limited to): the Iranian revolution of 1978–1979 that pitted a revolutionary vision of (Shi'a inspired) Islamic government against Saddam Hussein's secular–nationalist totalitarianism; the eight-year war between Iran and Iraq in which Saddam treated Shi'a as a fifth column; the 1991 Gulf war with its doomed Shi'a uprising in southern Iraq; the 2003 US invasion and occupation of Iraq and the rise of the various Sunni and Shi'a militias.[30] Discourse-based conceptualizations of sectarian identification thus point to the importance of external influences, economics, and shifting notions of modernity and nationalism, as well as to history, myths, and symbols as factors that create and sustain sectarianism in modern contexts.[31] They challenge researchers to move away from treating sectarianism as a thing-in-itself (and therefore from relying on taxonomies of church–sect–cult types) and back to sectarianism as a way of doing things, as a mode of being in the world, and as a discourse of identification.

A Narrative Identity Approach to Muslim Sects and Schools

Following these recent trends in the study of sectarianism, it becomes important to center the study of Muslim intra-religious divisions on the Muslims who adopt and articulate sectarian affiliations, and subsequently on the various institutions that perpetuate these affiliations (insofar as the institutions can be said to be accumulated products and reflections of particular kinds of Muslim sect identifications).[32] It must be borne in mind, however, that as a reflection of the (historically situated) human beings who cleave to them, intra-religious differences are not fixed, immutable, or eternal, but constantly changing, as is their salience in any given situation. Sectarian modes of identification turn out to be remarkably unstable, and related to innumerable circumstantial factors. Similarly, it is worth remembering that sect identification remains but one aspect of a larger, and malleable, patchwork of individual and group identifications—identifications that might include nationality, race, ethnicity, language, profession, family, and even geography (to give a far from exhaustive list). Religious and sectarian affiliations, therefore, must be approached as tangled up with these other kinds of identifications.

How, then, to study an unstable affiliation that is but one strand among many possible identifications? In this regard, the recent conversations among scholars of sociology, psychology, anthropology, philosophy, and literary theory about how human beings use narrative to form identities and interpret their experiences may prove useful in providing a methodology for approaching sect identification. In particular, the work of Margaret Somers captures some of the general insights of this line of inquiry: she builds on the idea that "it is through narrativity that we come to know, understand, and make sense of the social world, and it is through narratives and narrativity that we constitute our social identities."[33] That is to say: human beings find themselves "emplotted" in the midst of small- and large-scale narratives, relating to others as "characters" within those narratives, and navigating the roles that they choose to play with reference to the underlying "themes" and "plots" of such narratives. Such narratives feed into the individual and group identifications of human beings, allowing them to make sense of past, present, and future events through the lenses of the narratives in which they are emplotted.[34] Generally speaking, Somers argues for the idea that "all of us come to be who we are (however ephemeral, multiple, and changing) by being located or locating ourselves (usually unconsciously) in social narratives rarely of our own making."[35]

Adapting this view of narrative identity to the study of Muslim intrareligious divisions (and substituting, à la Brubaker and Cooper, the notion of "identity" for the more precise concept of "identification"), then, treats sect affiliation as one particular cluster of narratives (narratives among and related to many others) in which human beings find themselves emplotted.[36] As narratives, sect stories can be said to have particular themes and plots. Particularly vital to the sect narrative is the theme of salvation, a distinctive soteriology that the narrative offers to the emplotted. This salvation theme is tied to the plot of the sect narrative, which remains one of truth preservation set against the illegitimate forces that would seek to degrade, forget, or destroy those truths, and thus lead the community into damnation. And because the sect story itself is one of salvation by a particular group, participation in the sect—adoption of its worldview, practicing of its rituals, etc.—can become highly significant, even to the point where people might be willing to die for it.

The narrative identity approach, I believe, has much to commend it: first, it avoids essentializing sect affiliation by recognizing it as a product of human beings: a product that accumulates, changes, and develops—even breaks down—over time, and in accordance with the particular situations in which people deploy (or forget) it. Secondly, it allows for human agency within the social context of group affiliation,[37] viewing sect actors as both participating in a drama that goes beyond their individual selves and manipulating that drama through their participation in it.[38] Such a view opens the study of sectarianism to the possibility of "de-sectarianization," insofar as sectarian actors may decide for various reasons to stop participating in their sect narratives, thus downplaying the sectarian element of their identities. Thirdly, it recognizes sect identifications as part of the multiple, intersecting—and, in the context of sect affiliations, competing—identifications that constitute a person or social entity (that is, individuals and groups are involved in several narratives of being, all of which might affect each other to varying degrees).

Viewing sect affiliation as a kind of narrative identity thus permits the researcher of Muslim intra-religious divisions to inquire after the narratives, themes, plots, institutions, and characters that make up—collectively—what we consider to be any given *firqa* at any given moment, and in this way provides a potent methodology for the historical study of Muslim sectarianism in specific contexts. Taking a narrative identity approach to the study of Muslim sects and schools treats the question of how Muslims acquire, maintain, and manipulate their communal affiliations as a question of how the master narratives of Muslim sects and schools initially develop, how subsequent Muslims began to emplot themselves (or find themselves emplotted) in such narratives, and what such emplotments may have meant for them at the time. It also pays attention to the ways that the narratives of sect identification accumulated over time, became more refined, perpetuated themselves through institutions, frequently fragmented into sub-sects and schools, and sometimes disappeared altogether.

The job of the researcher who adopts a narrative identity model, then, is not simply to inquire into the grand sect narratives and their main actors, but also to investigate the extent to which specific persons understand the grand narratives to be relevant to and have implications for their particular situations. For example, by the narrative identity model, Shi'a are those who find themselves emplotted (and who actively emplot themselves) in a grand narrative of devotion to the family of the Prophet, the *ahl al-bayt*. This narrative casts the Imams as the legitimate leaders of humankind and true interpreters of what submission to God—*islam*—properly entails. For many Shi'a, an essential aspect of this grand narrative includes betrayals of the rightful Imams by Sunni Muslims in various ways: Abu Bakr and 'Umar's usurpation of 'Ali b. Abi Talib at the *saqifa* (the selection of Abu Bakr as the first Caliph at the covered portico—*saqifa*—of the Bani Sa'ida in Madina); or the martyrdom of Husayn b. 'Ali and his entourage at Karbala in 680 CE. Additionally, the grand narrative of Shi'ism might also include hope in a savior, identified by many as the Mahdi (the twelfth Imam), who will return at the end of time to "fill the earth with justice as it is now filled with injustice."[39] To be emplotted in these narratives (or to consciously emplot oneself in them through "rediscovering" or converting to Shi'ism) is one aspect of "being" Shi'a, and might entail a variety of activities, from passively hearing such narratives from birth or being surrounded by them during Muharram (the Shi'a period of mourning) and other important times to actively and fervently holding them to be true. In this sense, being emplotted in the grand narrative of Shi'ism becomes a means by which those who identify as Shi'a come to know, understand, and make sense of their social world.

Of course, simply knowing, understanding, or making sense of the social world through the lens of Shi'ism is but one aspect of the narrative identity model. Somers also directs our attention to these ways that people might find themselves emplotted in a narrative of Shi'ism that then enables said Shi'a to navigate and act accordingly in the world. For researchers, this active aspect of the narrative identity model poses questions about what and to what extent location in this grand narrative actually means for specific Shi'a in different places and times. Again, the level and kind of participation that particular emplotments entail will vary dramatically depending on time, place, and context: what the martyrdom of Husayn b. 'Ali implied for the Tawwabun (the "Penitents") in Karbala in 684 CE will certainly be different from what it implied to Iraqi Shi'a in Karbala in 1954, which will in turn be distinct from what it implied for the Mahdi Army occupying Karbala during the summer of 2004. But in all cases, emplotment in the narratives of Shi'ism has implications and consequences for those who thereby become Shi'a, and it becomes important for the researcher to investigate not only what the collective narratives of Shi'ism (the cumulative "traditions" of the various Shi'a groups) might recommend to adherents (for example, that they mourn for Husayn at Karbala), but also how those identifying as Shi'a respond to those recommendations (including how they mourn, and what they might understand themselves to be doing by mourning).

To give another example, a narrative identity approach to ISIS recruitment might examine how ISIS ideologues and recruiters employ a finite set of narrative themes to attract their various target groups (young men, converts, women, doctors, etc.), and how those themes then become internalized and reproduced by ISIS members. ISIS presents a particularly salient example of what a narrative identity approach might reveal insofar as the group appears to have achieved tight control over its narratives, combined with an impressive command of social media and recruiting outlets that disseminate them. Six broad themes seem to dominate ISIS's presentation of itself:

- belonging and camaraderie among the *mujahidun* (fighters)
- the Caliphate as a utopian social space
- merciful redemption for those who emigrate to the caliphate (and die as martyrs for it)
- divine justice under the ISIS courts
- victimhood at the hands of the caliphate's enemies (including the Assad regime, Americans, Russians, etc.)
- righteous warfare (usually articulated using the language of *jihad*) against those enemies[40]

Of course, these narrative themes mutually reinforce one another by pointing toward notions of earthly and ultimate salvation in the face of various enemies. Moreover, they are general enough that they can be fine-tuned to meet the larger needs of ISIS in specific cases of recruitment.

A researcher adopting the narrative identity approach to ISIS recruitment might profitably ask several questions of the ISIS narratives: Who controls the narratives, and how tightly? How are they tailored to attract different kinds of recruits? How do those persuaded by these narratives employ them to "make sense" of their new life in ISIS (and how do they position the "old" narratives of their lives in relation to the new)? What happens when recruits are no longer convinced by the ISIS narratives? As a specifically Sunni organization, when and how do narratives of sect fit into the overall narratives of ISIS?

Concomitantly, emplotment in the grand narratives of ISIS seems to strongly imply certain kinds of actions, depending on the individual(s) emplotted. Thus, ISIS uses the themes of righteous warfare, camaraderie, and redemption to attract fighters, primarily from among young Muslim men. In addition, the theme of utopia—especially the promise of marriage—seems to loom large in ISIS recruiting among young Arabs/Muslims outside Europe and America.[41] Unsurprisingly, when ISIS fighters speak of their involvement in the group, the themes of *jihad*, martyrdom, and brotherhood feature prominently in their discussions. Alternately, when ISIS needs doctors and other kinds of professionals, it stresses the themes of utopia (building a "true" and functioning Islamic society), divine justice (establishing their version of *shari'a*—Islamic law), and victimhood (how their work proceeds in spite of the efforts of the Shi'a, the Israelis, the Americans). In this way, active emplotment in one or more of the narratives of ISIS might imply either actively fighting as an ISIS soldier (or marrying one), or joining the caliphate to provide medical, legal, or technical services to it. In all cases, the different ISIS *da'wa* (outreach) wings in the organizations seem to tailor particular narratives to specific target groups depending on their needs. Important to note is how sectarianism proper—the notion of ISIS as a Sunni group fighting the Shi'a—is but one of many narratives that ISIS offers to its followers. Certainly, those who emplot themselves in the narratives of ISIS view some aspect of their affiliation in terms of sect, but sectarianism does not seem to be the only narrative. In such a way, the narrative identity approach allows for a more contextualized assessment of sectarianism as a factor in ISIS recruitment.

Narrative Identity and Sectarianization

There are several ways that the narrative identity approach to Islamic sectarianism might illumine the processes of "sectarianization" (the process by which conflicts in the Islamic world have morphed from non-sectarian to inter-sectarian) as well as "de-sectarianization" (the de-escalation or cessation of sectarian conflict). It should be reiterated, in conjunction with several of the other chapters in this volume, that inter-sectarian conflicts rarely if ever turn out to be "purely" sectarian. In other words, adherence to the grand narratives of Sunnism and Shi'ism is not enough in itself to cause conflict. Not only is sect affiliation but one aspect of an individual or group identity, but it is highly unstable over the long term and thus must be continually maintained in order to sustain itself.

How, then, might sectarianization happen? The narrative identity approach posits the "theme" of any given sectarian group as having something to do with salvation, and the "plot" (writ large) of these groups as revolving around the preservation of salvific truth from those who would degrade, forget, or destroy those truths. According to this model, in order for sectarianism to become active or hostile, a significant threat to the core truths of the group must be perceived and articulated in such a way as to be convincing to sufficient enough numbers of co-sectarians to make them act. In this manner, extra-sectarian factors come into play, as it is hardly enough for the mere existence of Sunnis vis-à-vis Shi'a or Shi'a vis-à-vis Sunnis to constitute a sufficient threat: those Sunnis or Shi'a must be shown to be doing something that imperils the truths of salvation (and their keepers) enough to warrant a violent reac-tion. Thus, they must be shown, for example, to be an economic, politi-cal, geographic, or demographic menace, or they must be cast, for example, as in cahoots with the forces of colonialism, Zionism, the "West," or indeed Satan himself.

Moreover, this must be done in a convincing manner—no mean feat, even for a skilled demagogue. I do not mean to reduce sectarianization to mere propagandizing (or to say that the threats themselves are not real, but "mere" constructions). Rather, I want to highlight the narrative aspects inherent in articulating an activist–sectarian stance that is capa-ble of motivating co-sectarians to violence. If this process bears close resemblance to what we might call propaganda, then it shows how labor-intensive and purposeful such processes must be to become successful in their aims. In this way, sectarianization, from the perspective of the nar-rative identity approach, would be the process by which actors identify and articulate threats in terms of and in relation to the grand narratives of the sect actors who perceive their sect to be under threat. Such an approach must also ask why and for what gain such actors choose to articulate such threats in terms of the sect narratives.

To my mind, the advantages of this approach consist in its ability to remain situation-specific while still drawing upon the accumulated traditions of any given sect. Thus, for example, when the Iraqi Sunni cleric Taha al-Dulaymi's anti-Shi'a rhetoric shifts from using the term *'ajam* (literally foreigners, but often indicating non-Arab foreigners, and thus Persians) to employing the term *rafida* (literally refusers, meaning those who refused to acknowledge the legitimacy of first three Caliphs, and thus a colloquial epithet for Shi'a in general), not only can we identify recent shifts from ethnicity-based anti-Shi'a narratives to religion-based anti-Shi'a narratives, but this shift can subsequently be anchored in the political and historical connotations that the term *rafida* carries with it.[42] This anchoring allows the researcher to make sense of how certain rhetoric draws upon medieval markers in modern ways, creating a sense of continuity with tradition. In this specific example, it casts al-Dulaymi as emplotted in several polemical traditions, the most recent of which draws upon Sunni polemics against Shi'a.

The study of Islamic sectarianism seems to be moving away from the obsessive categorizing that characterized Weberian–Troeltchian projects of previous decades and moving toward an understanding of sectarianism as a discourse and practice. Put another way, newer models of sectarianism are highlighting the process of sect creation and maintenance over the identification of traits that identify "types." The narrative identity approach to Islamic sectarianism accentuates the notion of sect-as-discourse, theorizing sectarianism as a process of location and navigation within narratives, and tying such locations to the process of identity formation. It is hoped that such a model might provide a bridge toward investigating specific moments of sectarianism and concrete instances of sectarianization.

5

INTERNATIONAL POLITICS, DOMESTIC IMPERATIVES, AND IDENTITY MOBILIZATION

SECTARIANISM IN PAKISTAN, 1979–1998

Vali Nasr

Since the Iraq War, sectarian conflict between Shi'a and Sunnis has emerged as a major fissure in Middle East politics—fueling conflicts in Lebanon, Syria, Iraq, and Yemen; a resurgence of extremism and the scourge of ISIS; and an escalation in tensions between Iran and Saudi Arabia, which has become the most significant clash between regional rivals in decades. From country to country, across the region, sectarian conflict is the thread that runs through each crisis, tying them into a strategic Gordian knot.

The common refrain in the West is that this is a fourteen-century-old feud we don't understand. Even US President Barack Obama said as much in his final State of the Union, calling the Middle East a place "rooted in conflicts that date back millennia." The not-so-subtle implication, of course, is that this is the kind of religious politics the West has long left behind. It is true that Shi'a and Sunni identities were formed centuries ago over a religious dispute. It is also true that Shi'a–Sunni clashes are nothing new. But sectarianism should not be dismissed out of hand as an ancient feud that defies modern logic. The violent paroxysm in today's Middle East is a modern phenomenon, a product of contemporary politics and priorities. Furthermore, it is playing out not in obscure theological forums but in the political arena.

Sectarianism today is a perfect storm—the product of a confluence of factors at play in the region. The first culprit in stoking sectarian conflict is Islamism. This modern-day ideology, born in the 1930s, calls for an ideal Islamic state built on the foundations of Islamic law and *shari'a*. The Islamic state is a utopian panacea that looks to religion to perfect modernity. But it is not a generic idea, as it requires harkening to either Shi'a or Sunni conceptions of Islam.

Shi'a and Sunnis each have their own methodology, interpretation, and practice of law. As such, there can be no such thing as a non-sectarian Islamic state. In a region in which Islam matters so much to politics, it is inevitable that the critical question then becomes "what Islam" and "whose Islam." The rise of narrower and more extreme forms of Islamism have only exacerbated sectarianism.

Sectarianism has become inextricably associated with the Middle East—and vice versa. But the first major conflict between Sunnis and Shi'a in recent history actually took place in South Asia. Sectarian violence in Pakistan soared during the final two decades of the twentieth century. In the following analysis, I map the sectarianization of Pakistani politics during that critical period, a process that has had dramatic regional and indeed international aftereffects.

* * *

Sectarian violence has risen phenomenally in Pakistan over the past two decades. It has extended beyond sporadic clashes over doctrinal issues between Sunnis, who constitute 90 per cent of the world's Muslims and 75–85 per cent of Pakistanis, and Shi'a, who constitute 15–25 per cent of Pakistanis, and metamorphosed into political conflict around mobilization of group identity.[1] It has developed political utility, and militant organizations that champion its cause operate for the most part in the political rather than religious arena.

The principal protagonists in this conflict are the Sunni Pakistan's Army of the Prophet's Companions (Sipah-i Sahaba Pakistan, SSP, established in 1984) and Pakistan's Shi'a Movement (Tahrik-i Jafaria Pakistan, TJP, formed in 1979) and its militant offshoot, the Army of Muhammad (Sipah-i Muhammad, SM, formed in 1991). They have waged a brutal and bloody campaign to safeguard the interests of their respective communities. Assassinations, attacks on mosques, and bomb blasts caused 581 deaths and over 1,600 injuries between 1990 and 1997.[2] One incident alone, a five-day "war" involving mortar guns, rocket launchers, and anti-aircraft missiles in a hamlet in northwest Pakistan in 1996, claimed over 200 lives and left several times that number injured.[3] The escalating violence cast a somber mood on the celebrations of the fiftieth anniversary of Pakistan's independence, which took place hours after a heated debate in the parliament over a new "anti-terrorism" law that was introduced to combat the problem. The conflict has had a debilitating effect on law and order, undermined the national ethos and the very sense of community in many urban and rural areas, and complicated democratic consolidation.

Sectarianism in the Pakistani context refers specifically to organized and militant religiopolitical activism, whose aim is to safeguard and promote the sociopolitical interests of the particular Muslim sectarian community, Shi'a or Sunni, with which it is associated. Its discourse of power promises empowerment to that community in tandem with greater adherence to Islamic norms in public life, as the religious sources and authorities of that community articulate them. These goals are to be achieved through mobilization of the sectarian identity in question and the marginalization of the rival sectarian community, largely through prolific use of violence.

The greater prominence of sectarianism in Pakistan's politics can be seen as a new phase in Islamist ideology and politics, especially among the Sunnis, one that is more militant and combines the demand for an Islamic state with a drive to marginalize religious minorities, especially the Shi'a. Sectarianism can, however, be better understood as a form of "ethnic" posturing: mobilization of group identity for political ends in lieu of class, ideology, or party affiliation.[4] Sectarianism is an enmeshing of the Islamist and ethnic discourses of power in a state wherein both are prevalent. Sectarianism is tied to Islamism in that the defining identity is elaborated in terms of Islam, and the ideological underpinning of Islamism also informs the politics of sectarianism, although sectarianism places greater emphasis on sectarian purity than the establishment of a universal Islamic orthodoxy. Still, the sectarian discourse of power and its underlying paradigm of politics are "ethnic"; they predicate participation in politics on group identity. Hence, whereas sectarianism in Pakistan displays far more concern for religious orthodoxy than confessionalism in Lebanon and Protestant and Catholic politics in Northern Ireland, the fundamental directives of their politics are not dissimilar. The Islamist veneer should not obfuscate the fact that at its core sectarianism is a form of religiopolitical nationalism. Therefore, our examination of its root causes is directly related to discussions of identity mobilization and ethnic conflict.

Some Theoretical Considerations

Identity Mobilization and Sectarianism

The two principal theoretical approaches in the social sciences to explaining ethnic mobilization have been primordialism and instrumentalism.[5] The first views ethnicity as a "subjectively held sense of shared identity," a "natural" phenomenon that is deeply embedded in human psychology and social relations.[6] Consequently, ethnic mobilization is integral to the political life of culturally plural societies, especially where class divisions are weak or absent. The second holds that ethnicity is adaptive in face of changing circumstances and serves as a tool in furthering the interests of political leaders and their constituencies. Both the primordialist and instrumentalist positions are relevant in explaining the rise of sectarianism. Sectarian identities could not have been politicized unless differences in beliefs, values, and historical memories compelled Shi'a and Sunnis to collective action. Still, these differences by themselves do not explain the rise in sectarianism and its role in society and politics. For most of Pakistan's history sectarianism has not been a political force. Differences between Shi'a and Sunnis have only recently become a notable divide in Pakistan's politics. Instrumentalist arguments, therefore, have greater utility in explaining sectarianism.

Instrumentalist explanations emphasize two causal factors: economic competition and the political opportunity structure. The first stipulates that competition over resources and wealth can serve as an impetus to ethnic mobilization if winners and losers are separated by identity or if identity mobilization holds the prospect of economic gain.[7] The second argues that identity mobilization is "social and political construction ... creations of elites, who draw upon, distort, and sometimes fabricate materials from the cultures of the groups they wish to represent in order to … gain political and economic advantage."[8] It follows that, if the structure of a political system permits the use of identity mobilization for political gain or rewards political leaders for engaging in identity politics, then the political system is likely to experience identity mobilization and conflict.[9]

The instrumentalist approach identifies "ethnic" leaders as primary agents in mobilizing identities. The choices and strategies they adopt in furthering their interests as well as the interests of their communities propel ethnic mobilization and conflict.[10] Ethnic mobilization is therefore a byproduct of political leaders' project of power and/or a facet of a community's drive for securing economic advantage.[11] Although relevant to the discussion here, especially insofar as the actions of Shi'a and Sunni leaders and organizations are concerned, the instrumentalist approach does not provide an adequate explanation of sectarianism, for it does not take into account the agency of international and state actors in identity mobilization.

International actors have generally been credited with determining the context for ethnic conflict, but not with directly mobilizing the identities involved in it.[12] Sectarianism in Pakistan provides a valuable case study in examining the relation between identity mobilization in one state and interests of other states in the international arena. The particular mix of Islamism and ethnic posturing that underpins sectarianism has found political relevance because it so effectively relates regional power alignments to specific political constituencies in Pakistan; it translates Iranian and Saudi/Iraqi competitions of power, on the one hand, and tensions born of the Afghan war, on the other, into Shi'a–Sunni struggles for domination. Thus, sectarian conflict in Pakistan highlights the importance of interplay of international and domestic political factors in giving rise to, entrenching, and even radicalizing identity cleavages. The high politics of international relations has shaped the low domestic politics of Pakistan.

Theories of ethnic conflict have generally treated the state as a passive actor in identity mobilization.[13] States fall victim to assertive ethnic forces that serve the interests of sub-state actors who use state institutions as the arena for their power struggles. The intensification of these struggles both signals and causes the weakening and ultimately the failure of the state. The case of Pakistan suggests that, far from being passive victims of identity mobilization, states can be directly instrumental in that process, manipulating the protagonists and entrenching identity cleavages. Identity mobilization here is rooted in the project of power of state actors, not of an elite or a community. These actors do not champion the cause of any one community but see gain in the conflict between the competing identities. This proposition allows the theoretical discussion to move beyond elite interests and primordial differences in explaining identity mobilization to look at state behavior in the context of the structure of state-society relations as a causal factor.

State Power and Identity Mobilization

The rise of sectarianism suggests that states with limited capabilities are more prone to manipulating cleavages of identity.[14] Such states are also less able to prevent other states from doing the same in their borders. The state in Pakistan is large and interventionist, but it enjoys only limited power and capacity.[15] It is greatly constricted in formulating coherent policies, and faces strong resistance to their implementation. Various private interests and social groups limit its reach into society and compromise its autonomy. It is able to exercise effective power only intermittently, and then more clearly vis-à-vis some social groups and with regard to certain policy choices. The state is therefore constricted by what Joel Migdal has termed "dispersed domination," circumstances in which neither the state nor social forces enjoy countrywide domination.[16] However, whereas the state is too weak to dominate, it is strong enough to manipulate, and can also use force to respond to challenges to national security or regime survival. It is a "lame leviathan," to borrow Thomas Callaghy's term in describing the state in Zaire/Congo.[17] That the state can use force at key junctures, however, does not compensate for limitations to state power and lack of effective domination.

Weak states cannot formulate and implement policies effectively (the final shape of their policies manifests the scope and nature of social resistance), and actions of state leaders often reflect "strategies of survival."[18] In fact, theoretical discussions of weak states have for the most part remained focused on explaining policy outcomes in the face of limitations to state power and capacity. The case of Pakistan expands the purview of the theoretical discussion to include examination of ways in which states can contend with limitations before them proactively and in enterprising ways.

Here, a weak state manipulates social and cultural divisions in order to gain advantage vis-à-vis social forces; a divide-and-rule strategy compensates for failure to build state capacity. This course of action does not make the weak state strong, but it gives it greater room to maneuver in the short run, albeit at the cost of undermining social cohesion and hence state interests in the long run. It also suggests that state actors are principal agents in identity mobilization and conflict in culturally plural societies, and that the manner in which politics of identity unfolds in a weak state is a product of the dialectic of state-society relations.[19]

International and Domestic Roots of Sectarian Conflict

The origins of the current spate of sectarian conflict in Pakistan can be traced to the intensification of regional politics after the Iranian revolution of 1979, the start of the Afghan war in 1980, and the Pakistani state's failure to prevent the political forces they unleashed from influencing its domestic politics. The Iranian revolution had a profound impact on the balance of relations between Shi'a and Sunni communities in Pakistan, and therefore on the country's politics as well. The Iranian revolution set in motion, first, a struggle for domination between the Pakistani state and its Shi'a population and, later, a competition for influence and power in Pakistan between Saudi Arabia and Iraq, on the one hand, and Iran, on the other, an extension of the Persian Gulf conflicts into South Asia. Both of these struggles for power helped mobilize and radicalize sectarian identities.

The Implications of Mobilization of Shi'a Identity

The Iranian revolution changed the character of both Sunni and Shi'a politics in Pakistan. Its impact on Shi'a was, however, more direct, and in turn influenced the politics of Sunni activism as well.[20] The ideological force of the revolution, combined with the fact that the first successful Islamic revolution had been carried out by Shi'a, emboldened the Shi'a community and politicized its identity. Soon after the success of the revolution in Tehran zealous emissaries of the revolutionary regime actively organized Pakistan's Shi'a, which led to the rise of the TJP and its various offshoots. Iranians were no doubt eager to export their revolution to Pakistan. The leadership of the revolution was also unhappy with

General Muhammad Zia ul-Haq, the military ruler of Pakistan, for having traveled to Iran in 1977–1978 to shore up the Shah's regime. In addition, after the Soviet invasion of Afghanistan in 1980 General Zia's government became closely allied with the USA, with which Iran was increasingly at loggerheads.

More important, Zia's regime was then in the midst of an ambitious Islamization project that sought to transform state institutions, laws, and policymaking in accordance with Islamic precepts. Pakistan's Islamization differed from Iran's own experiment in many regards. In fact, it was this competition between Shi'a and Sunni Islamisms—the Iranian and Pakistani models—that lay at the heart of Iran's posturing toward Pakistan and also provided Pakistan's Shi'a with a cause to rally around.

The Islamization package that General Zia unveiled in 1979, despite its claims of Islamic universalism, was in essence based on narrow Sunni interpretations of Islamic law and was therefore viewed by Shi'a as interference with their religious conduct and a threat to their sociopolitical interests.[21] In fact, the Islamization package produced a sense of siege among Shi'a that has since animated their militancy. They made their position clear when Zia's regime sought to implement Sunni laws of inheritance and the rules that govern the collection of the obligatory Islamic alms tax (*zakat*), which the state was charged to collect in the name of Islam, as the law of the land. Throughout 1979–1980 Shi'a mobilized in opposition to these laws. Their protests culminated in a two-day siege of Islamabad in July 1980. Faced with the strong Shi'a protest and significant pressure brought to bear on Pakistan by Iran, Zia's regime capitulated. It recognized Shi'a communal rights, thus legitimizing sectarian posturing, and exempted Shi'a from all those aspects of the Islamization package that contravened Shi'a law.

The Shi'a victory was deemed ominous by many in the ruling regime. The military was perturbed by the Shi'as' show of force, especially because Shi'a demonstrators had defied martial law with impunity thanks to Iranian pressure. Shi'a mobilization was therefore viewed as a potential strategic problem that was involving Iran in the domestic affairs of Pakistan. The formation of the TJP and its militant student wing in 1979, their assertive politics and emulation of the Iranian model, and the emergence of charismatic "Khomeini-like" leaders among the Shi'a, notably Arif Husaini, were also instrumental in convincing the ruling establishment of the threat that Shi'a mobilization posed to state authority, as well as to Pakistan's regional position.[22]

The state's capitulation to Shi'a demands in 1980 was seen by Zia's Sunni Islamist allies as nothing short of constricting their envisioned Islamic state and diluting the impact of Islamization. Shi'a protests had in effect reduced Islamization to "Sunnification," undermining the universal Islamic claims of the entire process. Sunni Islamists were not prepared to accept separate but equal domains for Sunnis and Shi'a. They argued that Pakistan was a Sunni state and its minorities had to live according to the norms and laws of the state, closely parallel to the way the Bharatiya Janata Party (Indian People's Party, BJP) argues against exemptions from civil laws afforded to Muslims in India. They also denied the legitimacy of Shi'a mobilization by arguing that Sunnism was Islam and, by implication, Shi'ism was outside the pale of Islam.

The organizational prowess of the TJP was meanwhile seen as a sign of hardening of Shi'a identity. Sunni Islamizers concluded that they would not be able to win over Shi'a and integrate them into their promised Islamic order, and that they exhibited "disloyalty" to Pakistan and its Islamic ideology. Thus, Zia and his Islamist allies developed a concerted strategy for containing Shi'a mobilization and limiting both Pakistani Shi'a and Iran's influence in Pakistan.

Pakistan initially sought to resolve the problem through diplomacy. For the better part of 1980–1981, foreign minister Agha Shahi, who favored conciliation toward Tehran, sought to dissuade Iran from meddling in Pakistan's domestic affairs and to enlist its support in pacifying the Shi'a.[23] However, Iran was implacable. Perturbed by the failure of the diplomatic initiative, Zia looked for other ways of contending with the "Shi'i problem." Due to successful social resistance to the state's policy initiative, combined with the intrusion of outside forces into the body politic, state leaders looked to mobilizing sectarian identities as a means of contending with the challenges before them.

This course of action also responded to the entwining of Shi'a mobilization with the pro-democracy movement and the channeling of its energies into opposition to martial law. In 1983 the TJP joined the multiparty Movement for Restoration of Democracy. The movement was formed by Benazir Bhutto's Pakistan People's Party (PPP) to oppose the military's domination of politics. Shi'a had been favorably disposed to the PPP ever since the 1970s.[24] By joining Bhutto's anti-Zia coalition the TJP further entrenched that support and tied Shi'a sectarian posturing vis-à-vis the state to the issue of democratization. The broad identification of the military regime with Sunnism and, conversely, Shi'ism with the pro-democracy movement gave sectarian identities new political significance. The military regime assumed that sectarianism would problematize the PPP's close affiliation with Shi'a. For in an environment of heightened sectarianism—which the military hoped would conveniently cast the struggle for democracy as one of Shi'a versus Sunni—the more numerous Sunni community would likely move away from the PPP. To this end the ruling military regime lent support to Sunni sectarianism and sought to use it as a means of balancing the PPP's base of support among the Shi'a with an anti-PPP Sunni one of its own.[25]

The Rise of Sunni Militancy

Zia's regime began its efforts to contain Shi'a assertiveness by investing in Sunni institutions in general, and Sunni seminaries in particular.[26] Curricular reforms in the seminaries opened the door for their graduates to enter the modern sectors of the economy and join government service. This change, it hoped, would entrench Sunni identity in the public arena and in various state institutions and government agencies. The state thus promoted Sunni Islamism only to confront the political and geostrategic threat of Shi'a Islamism.

With this aim in mind the state concentrated on strengthening Sunnism in areas where the "Shi'i threat" was perceived to be greatest. Much of this effort was undertaken by Pakistan's military and its elite intelligence wing, the Inter-Services Intelligence (ISI). Throughout the 1980s the military helped organize militant Sunni groups in Punjab and North-West Frontier Province and provided funding for seminaries in Baluchistan and North-West Frontier Province, provinces that abut Iran.[27] As one observer remarked, "If you look at where the most [Sunni] madrassahs [seminaries] were constructed you will realize that they form a wall blocking Iran off from Pakistan."[28] The military's involvement in sectarianism would grow over time as Sunni militancy developed organizational ties to the Islamist resistance in the Afghan war.

As part of this strategy, in 1988 the central government permitted marauding bands of Sunni activists to raid the town of Gilgit, the center of the Northern Areas of Pakistan, kill some 150 Shi'a, and burn shops and houses.[29] The government then proceeded to build an imposing Sunni mosque in the center of the predominantly Shi'a city. (If the

Northern Areas became a province, it would be the only one with a Shi'a majority.) In time this course of action gave rise to greater militancy and perpetuated the cycle of sectarian violence. The ruling establishment eventually found this strategy self-defeating. The mounting costs of sectarianism presented the state with serious problems once "the snake began to devour the snake-charmer," to use the Gramscian metaphor. State leaders did not find it easy to reverse the trend.

The state's efforts to contain Shi'a resurgence were complemented by those of Saudi Arabia and Iraq, who were also concerned about Shi'a activism in Pakistan and what they saw as Iran's growing influence there. In 1980 Iraq began a war with Iran that lasted eight years, and Saudi Arabia was wary of Iran's ideological and military threat and was leading a bitter campaign to contain Iran's revolutionary zeal and limit its power in the Persian Gulf region. Since then Saudi Arabia has sought to harden Sunni identity in countries around Iran, a policy that extends into Central Asia. Pakistan was important in the struggle for control of the Persian Gulf, as well as in the erection of a "Sunni wall" around Iran. Saudi Arabia and Iraq therefore developed a vested interest in preserving the Sunni character of Pakistan's Islamization. The two states began to finance seminaries and militant Sunni organizations, the primary beneficiary of which was the SSP.

The onset of the Afghan war further deepened Saudi Arabia's commitment to its Sunni clients in Pakistan. In fact, the funding that Saudi Arabia provided Afghan fighters also subsidized militant Sunni organizations in Pakistan, often through the intermediary of Pakistan's military. Afghanistan's Taliban and the SSP, as well as its offshoot in Kashmir, the Movement of the Companions of the Prophet (Harakat ul-Ansar), all hail from the same seminaries and receive training in the same military camps in North-West Frontier Province and southern Afghanistan that operate under the supervision of the Pakistan military. The most famous of these facilities was the al-Badr camp in southern Afghanistan, which was destroyed by the USA in 1998 in retaliation for the bombing of American embassies in East Africa. Since 1994 it has served as a principal training facility for the Taliban, SSP, and Harakat ul-Ansar. Similarly, Ramzi Ahmed Yusuf, convicted of bombing the World Trade Center in New York in 1993, was affiliated with a Saudi-financed seminary in Baluchistan that was active in the Afghan war but had also been prominent in anti-Shi'a activities in Pakistan. Yusuf is alleged to have been responsible for a bomb blast that killed twenty-four people in the Shi'a holy shrine of Mashhad in Iran in June 1994.[30]

The Saudi and Iraqi involvement in effect transplanted the Iran-Iraq war into Pakistan as the SSP and its allies and the TJP and its offshoots began to do the bidding of their foreign patrons. The flow of funds from the Persian Gulf continued to radicalize the Sunni groups as they sought to outdo one another in their use of vitriol and violence in order to get a larger share of the funding, turning sectarian posturing into a form of rent-seeking. Since 1990 Sunni sectarian groups have assassinated Iranian diplomats and military personnel and torched Iranian cultural centers in Punjab. Attacks on Iranian targets have been launched in retaliation for sectarian attacks on Sunni targets. By openly implicating Iran in attacks on Sunni targets and retaliating against its representatives and properties in Pakistan, Sunni sectarian groups have sought to complicate relations between Tehran and Islamabad and to portray Pakistani Shi'a as agents of a foreign power. When in September 1997 five Iranian military personnel were assassinated in Rawalpindi, the Iranian and Pakistani governments depicted the attack as a deliberate attempt to damage relations between the two countries.[31] The killing of twenty-two Shi'a in Lahore in January 1998 escalated tensions between the two countries further as Iran openly warned Pakistan about the spread of Sunni militancy.[32] The use of sectarianism to contend with the impact of the Iranian revolution thus produced a wider regional struggle for power that quickly went out of the control of the Pakistan state.

The Impact of the Afghan War

The Afghan war, meanwhile, helped aggravate the situation.[33] First, Saudi Arabia's role helped boost Sunni militancy in Pakistan—often in conjunction with elements in Pakistan's military—and limited Pakistan's willingness or ability to contain any Saudi exercise of power within its borders.[34] In addition, the Afghan scene itself was fraught with sectarian tensions as Shi'a and Persian-speaking pro-Iranian factions vied for power and position with the Saudi and American-backed Mujahedeen groups based in Pakistan. The rivalry between these groups and the competition for control of Afghanistan ineluctably spilled over into Pakistan. The advent of the Taliban only reinforced the linkage between regional power rivalries and sectarianism. Most notably, the escalation of tensions between the Taliban and the Iranian government in August–September 1998 set the stage for a wider regional Shi'a–Sunni conflict that will likely further animate sectarianism in Pakistan, control its ebbs and flows, and determine the extent and nature of the state's response to it.[35]

From the outset Pakistan's response to sectarianism was entangled with its own Afghan policy. For instance, in 1994–1996, while the government began to rein in Sunni militancy within Pakistan, which was by then deemed to be out of control, it was promoting it in Afghanistan and Kashmir. In 1994 the government launched Operation Save Punjab, which led to the arrest of some forty sectarian activists and sought to close seminaries to deny the TJP and SSP recruits.[36] Yet during 1994–1996 the government also organized militant Sunni seminary students into Taliban and Harakat ul-Ansar units for Pakistan-backed operations in Afghanistan and Kashmir. In the end, seminaries—and hence the SSP—thrived despite the crackdown. In fact, since the advent of the Taliban Sunni militancy has become more prominent. Increasingly, young activists are looking to the Taliban as a model. During a recent demonstration in Karachi, protesters taunted government leaders, proclaiming: "Do not think of us as weak. We have ousted Soviet troops and infidels from Afghanistan, we can do the same in Pakistan."[37] Containing sectarian groups therefore requires balancing Pakistan's military commitment to the Taliban in Afghanistan and the government's desire to maintain law and order within its borders.

The Afghan war was also important in other regards. The decade-long war flooded Pakistan with weapons of all kinds and ensconced militancy in its political culture, especially among Islamist groups. The "Kalashnikov culture" made sectarian conflicts bloodier and transformed militant organizations into paramilitary ones. The war also gave rise to powerful criminal networks in Pakistan that profit from trade in contraband and narcotics. The collapse of the state in Afghanistan led to the marked rise in production of heroin, which found its way to international markets via the Pakistani port city of Karachi.[38] The heroin production spawned important political relations which included Mujahedeen fighters, who used the narcotics trade to subsidize their war against the Soviet Union, tribal leaders, Pakistani military commanders, and criminal gangs in Pakistan. The narcotics trade eventually produced formidable criminal networks whose reach extends through the length of the country, from the borders of Afghanistan in the north to the port city of Karachi in the south. The relation between criminal networks and militant activists first surfaced in Afghanistan itself. There, political and economic ties with some of the Afghan Mujahedeen units worked in largely the same manner as those seen between drug lords and leftist guerrillas in Latin America.

Over time the drug trade developed ties with sectarian organizations, replicating in Pakistan the economic and political relationship that had already developed in Afghanistan between militant groups and drug traffickers. Many of the Afghan Mujahedeen fighters who became tied to the narcotics traffic have also been involved in sectarian conflict. The Mujahedeen thus helped forge linkages between their Pakistani sectarian allies and their partners among drug traffickers. The drug trade, in addition, found sectarian violence a useful cover for its criminal operations. Sectarian organizations have accepted this pact with the devil for the most part because it has been financially beneficial and has provided them with expertise and resources in perpetuating violence. There are also cases where the criminals have actually set up sectarian organizations as fronts for criminal activity.[39] Criminal networks have thus become deeply embedded in the politics of sectarianism, and their financial, political, and criminal interests in good measure control the ebbs and flows of sectarianism. The result is an Islamization of criminal activity and a criminalization of segments of Islamism in Pakistan.

The authorities in Pakistan find it difficult to crack down on activities that are associated with organizations that operate in the name of Islam and claim to be defending its interests. Police action against criminals is seen as harassment of the true servants of the faith, and thus faces resistance from local communities. In addition, since sectarianism involves religion, sectarian activists have had the tacit support of some larger national parties that have routinely used their influence to protect sectarian activists from prosecution. By associating themselves with sectarianism, criminal organizations, particularly smaller criminal networks, have benefited from that protection. The participation of criminals in sectarian conflict has escalated the violence, for hardened criminals have been more willing to attack mosques and people at prayer, and have generally been more willing to kill. The rising power of narcotics trade has therefore fanned the flames of sectarianism.

Consequently, the state's control over both sectarian and criminal forces has been weakened. Its ability to contend with violence has been restricted. And in many places in the country the combined forces of sectarian and criminal organizations have eliminated state authority altogether and replaced it with local political control rooted in criminal activity and sectarian politics.

The Predicament of a Weak State

While intensification of regional conflicts was instrumental in giving rise to sectarianism in Pakistan, the vicissitudes of Pakistani politics decided the direction that this form of identity mobilization has taken and the role it has come to play in state-society relations. Sectarianism has increased as the center in Pakistan has weakened. Its raging violence manifests the debility of state institutions. Throughout the 1980s a bloody ethnic war escalated in Pakistan's southern province of Sind.[40] The ethnic conflict posed a serious threat to political control of ruling governments both under Zia and the democratically elected prime ministers who succeeded him after 1988. This trend has proved particularly problematic for democratic consolidation. Weakness at the center limited the ability of the governments of Benazir Bhutto (1988–1990 and 1993–1996) and Nawaz Sharif (1990–1993 and 1997–1999) to reform the economy, restore law and order, and manage delicate relations with the military.[41]

The weakening of the center has also led to greater assertiveness of local powerbrokers—the landed elite and their networks of strongmen, for the most part.[42] The Pakistani state has since its creation relied on these local powerbrokers to govern the rural areas.[43] As the center weakened over the years, especially after 1988, and competition between ruling governments and their oppositions grew more intense, the landed elite became more autonomous, and the state's authority in rural areas dwindled. In Punjab and North-West Frontier Province an important space—liberated zones of sorts—was created in which sectarian organizations and criminal elements could operate. In many instances the landed elite has provided protection for the burgeoning sectarian and criminal networks. In these cases, it has received financial benefits from criminal activities and used sectarian forces as private militias.[44] As state authority has begun to retract from the rural scene, the power structure associated with the landed elite has acted as the de facto local government. Here, sectarian forces have served as the much-needed organizational muscle of the ascendant rural power structure. The Islamic veneer of sectarian groups has conveniently served to legitimize the authority of the local power structure and limit the ability of the state to infringe upon it. The rise in the political fortunes of the local powerbrokers has therefore occurred under the cover of sectarianism and helped entrench it in politics.

This trend has been helped by the fact that the levers of power have become increasingly ineffective. This ineffectiveness is most evident in limitations before the powers of the police, the force most immediately concerned with containing sectarian violence. The police in Pakistan is not an effective force; it is corrupt, weak, and ill-equipped. According to one estimate, there are five times as many Islamist militants in the country as there are policemen.[45] There is even evidence that sectarian forces have infiltrated the police force.[46] The ineffectiveness of the police became clearly evident in October 1996 when it was barred from entry into the village of Thokar Niaz Beig in Punjab, where the militant Shi'a SM is headquartered and maintains a large cache of arms. In May 1997 the police force was dealt yet another blow when the officer investigating the torching of Iranian cultural centers in January 1997 was assassinated. Since the assassination the police actually appear to fear confrontation with sectarian groups, and officers have apologized to sectarian groups for their past "misdeeds," that is, the arrest and prosecution of activists.[47] The message of the assassination was also not lost on judges, who are proving unwilling to convict sectarian activists for fear of reprisals.[48] In addition, since provincial authorities control the police, it is difficult for the center to rely on it to contend with sectarian violence.[49] The problem is compounded when larger national parties or landlords who protect sectarian elements use their power and position to prevent police action. The governments at the center and in the provinces are compelled to restrain the police in the interests of maintaining parliamentary coalitions.

Consequently, when violence reaches a critical stage, the military has stepped in to restore order. In 1992 in Peshawar, in 1995 in Pachinar, and in August 1997 and March 1998 in North-West Frontier Province the military intervened to end the violence. However, these operations were limited; the military merely imposed a ceasefire and ended the bloodshed. If the military were to participate in disarming militant organizations and rooting out sectarianism—which some elements in the military have helped organize—it would need a broader mandate and would need to be allowed to assume a greater political role. That solution would not be in the interests of democracy. This dilemma became clear in

August 1997, when the government pushed through the parliament a draconian anti-terrorism bill. The bill gave broad powers to the government and police to arrest and try suspects without due process and in contravention of civil rights stipulated in the constitution.

In the towns and hamlets of rural Punjab sectarianism has also served the interests of a different social stratum. Throughout the late 1970s and the 1980s, owing to population pressure and labor remittances from Persian Gulf states, the urban centers of Punjab grew in size, and new ones developed on the edge of agricultural lands.[50] Urbanization has changed patterns of authority, especially because these urban developments have been dominated by the Sunni middle classes and bourgeoisie, traders and merchants who are tied to the agricultural economy but are not part of the rural power structure. Increasingly, the burgeoning Sunni middle classes have demanded a say in local politics and have thus challenged the political control of the landed elite. In these areas of Punjab, such as Jhang and Kabirwala, where Shiʿa landlords hold power over Sunni peasants, the rising Sunni middle classes have emphasized sectarian identity in the manner described by instrumentalist theories as a means of weakening the Shiʿa landed elite. Hence since 1986 urban areas in the Jhang district of Punjab, where Shiʿa landlords and Sunni middle classes now compete for the allegiance of Sunni peasants, have been the centers for militant seminaries and the scene of most of the sectarian violence.

The Sunni middle-class support for sectarianism in Punjab reinforces the effect of sectarian organizations' alliances with other local powerbrokers to extend the purview of Sunni militancy from towns to villages. The sectarian forces have used these circumstances to further weaken the state's presence at the local level, combining their attack on the state with their desired purge of Shiʿa. Between January and May 1997 the SSP assassinated seventy-five Shiʿa municipal officials and community leaders. Although the attacks had sectarian coloring, the targets were also agents of the state.[51] The purge of Shiʿa local officials was designed to open the way for appointment not only of Sunnis, but of officials who would be more favorably disposed toward strengthening the rising local power structure. The attack on the state was unmistakable.

The response of Shiʿa landlords with few exceptions has been to gravitate toward right-of-center parties, most notably the Pakistan Muslim League (PML). They concluded that, whereas traditional religious and feudal ties could keep their Shi'a peasants in check, association with the PML was necessary to placate their Sunni constituents. As they became more powerful within the PML and were able to limit somewhat the party's support for Sunni sectarianism, their positions within their constituencies strengthened. Shi'a landlords thus created sectarian bridges and protected Shi'a interests in the PML, but did not eliminate sectarianism.

Demographic changes in Karachi have been similarly instrumental in sectarian identity mobilization in that city. In recent years the number of Pathans—from North-West Frontier Province and Afghanistan—in Karachi has grown markedly. This community has been closely tied to both Sunni orthodoxy and militancy, and has benefited more directly from the legal as well as illegal financial linkages that have been spawned by the Afghan war. Pathan ascendancy eventually precipitated conflict with Muhajirs, the dominant ethnic community in the city.[52] Since the advent of this conflict in 1985 sectarianism has served the interests of Pathans and the financial networks that are tied with them, for it can draw a wedge between Shi'a and Sunni Muhajirs and weaken the hold of the dominant Muhajir party (MQM), many of whose leaders are Shi'a, over that community. By redefining the main axis of conflict in Karachi as sectarian rather than ethnic, Pathans hope to reduce resistance to their growing political and economic presence there.

In many ways Pakistan has become an archipelago of stability. The state's power exists in pockets and regions and is absent in others. The state has, as of late, begun to view this development with alarm. Not only does it not look favorably on limits to its power and reach, but the shrinkage of state power in the rural areas can translate into unmanageable sectarian conflict and criminal activity, and weaken Pakistan in its regional power struggle with its perennial nemesis, India.

The state helped foster sectarian conflict in the first place, but because of its gradual weakening has been slow to control it, particularly because in Pakistan the rise of sectarian conflict has coincided with democratization. The fragility of democratic institutions combined with intense competition between political parties and actors has further eroded state power and created circumstances that are particularly conducive to sectarian conflict. For, just as state institutions have dithered in stymieing the tide of sectarianism, various political actors have followed the example of state leaders in the 1980s in manipulating sectarian identities to serve their interests. Problems of democratic consolidation have consequently helped ensconce sectarianism in the political process.

Sectarianism, Weak Democracy, and Crisis of Governability

The first three general elections after the return of democracy to Pakistan, in 1988, 1990, and 1993, failed to produce viable parliamentary majorities. The election of 1997 was the first to give a strong majority to one party, Nawaz Sharif's PML. The management of parliamentary coalitions therefore became central to national and provincial politics. The competition between rival coalitions placed a premium on every member of the national and provincial assemblies. Government and opposition parties went to great lengths to curry favor with them. Fringe parties and independents benefited most from these circumstances, as they were able to exert power and influence beyond what their numbers warranted.

The first three elections also gave the opposition party direct or indirect control of some provinces. Since many police and judicial powers lie with the provinces, the center found it difficult to control sectarian violence, and the provinces—and, many in Pakistan argue, the military—found it prudent to use the instability created by the violence to weaken the central government.

Sectarian parties and their allies exploited these circumstances to pursue their activities. After 1988 representatives associated with sectarian parties, and after 1990, when the SSP ran candidates of its own and won seats to national and provincial assemblies, members of sectarian parties could exert significant influence. For instance, the PPP had to give the SSP a provincial ministerial position in the Punjab provincial cabinet between 1993 and 1996 in order to get the party's support and deny it to the PML. The ruling parties turned a blind eye to sectarian activities and in essence gave the activists immunity from prosecution for criminal and violent acts. The SSP member of Punjab's cabinet between 1993 and 1996 had eight cases of murder registered against him.[53] Not until the PML handily won the 1997 general elections and gained control at the center as well as in Punjab and North-West Frontier Province—and was thus relieved of the considerations that had hitherto governed its position on sectarianism—did the government begin to crack down on sectarian forces in earnest. It arrested 1,500 activists between February and May 1997, closed a Shi'a seminary for sectarian activities in July, pushed through parliament a new anti-terrorism law in August, and rounded up more activists after the resumption of sectarian violence in January 1998.[54] It has become apparent that effective governance at the center, which is directly tied to the question of state power, is necessary for contending with sectarian violence. Moreover, the fortunes of sectarianism are tied to those of democratic consolidation. Still, the scope of the problem extends beyond the crisis of governability that followed democratization. For this crisis provided opportunity and encouragement to politicians to use sectarianism in the manner first used by state leaders, to serve their political ends as well as to shore up government authority. The pattern of decision making of Benazir Bhutto's government between 1993 and 1996 is particularly instructive in this regard.

During her second term of office (1993–1996) Benazir Bhutto's government looked at the problem of sectarianism differently. She followed the policy of exchanging immunity from prosecution and freedom of activity for sectarian forces for their support, but began more directly to use sectarianism to the advantage of her own government. At the time, her party still enjoyed strong support among Shi'a, and the TJP was tacitly allied with her party. Confident of Shi'a support, she began to explore the possibility of making inroads into the Sunni vote bank. Her main success in this regard was the Party of Ulama of Islam (Jamiat-i Ulama Islam, JUI). The JUI made a deal with the PPP as a result of which it received access to important aspects of government policymaking. The JUI has had close organizational and political ties with the SSP; its prominence in government therefore translated into protection for SSP activists.

Because Benazir Bhutto was viewed as secular and lacked Islamic legitimacy, and because her government was in dire need of such legitimacy, she was overreliant on the JUI. Initially Shi'a accepted her deal with the JUI in the hope that she would rein in the JUI and its sectarian allies. However, she was unable to control them, and instead the JUI began to use government resources to support the SSP. This failure began to alienate the PPP's Shi'a supporters.

From 1994 onwards it became increasingly evident that the government not only was incapable of reining in the JUI and SSP, but was actually fanning the flames of sectarianism. In local elections in the Northern Areas, a predominantly Shi'a area, in 1994 the TJP won six seats, and the PPP came in second with five. The TJP proposed an alliance with the PPP that would be led by the TJP; the vice-chairmanship (highest elected office) of the territories would be held by the TJP. The PPP refused, demanding that it lead the alliance and occupy the major administrative positions.[55] The PPP eventually got its way, took over all the major offices, formed the ministry in the Northern Areas, and denied the TJP control in its stronghold. The PPP's victory, however, came at the cost of a breach with the TJP. Shi'a, who were already perturbed by the PPP's alliance with the JUI, began to view Bhutto as only nominally pro-Shi'a but in reality unfavorably disposed toward their interests. The TJP was particularly disturbed by the tussle over control of the Northern Areas because the victory there had been the party's only strong electoral showing and its first opportunity to exercise power. The TJP flatly refused to accept the PPP's claim to represent Shi'a, viewing such an outcome as detrimental to its own interests. To make its point of view clear, the TJP held a large anti-PPP rally in Lahore, the first open sign of Shi'a unhappiness with Bhutto, and therefore viewed with alarm by her government.

The government, however, preferred divide-and-rule strategies to addressing Shi'a concerns and accommodating the TJP. Bhutto turned to the more militant SM, forming a tacit alliance with the most sectarian element among the Shi'a. Having lost the TJP's support, with Shi'a landlords gravitating toward the PML, the SM was the only Shi'a organization to which the PPP could turn in hope of maintaining a foothold in Shi'a politics. Bhutto was also hoping to use the SM to undermine the TJP's position within the Shi'a community. The PPP was borrowing a page from Indira Gandhi's strategy in India's Punjab province. There, in the early 1980s, the Indian prime minister had used Sikh militants to undermine the moderate Sikh party, Akali Dal, which the Congress Party had alienated. Similarly, in Pakistan's Punjab, support for the militant elements constricted the moderates but also helped fuel the cycle of violence. By 1995 the PPP government found itself in the position of actively supporting the most militant sectarian forces on both sides: the SSP through the JUI and the SM in order to weaken the TJP and maintain a foothold in Shi'a politics. Serving its immediate interests, Bhutto's government thus resorted to pulverizing civic order and promoting violence. For this reason the TJP began to move in the direction of the PML. In March 1995 it joined efforts by the National Reconciliation Council (Milli Yikjahati Council) to contain sectarian conflict, which for the TJP meant containing the SM as well as the SSP.

The mainstream Sunni Islamist parties and Islamist elements in the PML had formed the council in order to end sectarian conflict. It also enjoyed the support of the Shi'a landed elite and the TJP. The Islamist parties believed that the violence was damaging their cause and would eventually provide the government and the military with the excuse they needed to crack down on all Islamist parties. The council hoped to show that sectarian conflict did not enjoy the support of mainstream Islamist parties and to dissociate Islamist politics from sectarianism. Since both the JUI and the TJP were on the council, it was hoped that they would cooperate in reining in the SSP and SM.

The council sought to defuse sectarian tensions by focusing attention on what all Islamist parties shared: the demand for an Islamic state. Bhutto viewed such a consensus as dangerous to her interests. If Islamist parties were able to cobble together a united front that would focus its energies on the demand for an Islamic state, they could pose a threat to her government and lay the grounds for a strong Islamic electoral alliance in the next elections.[56] Bhutto concluded that it would be better for Islamist parties and their constituencies to fight each other and spend their energies in sectarian conflict rather than challenge the existing political order. The PPP government therefore actively worked to undermine the council. With the government's prodding, the JUI distanced itself from the council, and the SSP and SM resumed their violent attacks, effectively ending the council.[57]

This development was viewed with alarm in all circles, and especially among the Shi'a, who began to view the PPP as detrimental to their interests. Bhutto's brinkmanship between 1993 and 1996 alienated the Shi'a community, TJP, and Shi'a landed elite, all of whom went over to the PML. She was never in a position to control Sunni Islamist or sectarian parties, but in attempting to control them she lost the one constituency that since 1970 had been committed to the PPP. Bhutto's strategy in turn provided the PML, which had been more closely associated with Sunni interests, with inroads into the Shi'a vote.

In Pakistan, problems facing consolidation of democracy have further weakened the center, creating space for sectarianism to grow and to use the political process to its own advantage. Faced with competition for power, the political leadership has used sectarianism as a political tool, as have elements in the military, the landed elite, and criminal networks. The manner in which state leaders manipulated cleavages of identity in the 1980s has thus increasingly become institutionalized in the political process.

Conclusion

Mobilization of sectarian identities in Pakistan has produced an important fault line in the country's politics with broad ramifications for law and order, social cohesion, and ultimately government authority and democratic consolidation. The manner in which largely theological differences between Shi'a and Sunnis have been transformed into a full-fledged political conflict provides new insight into the root causes of identity mobilization; most notably, it includes international and state actors in theoretical discussions. It also relates the question of state capacity and power, internationally as well as domestically, to identity mobilization and thus provides the basis for broader frameworks for examining it in the Third World.

States operate in two intersecting arenas, the world and the domestic. The relative strength and weakness of a state determines whether or not international forces will be able to pursue their interests in its body politic. Weak states are susceptible to intrusion of outside forces and can become the arena for competition between international actors. That intrusion can affect social mobilization and polarize politics along identity lines. The resultant conflicts then become proxy wars between outside forces.

Weak states are not likely to contend quickly or effectively with the consequences. Conversely, the structure of their politics is likely to entrench the divisions as state leaders, and eventually some politicians, manipulate the emerging cleavages to further their interests. These actors are not directly associated with, do not speak for, and do not lead the identities they help mobilize. Hence their fortunes are not directly tied to identity mobilization, and they do not use it as a means to power in the manner explained by instrumentalist theories (although that explanation still holds true for sectarian activists). The interests of these actors are rather served most immediately by the conflict and violence that follow identity mobilization. This pattern of action is a response to limitations before state power and capacity. It follows that weak states are not simply victims of identity mobilization, but manipulate it and can thrive on it. For the state, however, this victory is only pyrrhic, for it gains momentary advantage vis-à-vis social forces at the cost of social division, violence, and political turmoil.

I would like to thank the Harry Frank Guggenheim Foundation and the American Institute of Pakistan Studies for their support of fieldwork research and Mumtaz Ahmad, Muhammad Qasim Zaman, Suhayl Hashmi, and anonymous reviewers for *Comparative Politics* for their suggestions. The findings of this chapter draw on personal interviews with politicians, government officials, police and military officers, and members of Sunni and Shi'a sectarian organizations.

6

SECTARIAN RELATIONS BEFORE "SECTARIANIZATION" IN PRE-2003 IRAQ

Fanar Haddad

Introduction

A fairly common view holds that the intensity of the entrenchment marking Sunni-Shi'a relations in the Middle East today can be traced back to
2003. To be sure, there can scarcely be any exaggerating the impact of
that year on modern sectarian relations in the Middle East and beyond.[1]
However, one exaggeration in that regard is the assumption that 2003
marks the dividing line between a "sectarian" and a "non-sectarian" Iraq
(or broader Middle East). While 2003 was indeed pivotal in elevating the
political relevance of sectarian identity to unprecedented levels, many of
the processes and dynamics that were set in motion by the political
changes of that year were the result of cumulative factors that had been
developing over several generations.

For example, 2003 can be regarded as something of a Copernican
moment in modern sectarian relations in that the Arab world was forcefully confronted with a political landscape that did not revolve around

Sunni Arabs. Yet, the political actors empowered in Iraq were not the products of regime change: the existence of Iraqi sect-centric Shi'a political actors, their attachment to identity politics, and the regional and international positions toward such a reconfiguration of Iraqi politics were all rooted in factors pre-dating 2003. Whilst there are qualitative differences between the pre- and post-2003 eras, there are likewise continuities between the two, and to fully understand the events of the past thirteen years one must closely examine them.

The central aim of this chapter is to highlight the pre-2003 roots of post-2003 "sectarianization" in Iraq. In doing so, my hope is to highlight that the sectarian competition we are witnessing in Iraq today, and elsewhere in the region, is not simply a product of the fact of sectarian plurality in and of itself; it is more a product of the emergence of the modern nation-state, and is related to contested political dynamics to do with nation-building, national identity, the (mis)management of sectarian plurality, and, ultimately, state legitimacy. Failure to account for the more subtle forms of sectarian entrenchment and sectarian politics characteristic of the pre-2003 era not only distorts our understanding of post-2003 dynamics, but has a similarly detrimental effect on proposed solutions. Likewise, believing the fiction of a supposedly "a-sectarian" or "non-sectarian" or "pre-sectarian" pre-2003 Iraq carries the risk of repeating the mistakes of the past in the years ahead.

"Sectarianism": Incoherent Terminology Leads to Incoherent Conclusions

Before discussing sectarian relations in pre-2003 Iraq and the roots of post-2003 "sectarianization," it is essential to establish some form of lexical clarity—something that is sorely missing in discussions of "sectarianism"/*ta'ifiyya* and sectarian identity.[2] After all, if one of our purposes is to revisit the notion that 2003 separates a "sectarian" from a "non-sectarian" Iraq, then we should at least be clear what the characteristics of each would entail. Indeed, the notion of a "non-sectarian" pre-2003 Iraq is largely facilitated by the ambiguity that marks the vocabulary of the study of sectarian relations: what makes a person, era, policy, position, or anything else "sectarian"? And what exactly is "sectarianism"?[3] Is it something that is felt, or is it a policy that is practiced and instituted? Does being "sectarian" necessarily imply feelings of sectarian hatred, or can it also refer to varying degrees of perhaps non-belligerent sect-centricity? Is "sectarianism" a social, religious, or political issue?

Surveying the field, one finds that the terminology is left largely unde-fined, with various writers and scholars seemingly assuming that their readers and peers share their understanding of what "sectarianism" (and, by extension, "sectarian") means. Some scholars have, however, attempted to formulate a clear definition of what "sectarianism" entails, but seldom have such attempts yielded comprehensive results, let alone consensus on the term's meaning.

Whether through explicit definition or through inferred meaning one can identify several ways in which the term "sectarianism" (and its Arabic equivalent, *ta'ifiyya*) is used. Firstly, it is used by some in an expan-sive manner to refer to much if not all that is related to the assertion of sectarian identities without clarifying the boundaries between legitimate or benign assertions of sectarian identity and those that constitute exam-ples of "sectarianism."[4] Absent such a clarification, this approach carries the risk of criminalizing otherwise legitimate manifestations of sectarian identity by associating them with an inherently negative but hopelessly vague "sectarianism." In some cases this same expansive approach sees the terminology's coherence further reduced by using "sectarianism" to refer to antagonisms between any sub-national identities, be they reli-gious, sub-religious, ethnic, or even class and regional identities.[5] A sec-ond approach sees scholars taking "sectarianism" to mean varying forms of sect-centricity.[6] Needless to say, what may be considered sect-centric covers a vast spectrum from social or intellectual insularity all the way to belligerent mobilization against the sectarian other. For such a broad spectrum to be subsumed under one emotionally charged and value-laden term such as "sectarianism" seems impractical and inaccurate.

Thirdly, in other works "sectarianism" is understood as a byword for the Lebanese political system, or any other political system that institu-tionalizes sectarian identities.[7] This approach is perhaps too restrictive in that it solely focuses on institutional politics, thereby excluding society, religion, sectarian dogma, and individual agency from discussions of "sectarianism." Similarly, scholars who confine their understanding of "sectarianism" to the confluence between sectarian identity and politics (regardless of whether this is formally institutionalized or not)[8] exclude potentially non-political manifestations of sectarian tension or sectarian hatred such as those one encounters in theological sectarian polemics.

A fourth approach to the terminology finds scholars avoiding singular definitions and instead attempting to offer multi-faceted descriptions of what constitutes "sectarianism," often with the aid of a typology of various "sectarianisms."[9] Finally, an oft-encountered approach to "sectarianism" is one that explicitly or implicitly takes it to mean the sect-based equivalent of racism.[10]

In short, the word "sectarianism" has not only eluded definition but has led to a definitional free-for-all precluding a common understanding of what "sectarianism" is, thereby complicating the study and understanding of the dynamics of sectarian identities and sectarian relations. The field is further skewed by the fact that the only definitional point on which there seems to be a measure of (perhaps misplaced) consensus is that "sectarianism," however defined, is a phenomenon regarded with pronounced negativity.

This duality of negativity and indefinability that so characterizes common approaches to "sectarianism" is not simply a matter for pedants to obsess over; rather, it is an issue of some import given the practical implications of leaving undefined an expression that so pervades policy discussions of a Middle East more polarized than ever by sectarian identities. In the first place, its lack of definition and clear contours allows the term to divert analytic focus away from underlying issues such as economic, class, local, or political factors in favor of focusing on a mercurial "sectarianism."[11] Secondly, its indefinability endows it with a shape-shifting quality that allows the term to apply to a vast spectrum of issues relating to sectarian identities. Thirdly, and more importantly, this boundless way in which the term is used becomes dangerous when coupled with its widely assumed negativity: time and again we have seen the term "sectarianism" being utilized as a tool with which regimes and conservative social elements can exclude perceived threats.

From Iraq to Syria to Bahrain to Saudi Arabia and beyond, the ready-made charge of "sectarianism" is easily and effectively leveled at political and social opponents in an effort to isolate and delegitimize them. In practice the charge of "sectarianism" in such cases is often little more than an implicit reference to the sectarian otherness of political and/or social rivals; yet, ill-defined and incoherent as it remains, the charge of "sectarianism" is one that easily finds a receptive audience in broader society, reflecting the fact that there is a significant body of opinion that is ever-ready to believe that the sectarian other is guilty of an undefined (yet undoubtedly nefarious) "sectarianism." Over time this dynamic has helped turn sectarian plurality into sectarian division amongst sections of the public in several countries suffering from heightened sectarian entrenchment today. Finally, and most relevant to this chapter, an inescapable implication of the incoherence of our approaches to "sectarianism" has been a concomitant incoherence in our understanding of the subject and in our proposed cures for those areas marked by heightened sectarian competition.

All of which brings us back to the imagined 2003 boundary between "sectarian" and "non-sectarian" Iraq. These are a direct product of our convoluted approach to "sectarianism": if we restrict our understanding of "sectarianism" solely to violent sectarian conflict, widespread sectarian hatred, and the empowerment of sect-centric political actors, then 2003 undoubtedly becomes the moment separating a "sectarian" Iraq from a "non-sectarian" one. But that would be to adopt an absurdly restrictive conception of "sectarianism" that obscures the dynamics of sectarian relations and sectarian competition that are in fact far broader than just the extreme manifestations of violence and active hatred.

To illustrate, if we take "sectarianism" to mean, alongside the headline-grabbing extremes witnessed over the past thirteen years, sect-centric bias, prejudice, stereotypes, or institutional discrimination, then "sectarianism" in Iraq (and other parts of the Arab world) was alive and well long before 2003.

Intersections

Here the largely ignored parallels between the study of sectarian relations and the study of race relations are instructive. As already mentioned, some scholars do approach "sectarianism" in a manner suggesting that it is the sect-based equivalent of racism.[12] This is a potentially fruitful framework for the study of sectarian relations, but there remains a significant discrepancy between the two fields. The literature on race, race relations, and critical race theory is far more mature and sophisticated than what has so far been produced on sectarian relations in the Middle East. For example, it takes into account not just the vulgar manifestations of racism such as racial violence or active racial discrimination but also draws our attention to the more subtle underpinnings of racism such as institutional racism, structural racism, and the role of law and power in race relations.

If we are to understand "sectarianism" as the sect-based equivalent of racism, then the study of sectarian relations must match the sophistication of the study of race relations. The reality is that the complexity of sectarian relations mandates that our understanding of "sectarianism" cannot be restricted to just sectarian violence or active sectarian hatred any more than a plausible understanding of racism could be restricted to its physically violent manifestations. Such a restrictive approach blinds us to the more subtle aspects of sectarian or race relations, and completely blinds us to the role of power relations, economic conditions, personal and group bias, memory, and prejudice.

One of the many interesting insights and parallels one gleans from the study of race relations relates to the subtleties of racism. For example, several scholars have highlighted the sometimes incidental relation of physical appearance (for example, skin color) to racial prejudice. Several paradigms in the study of contemporary racism ("new racism," "cultural racism," and "color-blind racism," for example) avoid linking physical appearance with the ordering of social hierarchies, opting instead to focus on people's cultures as perceived and essentialized by more dominant others. As Steve Garner argues:

> Racialization has to do with homogenizing groups, de-historicizing and not seeing their struggles, reducing their distinctiveness and viewing them as bearers of particular kinds of cultural norms. You can make "race" without talking explicitly about physical appearance, but not without prior visual filtering.[13]

If we substitute "race" with "sectarianism" and then substitute "physical appearance" with "sectarian dogma," the parallel becomes obvious. Sectarian identities, solidarities, and grievances are not necessarily rooted in religious or dogmatic issues, nor are they always manifested in spectacular fashion. Sectarian prejudices and sectarian division can be manifested in subtle, unintentional, even subconscious ways, as I will discuss shortly. In the era of the nation-state, sectarian competition in the single nation-state is just as likely, if not more likely, to be animated by contested national truths rather than religious ones, thereby rendering a country's sects into loosely defined collectives that may often be perceived more along economic or regional lines than strictly according to sectarian affiliation.[14] Furthermore, just as sectarian competition comes to be more focused on the profane, so too do the contours of sectarian identities and sectarian prejudices—as illustrated by the fact that modern sectarian dynamics in Iraq and elsewhere are intensely influenced by considerations of class, region, and ethnicity. Whilst strictly religious sectarian polemics were never completely absent, a far more familiar pattern in the twentieth century was for sectarian exclusion to question a person's or a group's national loyalty, Arab ethnicity, and to disparage cultural habits, norms, and values rather than picking on the finer points of jurisprudence.

In short, feelings of sectarian victimhood and the existence of sectarian division can be nourished by far less than the *takfiri* suicide bomber or the institutionalization of identity politics.[15] Sectarian dynamics can and have been manifested in complex and subtle ways, such as through the intertwining of sectarian identity with class, tribal, and regional considerations.[16] A notable illustration of this can be found in the structures of power that underlay the Ba'ath Party. Commenting on sectarian relations in the late 1970s, Marion Farouk-Sluglett and Peter Sluglett noted:

> It seems almost unnecessary to point out that, given the shaky social basis of the regime, the fact that most of the members of the Revolutionary Command Council came from [western Iraq] is because they are the friends and kin of those already there, rather than because they attend the same mosque. … Ba'thist ministers and technocrats, while acknowledging the importance of [connections], would be astounded at any suggestion that they owed their position to their sectarian affiliation.[17]

Another good illustration of the subtleties of pre-2003 sectarian dynamics and how influenced they were by the intersection of sect, class, and regional dynamics can be seen in the example of the *shrug* and in popular prejudices against them. Conventional wisdom has it that the word *shrug* (sing. *shargawi* or *shrugi*) was originally a term used to refer to those from east of the Tigris, specifically those from the southeast. In this reading the term derives from *sharq* (east). In any case, over the course of the twentieth century, and due in no small part to massive rural-to-urban migration, the term came to be associated with the working class, particularly those from the southern governorates.[18] The term also acquired derogatory connotations relating to uncouthness, poverty, ignorance, and sometimes criminality. With time the word *shrug* was used to refer derisively to the capital's working classes, particularly those who hailed from the south. The term also came to be used more broadly to refer to southerners in general. The fact that the vast majority of these are Shi'a lent a sectarian dimension to the term, in that it was implicitly referring to Shi'a—or at least a certain *kind* of Shi'a.

The centrality of class and regional dimensions to this phenomenon is illustrated by the fact that middle-class Baghdadi Shi'a were not averse to labeling their southern compatriots/co-religionists with the derogatory term. Even southern Sunnis had to contend with the label.[19] Nevertheless, regardless of the drivers and intentions, the *perception* existed amongst the Shi'a working classes and amongst Shi'a southerners that their lot was a poor one dictated by their sectarian otherness and that they were collectively marginalized *as Shi'a* who were derisively labelled as *shrug*. The point is that just as Steve Garner argues that one can make "race" without explicitly talking about physical appearance, one can "make sectarianism" without talking about sects per se.[20]

The preceding should not be taken as an argument for a perpetually divided Iraq. Nor does it negate the realities of coexistence, intermarriage, or cross-sectarian nationalist sentiment. To do so would be to insist on a monochrome picture of sectarian relations in pre-2003 Iraq, an approach that paves the slippery slope toward the false dichotomy of a sectarian/non-sectarian Iraq. Outlining the contours of a "sectarian issue" does not imply that it is the sole feature of Iraqi society. Nor does it follow that the "sectarian issue" is perpetually relevant. Similarly, discussing race relations or referring to racial tensions in the United States does not negate the facts of racial coexistence, interracial marriage, or the fact that an African American sits in the White House. Whether we are discussing American or Iraqi society, race relations or sectarian relations, it seems self-evident that people are neither perpetually at one another's throats nor forever in each other's embrace. Between the two extremes lies a broader spectrum that will tilt more one way than another depending on context. It is this ever-fluctuating context that dictates the trajectory of a society's racial or sectarian dynamics.

Sectarian Relations and the Iraqi Nation-State

It is crucial to distinguish sectarian relations in the age of the nation-state from what they were prior to that. It is only with the advent of the nation-state that people developed a sense of ownership of and entitlement to the polity. Prior to that, political authority was, for the vast majority of people, distant, alien, and exogenous to local identities. There was no pretence to anything we would recognise as citizenship, and as such there was no pretence on the part of political authority to being an embodiment of "the people."

Likewise, the vast majority of people did not expect a say or a share in political power, and only seldom mobilized, on the occasions that political authority seemed unduly oppressive or suddenly vulnerable.[21] The nation-state completely altered perceptions of self and other and toward political power. With the nation-state came notions such as citizenship, economic and political rights, and the notion that "the people" owned and were entitled to a share in the body politic. As the concept of the nation-state took root, there was a growing expectation that it would reflect "the nation." As such, the boundaries separating the national "us" from outsiders hardened in people's perceptions, and asymmetric power relations between communal groups within the nation-state came to be more contested and were not as readily accepted as inevitable in the way they may have been previously.

One of the consequences of these developments is that the nation-state created a new, profane, and far more tangible plane on which sectarian identities were formulated and in which they competed. Rather than disputes over religious truths or local rivalries, as had been more often the case in the past, the nation-state meant that sectarian relations were increasingly animated by contested *national* truths and contested access to and ownership of the body politic. Indeed, one could argue that with the advent of the Iraqi nation-state in 1921, Sunni-Shi'a relations came to be imagined on two overlapping levels: at the level of the nation-state and at the global Islamic level; the national and the transnational— or, more precisely, the national and the religious.[22]

This duality is highlighted by the differences one notices when comparing Sunni-Shi'a competition between people hailing from different countries and Sunni-Shi'a competition between compatriots. In the case of the former, they are far more likely to debate religious truths. This is to be expected, given that religion and religious identity form the only mutually claimed site of competition between Sunnis and Shi'a of differing nationalities. In the case of Sunni and Shi'a compatriots, in contrast, we are far more likely to see them clash over national truths (demographics, national history, entitlement within the nation-state, and the like) in addition to, if not instead of, religious ones. This increases the porousness of what one may perceive as being "sectarian" and facilitates the overlapping of sectarian identity with politics, policy, economics, and national memory. Needless to say, this national framing of sectarian identities is more immediate, and can be more flammable, than the purely religious frame in that it has a more tangible impact on individual interests.

Mismanagement of Communal Plurality

Competing sub-national groups—be they religious, sectarian, racial, tribal, or class based—are features of all nation-states. As such, sectarian competition in Iraq or clashing conceptions of the nation-state are only remarkable to the extent that they have been mismanaged over the better part of a century.

The cumulative effects of this mismanagement were laid bare in 2003 when the extent to which state legitimacy had been contested was demonstrated by the varying reactions to the US invasion of Iraq and the rise of sect-centric political actors who sought to capture and redefine the state. While the occupation can be given much of the dubious credit for empowering these sect-centric political actors and for institutionalizing ethno-sectarian politics in Iraq, we should nevertheless ask why these sect-centric political actors existed in the first place, why they were so well placed for political gain in 2003, and why Arab Iraq was so susceptible to identity politics after regime change. The answers to these questions are almost entirely to be found in pre-2003 Iraqi history and the mismanagement of communal plurality.

When surveying Iraqi sectarian relations between the state's establishment in 1921 and 2003, one notices four characteristics. Firstly, sectarian relations prior to 2003 were far more a subject of state—Shi'a rather than Sunni—Shi'a relations. Prior to 2003, and unlike their Shi'a compatriots, Sunnis did not have an active sectarian identity that could serve as a mobilizer or that demanded validation or expression—certainly not in any manner that would parallel the contours of (some forms of) Shi'a identity in pre-2003 Iraq.[23] Secondly, Iraq had a "sectarian issue" that was chiefly related to Shi'a political representation, the institutional extent of organized Shi'ism (both politically and religiously) and the limits of Shi'a identity in the public sphere. The relevance of this "sectarian issue" varied considerably over time, but it nevertheless existed as evidenced by the continuous presence of Shi'a-centric issues, mobilization, political organizations, and eventually militants as well. The relevance of a country's sectarian question is difficult to measure at any particular time given the multiplicity of actors, views, and drivers, and the fluidity of the perceptual factors that lie at the heart of issues relating to identity. Perhaps one way to gauge its relevance would be to examine how easily political and social issues can be sect-coded at a given time; that we refer to a "Sunni demonstration," a "Shi'a protest," or a "sectarian conflict" highlights the existence of sectarian fault lines and reveals much about power relations at a given moment.[24]

The third characteristic of sectarian relations in pre-2003 Iraq was that the nation-state was not in question, even if the state structure was at times. Sectarian competition unfolded in the name of and within Iraq and Iraqi nationalism. At no point did any significant sect-centric actors aspire to secession or seek to alter borders. The fourth characteristic is perhaps the most important when considering the mismanagement of sectarian relations in pre-2003 Iraq: the paradoxical way in which sectarian plurality was framed. While sectarian plurality was always accepted—celebrated even—as a defining fact of Iraq, sectarian identity and its expression were viewed in a negative light, to the point of criminalization, largely due to the fact that the dominant discourse framed sectarian identity (and more so its assertion) as being detrimental to national unity.

This awkwardness toward sectarian plurality extended far beyond Iraq's sectarian divide, and can be seen with regard to the pre-2003 state's relations with different groups generally. There are several possible explanations for this, relating to anti-colonialism, the way Arab nationalism evolved over the course of the twentieth century, and, above all, the ever-intensifying authoritarianism of the twentieth-century Iraqi state.

Commenting on the post-colonial state in general, Milton Esman argues that anti-colonialists often felt it necessary to build a united and clearly distilled "us" to stand against foreign rule. Intentionally or not, this often meant that minorities or out-groups had to dilute their identity, the better to be assimilated into the supposedly indivisible nation. A differentiated identity thereby often came to be regarded as a potential indicator of "dual loyalties" and a threat to national unity; out-groups were therefore discouraged or forbidden from asserting a differentiated identity—culturally and, even more so, politically.[25]

Exclusionary Nation-Building

In the case of Iraq, the roots of this issue extend back to the Mandate period and the establishment of the state, when patterns and mechanisms were set in motion with far-reaching consequences for Iraq's political development and national cohesion.[26] These dynamics only deepened over time with the expansion of the state and the intensification of its authoritarianism. In Hamit Bozarslan's words, the instability and upheavals of twentieth-century Iraq helped lead to the "redefinition of ethnic, religious and political 'otherness' as potential expressions of enmity, betrayal and 'vital threats' to the nation."[27] At heart, what we see in twentieth-century Iraq is a history of exclusionary nation-building that was based on problematic and coercive understandings of "unity" and "pluralism" that were used to exclude dissenters whose nonconformity was regarded as a threat to the body politic. From the exclusionary and discriminatory Nationality Law of 1924[28] to Arabization policies[29] to the way concepts such as *shu'ubiyya* and *taba'iyya* were used,[30] we repeatedly find the twentieth-century Iraqi state marginalizing or excluding citizens on the basis of their identities and/or their political views.

The Sectarian Taboo[31]

The subject of sectarian identities and sectarian relations was always regarded as something of a taboo. As early as 1950 the British ambassador to Iraq noted that "the struggle [between Sunnis and Shi'a] remains a partially hidden one, of which both sides are vaguely ashamed and which both would like to see resolved without an open political clash."[32] Indeed, it would not be going too far to say that in pre-2003 Iraq the terms "Sunni" and "Shi'a" were regarded by many as being distasteful, if not unmentionable—perhaps due to their uncomfortable proximity to the porous and shape-shifting ill of "sectarianism."[33]

This suppression of issues relating to sectarian relations inevitably entailed a degree of implicit vilification of assertions and expressions of sectarian identities. It is crucial to note that the impact of this was felt differently by Sunnis and Shi'a: as already mentioned, Sunni identity did not exist in any meaningful way in pre-2003 Iraq, meaning that the assertion of a specifically Sunni identity was seldom if ever an issue. Unsurprisingly, this meant that the question of "sectarianism" was one disproportionately associated with Shi'a. Thus to stigmatize sectarian identities in pre-2003 Iraq was not to equally stigmatize Sunni and Shi'a identities, since the former did not have the cultural differentiation or the heightened self-awareness that the latter did.

In many ways, the pre-2003 state's stance toward "sectarianism," and the fact that, intentionally or not, it adversely affected Shi'a identities and Shi'a self-assertion, was one of the key drivers behind the emergence of a sect-centric Shi'a political culture that was to grow over the course of the twentieth century until it eclipsed other forms of political activism before flourishing in the post-2003 environment that so privileged identity politics.

To be clear, what is being described is not a clash pitting Shi'a against a "Sunni state." Rather than Shi'a being "reluctant Iraqis" fighting against Sunni overlords, these tensions were a result of the fact that since state establishment in 1921, and unlike their Sunni compatriots, significant sections of Shi'a society had a politically salient and culturally autonomous sectarian identity that demanded recognition and that grated against the modern state's homogenizing impulses and its attempts to include them through dilution. It is not that the Iraqi state wanted to turn Shi'a into Sunnis. Nor was the state anti-Shi'a per se. Rather, it was more a case of the pre-2003 state being suspicious of those whose lives and identities were embedded in Shi'a social and religious structures (some of which have a transnational element) that provided parallel truths regarding Iraqi history, the Iraqi self, and the Iraqi nation—truths that the Iraqi state felt it needed to exercise a monopoly over.

The nature of the state's antagonisms with and suspicions of organized Shi'ism are perhaps best summed up by the former minister of the interior, Sa'dun Shakir, who remarked that "the *hawza* [Shi'i religious seminary] was essentially established to distribute money and separate the [Shi'a] people from the state."[34] This comment says much about what the state would have regarded as "good Shi'a," and indeed social and political mobility were readily available to those Shi'a who were less embedded in Shi'a social, religious, and political structures. It is worth re-stating that there was no discernible Sunni equivalent of any significance.

Likewise, prior to 2003 the political culture of sect-centricity was very much the preserve of the Shi'a. Even Sunni religious movements framed their actions in Islamic rather than Sunni terms: there was no "*Sunni* victimhood" or "*Sunni* issues" to champion. In contrast, there are many instances of Shi'a politicians, leaders, and organizations advocating for specifically Shi'a issues from the earliest days of the modern Iraqi nation-state. For example, as early as April 1922 we find Mahdi al-Khalisi—a militant though far from marginal Shi'a cleric known for his opposition to the government—making a series of political demands that, alongside demands for complete Iraqi independence from Britain, included calls for half the cabinet and half of all government officials to be Shi'a.[35]

Similarly, in the 1920s we also see the emergence of the short-lived and avowedly Shi'a-centric al-Nahdha Party, which championed the cause of Shi'a rights and Shi'a representation.[36] Another example can be found in the People's Pact (*Mithaq al-Sha'ab*) of 1935. Addressed to King Ghazi, this document was signed by tribal and religious leaders from the mid-Euphrates and by Shi'a lawyers in the capital demanding, amongst other issues unrelated to sectarian relations, that Shi'a be better represented in government and that Shi'a jurisprudence be represented in the judiciary.[37] The lack of a Sunni counterpart to such activism accentuated the association of "sectarianism" with Shi'a.

To be clear, there is nothing inherently wrong or problematic with sect-centricity, particularly when one considers how broad a spectrum it encompasses. In any case, the above examples do not negate the existence of other strands of Shi'a opinion and political activism. Nor should they be taken as proof of hostility or interminable division. Rather, what these examples reflect is the existence of a latent resentment against the pre-2003 state on the part of many Shi'a. Regardless of whether this was a result of reality or mere perception, the fact remains that, throughout pre-2003 Iraq's existence, some sections of Shi'a society firmly believed that they were treated as second-class citizens whose sectarian identities were suppressed and whose political representation in no way matched their demographic weight. Indeed, this resentment was acknowledged by Iraq's first monarch, Faisal I, who, writing in 1932, argued that what disadvantage existed amongst Shia was the result of structural and historical reasons rather than sectarian considerations, but that this had, nevertheless, "led this majority [the Shi'a] … to claim that they continue to be oppressed simply by being Shi'a."[38]

The Emergence of Sect-Centrism

It is this belief that led to the emergence of sect-centric Shi'a political movements. To begin with, these were rather marginal and were overshadowed by other more popular movements, such as the Iraqi Communist Party, which fought in the name of broader conceptions of social justice beyond the prism of sectarian identity. Over the decades, however, several factors emerged to reverse this. Firstly, the state's everincreasing authoritarianism was accompanied by an intensification and hardening of Shi'a activism, both qualitatively and quantitatively.[39] This accentuated the state's suspicions of political Shi'ism and of the mobilization of Shi'a identity, which in turn served to deepen Shi'a resentment and broaden the base of Shi'a-centric movements.

By the 1970s Shi'a political activism was becoming more outspoken, resulting in increasingly violent confrontations with the state. This escalation was partly shaped by the regional environment and deteriorating relations with Iran, a trend that was only accelerated by the Iranian revolution of 1979. The demise of Arab nationalism and communism as significant political forces and the emergence of the Islamic Republic (and regional Islamist movements in general) further explain the growing relevance of Shi'a-centric movements to the organized opposition within Iraq and beyond. Beginning in the 1980s, but particularly in the 1990s, the opposition-in-exile came to be heavily dominated by Kurdish ethnocentric and Shi'a sect-centric movements, both of which were viewed with intense suspicion by those Iraqis who subscribed in one way or another to the state's centralizing and homogenizing visions of Iraqi nationalism.[40]

These trends were amplified during the sanctions period of 1990–2003. The hardships of those years created sociopolitical realities that were to prove conducive to the institutionalization of identity politics in 2003. Nowhere was this more evident than in the opposition-in-exile, which even before the 1990s had seen the elevation of a once-marginal culture of political sect-centricity to a position of dominance in the non-Kurdish opposition to Saddam Hussein's regime. This sect-centricity was founded on the belief amongst Shi'a that they were uniquely victimized by the Ba'ath regime, coupled with an equally strong sense of entitlement based on their politically underrepresented demographic weight. Whilst such convictions pre-date the 1990s, they were significantly accelerated during the sanctions years as a result of several factors: the legacy of the Iran-Iraq war and the empowerment of political Shi'ism in Iran; the Gulf war and particularly the Shi'a uprisings that followed in 1991; the social impact of the economic sanctions and the mass migration witnessed throughout the 1990s; and finally, the increased involvement and interest of foreign patrons in Iraqi opposition movements.[41]

It is worth highlighting here that the post-2003 "sectarianization of Iraq," which is often solely blamed on the occupation authorities, had several more authors, not least of whom were the newly empowered Iraqi political elites. Long before 2003 we find a mutually reinforcing affinity between how Iraq was imagined in US policy and the Iraqi opposition's sect-centricity and ethnocentricity. The simplistic three-way division of Iraq into oppressive Sunnis and victimized Shi'a and Kurds was adopted—cynically or otherwise—by much of the Iraqi opposition-in-exile and by their foreign patrons. This was perhaps to be expected, as the Iraqi opposition, particularly by the 1990s, was largely the product of ethnocentric and sect-centric movements: Kurdish nationalists and Shi'a-centric political actors whose politics were deeply embedded in their senses of communal victimhood and communal entitlement. Such forms of sectional advocacy, whilst being perfectly legitimate, and at times necessary, in any political system, were elevated to the defining principle of national politics after regime change. This elevation was not simply the product of American calculation: it reflected the nature of the newly empowered political elites and their evolution over previous decades; indeed, some of the most important actors in the Iraqi opposition had advocated the adoption of ethno-sectarian quotas from as early as 1992.[42]

The rise in sect-centricity was not restricted to exiles. Both in Iraq and beyond, the 1990s saw the withering away of a hitherto deep-seated aversion to discussions of sects and "sectarianism" and the mainstreaming of more assertive forms of Shi'a identity.[43] Consequently, while the exiled opposition lacked a social base, and often even lacked name recognition within Iraq, by 2003 their sect-centricity and attachment to varying forms of identity politics resonated with a significant body of Shi'a opinion. This was illustrated immediately after the fall of the regime through the abundant displays of popular religiosity and the triumphalist assertion of Shi'a identity.

The relevance of Shi'a sect-centricity would soon be reflected in the electoral process: for a certain Shi'a constituency, regime change was not just Iraq's liberation from tyranny, but the moment of their deliverance as a sectarian group within Iraq. To this mindset, 2003 was a unique opportunity through which to ensure the empowerment of Shi'a-centric political actors, thereby validating the Shi'a's senses of entitlement and victimhood by translating their demographic weight into political dominance. This partly explains the sweeping success of the United Iraqi Alliance—the grand Shi'a electoral coalition—in the December 2005 elections. As reported at the time by the International Crisis Group:

> Even secular Shiites appear to have voted for the UIA rather than for the available alternatives. ... In the words of a western diplomat, they may well have voted "against the hijacking of a historical opportunity for the Shiites."[44]

While it is necessary to acknowledge the pre-2003 roots of post-2003 sectarianization, it is equally important to guard against tautologies that predetermine the institutionalization of identity politics after regime change. Sect-centric political actors and those sections of society that were receptive to them were one voice amongst many in 2003. Even if we were to make the fairly safe assumption that theirs formed the broadest and most organized position along Iraq's immediate post-invasion political spectrum, we should be mindful of the fact that this position was empowered and privileged in the new Iraq as a result of US policy and the evolution of diaspora politics.

With hindsight one can argue that the course taken after 2003 was not inevitable, but was always likely: conditions in Iraq, the country's divisive history, and the nature of the Iraqi opposition-in-exile made identity politics the path of least resistance for returning Iraqi politicians in search of a constituency, and for American policymakers trying to manage the ill-conceived occupation of Iraq. Indeed, more than just the path of least resistance, the appeal to Shiʻa-centricity reflected the long-held sect-centricity of many of the most seasoned opponents of the former regime and the depth of sect-centricity in significant sections of Shiʻa society. As such, one could argue that the drivers of Shiʻa-centric politics came from both above and below: it was championed by Shiʻa elites and by US policy, but it also fed off preexisting social divisions, fears, and aspirations. That Shiʻa are the long-oppressed majority who should rule Iraq was not an idea invented by US policymakers, nor was it the preserve of Shiʻa-centric politicians in exile; rather, for many Shiʻa it was a long-held article of faith dating back to the foundations of the modern Iraqi state. Unsurprisingly, it proved problematic in post-2003 Iraq in that its main practical implication was Shiʻa ascendency (through demographic weight) rather than sectarian equality. As such, it has proven incompatible with and resistant to an a-sectarian or sect-blind approach to Iraq: for those who are implicitly or explicitly Shiʻa-centric in their politics, a sect-blind approach would be rejected for fear that it would squander the Shiʻa's demographic advantage and that it would stifle the expression of Shiʻa identities.

2003 and the Emergence of Sunni Identity

Prior to 2003 Sunnis in Iraq seldom had much reason to perceive themselves in explicitly sectarian terms. They never felt threatened or persecuted as Sunnis; not in their relations with the state, not in how the threat of political Shiʻism was viewed, and not even during the Iran-Iraq war.

The power relations that underpinned state-society relations granted Sunnis enough ontological security to allow them to see themselves as more or less "sect-less": they were "normal" Iraqis and "normal" Muslims with no need for hyphenation or sect-coding.[45] In this, they reproduced the dominant discourse's vilification of sectarian identities and sectarian expression, and were particularly receptive to the state's demonization of Shi'a-centric political actors, who were relentlessly framed as traitors and as agents of Iranian enmity. Until 2003 Sunni Arab Iraqis enjoyed the identity security that arises from the conviction that "we" are the *Staatsvolk* whose identity is validated in the daily reproduction of power relations.

This lent them a degree of obliviousness to the realities of sectarian privilege—real or perceived—and to Shi'a sect-centricity. Prior to 2003 many Sunnis had never encountered or even known of the existence of an alternate Shi'a-centric narrative of Iraqi nationalism. For many if not most Sunnis, a differentiated and explicitly Shi'a political consciousness was an alien and irredeemably negative notion that was only visible when it was highlighted by Saddam's regime as evidence of pro-Iranian treason. Even the Shi'a's demographic strength—the bedrock of their sense of victimhood and entitlement—was something of an alien concept to Sunnis, many of whom would in no way have perceived Baghdad as anything even approaching a Shi'a-majority city.[46] After regime change many Sunnis contested not just the Shi'a's demographic weight but even the notion that Sunnis are a minority at all.[47]

Suddenly Sect-Coded: The Shock of Recognition

In 2003 the power relations that had sustained the Sunnis' sense of being "sect-less" were disturbed. Suddenly they were sect-coded, implicitly vilified, and reduced to minority status. Regime change forced Sunnis to reimagine themselves as a sectarian group, both as a response to the political empowerment of Shi'a sect-centricity and in order to be relevant in a system fundamentally based on identity politics. Unsurprisingly, the Sunni identity that emerged from this was significantly driven by antagonism toward the post-2003 order. To a significant body of Sunni opinion, the new Iraq was inherently contentious. For reasons already discussed, while pre-2003 dynamics had left many Shi'a more receptive to identity politics and sect-centricity, the pre-2003 legacy predisposed Sunnis to regard the sectarian frame as alien and threatening.

Elevating ethno-sectarian identities and communal victimhood into the founding principles of national politics not only disadvantaged Sunnis due to their demographic weakness and their lack of sectarian self-awareness, sect-centric organizations, and structures, but struck many of them as somewhat alien, if not downright sinister. Worse, perhaps, was having to accept political figures who had long been framed as the epitome of treason and duplicity: Kurdish separatists and Iranian-sponsored Shi'a Islamists. As succinctly argued by Harith al-Qarawee, the pre-2003 state had convinced Sunnis that they were confronted with three major threats: foreign occupation; Kurdish separatism; and political Shi'ism:

> In 2003 Sunni Arabs woke up and saw these three enemies—the occupiers, the Kurdish nationalists and the Shi'a Islamists—sitting together and setting the rules for the new Iraq.[48]

Perhaps a more basic obstacle facing Sunni acceptance of the post-2003 order was that it carried an overt sense of Shi'a ownership that made it difficult for Sunnis, unaccustomed as they were to thinking of themselves as a sectarian group (much less as a minority one), to subscribe to a new national mythology based on the symbols and narratives of what would formerly have been considered an out-group. That in some cases these symbols and narratives excluded if not vilified Sunnis made their acceptance of the realities of post-2003 Iraq all the more difficult.[49] As such, despite their long-held aversion to the assertion of sub-national identities, Sunni opponents of the post-2003 order had to become as sect-centric as the system they derided for its sect-centricity.[50]

It is in this contentious and defensive context that a coherent sense of Sunni identity began to emerge in Iraq. As a result, it is chiefly characterized by a profound sense of victimhood and deep resentment toward the post-2003 state. This has propelled a spectrum of Sunni rejection ranging from begrudging acceptance of the new order to armed rebellion against it.[51] The centrality of rejection to post-invasion Sunni identity has proved problematic in that Sunni leaders have often found themselves seeking a greater share of a system that many of their constituents deem illegitimate and whose demise they would welcome. It has also fostered a pronounced ambivalence amongst some sections of Sunni society toward anti-state violence.[52] Furthermore, there is also the danger that Sunni rejection of the post-2003 order may ultimately translate into an alienation from the Iraqi nation-state, something already seen on the most extreme end of the spectrum of Sunni rejection in the form of ISIS. Likewise, and particularly at times of heightened tension, the line separating Sunni rejection of empowered political Shi'ism from outright anti-Shi'ism can easily be blurred.[53]

No End in Sight

The central contention of this chapter is that a coherent understanding of post-2003 sectarian relations necessitates an understanding of pre-2003 sectarian dynamics. Sectarian relations have undergone previously unimaginable changes over the past thirteen years, but in large part these are the result of and have built on cumulative processes that had been in motion for several generations. While there was nothing inevitable about the unprecedented sectarian entrenchment that has marked post-2003 Iraq, several factors made it more likely:

(1) Post-2003 Iraq had to contend with a legacy of failed nation-building and a persistent mismanagement of communal plurality. This in turn led to varying degrees of sect-centricity amongst elites and masses and to divergent, sect-coded visions of Iraqi nationalism and Iraqi history.

(2) The way regime change was executed and the politics and backgrounds of those who were empowered made 2003 all the more divisive and made the reactions to the political changes of that year all the more extreme.

(3) The failures of the occupation and of successive Iraqi governments facilitated the downward spiral toward civil war that further perpetuated sectarian entrenchment.

The drivers behind these processes were no less complex, with local, national, regional, top-down, and bottom-up factors interacting in a cyclical fashion that endowed the accelerated sectarianization of Iraq with self-perpetuating and contagious qualities that were to spread across the region.

This "sectarianization" process is not restricted to the institutionalization of identity politics or to the empowerment of sect-centric actors; it also encompasses the reactions to these events and the dynamics and processes that they set in motion. Within Iraq we see an as-yet-unresolved tension between Shi'a-centric state-building and Sunni rejection. The horrific violence that has accompanied this process has further justified and normalized the logic of sectarian entrenchment and accentuated the competition of sect-centric senses of victimhood and entitlement.[54]

Beyond Iraq, we see similar dynamics in that regional powers and regional non-state actors have fueled and taken part in the Iraqi contest between Shi'a-centric state-building and Sunni rejection. Consequently the prism of sectarian identity has increasingly overlapped with regional geopolitics, or at least with how these are framed.[55] This process of regionalization was accelerated by the fact that the birth of the new Iraq perfectly coincided with the emergence of social media.[56] The evolution of these trends between 2003 and 2011 meant that the Arab uprisings unfolded in a less than benevolent regional environment, as has been most tragically and devastatingly illustrated in the case of Syria.[57]

What the sectarianization of (firstly) Iraq and (then) the region has meant in practice has been that sectarian identity has had an inordinate and seemingly ever-expanding capacity to inhere in how people perceive their social and political horizons, as evidenced by the fact that ever-wider social and political phenomena succumb to sect-coding today. At times this has seen tragedy turn into farce, as in the extension of sect-coding even to children's toys. In 2011 several videos emerged of a toy gun that, when fired, emitted a command to strike Aisha, the Prophet's wife and a subject of intense Sunni-Shi'a disagreement. The videos informed viewers that this was but a part of Shi'a machinations against the Sunni world. The issue gained enough traction for it to be raised on satellite channels, at pulpits across the region, and even in the Egyptian House of Representatives, where the toy gun was presented as evidence of the pernicious spread of Shi'ism and of its relentless hatred of all things Sunni. The tragicomic truth behind the sect-coding of the offending toy is that what was so readily believed to be evidence of the evils of organized Shi'ism turned out to be a case of poor English: rather than exhorting children to strike Aisha, the sound that the toy actually emitted was, "Go, go, go, pull over and save the hostages."[58]

As ridiculous as this episode is, it nevertheless illustrates the extent to which sections of Arab societies across the region have, since 2003, become prone to sectarian entrenchment, and how deep the mistrust has grown toward the sectarian "other" amongst them. The hypersensitivity of sectarian identities in several parts of the post-2003 Arab world is fundamentally related to the perceived balance of power between sect-centric political actors within individual countries and across the region. While this was always contested, it was only truly upset in 2003, when the structures of power were dismantled in Iraq and a sect-centric righting of historical wrongs was attempted. The misguided way in which this unfolded and the vicious reaction it elicited have spawned a web of interrelated tensions and conflicts that have fundamentally reshaped the region.

While some Iraqis may have hoped for 2003 to be the moment that would usher in a clean slate in which the tensions and "sectarianism" of the past would finally be resolved, what has instead happened is that the cumulative cost of failed nation-building and the mismanagement of communal plurality has only been amplified by the mistakes and failures of the past thirteen years and by the aggressive reaction to the upending of the pre-2003 balance of power between sect-centric actors. With the current Iraqi state's cautiousness about Sunni identity now rivalling that of the *ancien régime* toward Shi'a identity, and with the interweaving of multiple sect-coded conflicts and tensions within Iraq and across the region, the post-2003 sectarianization of Iraq and its immediate sur-roundings seems to be a process that is far from over.

7

THE SHATTERED NATION

THE SECTARIANIZATION OF THE SYRIAN CONFLICT

Paulo Gabriel Hilu Pinto

In this chapter I map the sectarianization of the Syrian conflict, a process that has unfolded on multiple levels: top-down (state generated); bottom-up (socially generated); outside-in (fueled by regional forces); and inside-out (the spread of Syria's conflict into neighboring states).

The appalling violence of the Syrian war, distributed along largely sectarian lines; the Assad regime's claim that it is protecting "religious minorities" from a Sunni Islamist uprising; and the consolidation of openly sectarian groups such as Jabhat al-Nusra (the Nusra front) and, in a more dramatic way, ISIS, as key actors in the conflict—all of these factors have led to the consolidation of sectarianism, for many observers and participants, as the interpretive key to the Syrian tragedy. Upon closer observation, however, the situation appears much more complex and indeterminate than the narratives about the "inherent hostility" between a radicalized Sunni majority and the other religious groups in the country allow.

While it is undeniable that the Syrian protesters mobilized religious references from the beginning of the uprising, they did it within the discursive limits of a religious nationalism that was elaborated and fostered by Bashar al-Assad's government itself. Their early demands were framed in universalistic political terms, such as the reform—or the end—of the Bashar al-Assad's rule, the restoration of freedom (*huriyya*) and "dignity" (*karama*). To be sure, sectarian tensions were not unknown in Syria and, indeed, had been on the rise since 2006, due mainly to the impact of the sectarian violence ravaging neighboring Iraq on the growing discontent of Syrian Sunni Muslims with Bashar al-Assad's religious policies. But sectarian tensions are not the same as sectarianism, which can be defined as the political mobilization of religious differences as a framework for the distribution of rights, privileges, and/or violence among a certain population.[1]

"Sectarianism" thus has no explanatory power to make sense of the Syrian conflict. It is, rather, a political tool that was shaped and fostered by many actors in the conflict. To analyze how sectarianism emerged as a discursive and practical framework in the Syrian conflict, I will examine the religious context upon which it was constructed; the agents of sectarianism and their strategies of fostering it in order to get or maintain power; and the political and social context that enabled sectarianism to become a major idiom through which political projects were expressed and violence was distributed in a situation of generalized armed conflict.

The Deployment of Religious Idioms in the Syrian Uprising: Religious Nationalism and State Sectarianism

When it began in 2011, the popular uprising against the regime mobilized the regions of the country that had been marginalized and impoverished by the decade of neoliberal economic reforms fostered by Bashar al-Assad: the agricultural regions (Euphrates, Hawran, Idlib, and Hama), the coastal areas (Baniyas, Latakiya), and the industrial city of Homs. While anti-government protests did take place in Damascus and Aleppo in February and March of 2011, both cities remained relatively calm during the first year of the uprising, even becoming the stage of several pro-Bashar demonstrations.[2]

As early as January 2011 there were demonstrations of discontent with the Assad regime,[3] such as episodes of civil disobedience and even self-immolations.[4] In February 2011 hundreds of people protested in

Damascus, chanting "The Syrian people will not be humiliated" after traffic police officers assaulted the son of a merchant in the Hariqa district.[5] Throughout that month, anti-government protests were violently dispersed by the security forces. The first episodes of civil unrest were met by both violence from the security forces and nonchalant scorn from Bashar al-Assad himself. In an interview with the *Wall Street Journal* at the end of January 2011, Assad compared the protesters in the Arab world with "microbes" and assured the interviewer that Syria was "stable" because, according to him, the government was "closely linked" to the people's beliefs.[6] Ironically, it was exactly the overzealous repression by the security forces that ignited an uprising on a national scale.

The arrest and torture in March 2011 of fifteen students, between ten and fifteen years old, for writing the slogan of the Tunisian revolution—"al-Shaʻb yurid isqat al-nizam" (the people want the downfall of the regime)—on their school's wall in the southern town of Derʻa sparked a series of mass protests that are widely considered to mark the "beginning" of the Syrian uprising. In a rapid succession of events, local solidarity with the families affected by the arrests transformed personal grievances against the state into political indignation against the Assad regime. By March 25 the whole central area of the town was under the control of the protesters. The Syrian army only regained control after a large military operation at the end of April.

Once Derʻa fell back under the regime's control, other towns and cities—such as Baniyas, Jeble, Latakiya, Idlib, Hama, Homs, Raqqah, and Dayr al-Zur—became centers of anti-government civil protest, sometimes even escaping governmental control and becoming self-ruled areas. After a cautious beginning, the demands for "reform" were displaced by more emphatic demands for dignity (*karama*) and freedom (*huriyya*). In this process, the Syrian protesters appropriated the slogans of the Tunisian and Egyptian revolutions, and started to create their own vocabulary for demanding political change and the end of the authoritarian rule of the Assad regime.

The Syrian uprising was marked by the widespread use of religious spaces, symbols, and vocabulary by the protesters. In the demonstrations, political slogans demanding freedom, justice, or the end of the Assad regime were combined with the chanting of "Allahu Akbar" (God is great) and "La ilah illa Allah" (There is no god but God), which expressed the use of shared religious vocabulary by the protesters.

Because the protesters could not take continuous hold of open urban spaces, mosques became the only spaces where they could gather and organize out of sight of the security forces.

This deployment of religious vocabulary and symbols to express political opposition to the Assad regime reflected the importance of Islam as a moral framework for action in Syrian society. The regime promoted a form of religious nationalism to gain the support of pious Muslims, as international pressure mounted on Syria following the assassination of Lebanese prime minister Rafiq al-Hariri in 2005, leading to the withdrawal of Syrian troops from Lebanon.

In contrast to the secular nationalism of early Ba'ath rule, Hafez al-Assad, who ruled Syria from 1970 until his death in 2000, used religious symbols to gain the support of Syria's majority Sunni Muslim population, especially following the massive military repression his regime unleashed against the revolt led by the Syrian Muslim Brotherhood against his rule (1979–1982). This was limited mainly to periods of heightened religiosity, such as Ramadan. The accession of Bashar al-Assad saw a new religious nationalism, and the construction of a "pious" persona for the Syrian dictator. Images of Bashar praying, holding a Qur'an, and kissing it became conspicuous not only in the official media, but throughout the country's urban landscape.

The regime's deployment of religious symbols and vocabulary led to a reconfiguration of the nationalist discourse fostered by the Syrian state. Billboards displaying a picture of Bashar al-Assad with a map of Syria with the colors of the national flag and the sentence "Allah yahmiki ya Suriya" (God protects you, O Syria) were erected all over the country. Assad uttered this phrase during a speech at the University of Damascus, and it became part of the official state discourse with the aim of whipping up nationalistic feelings in the population. Indeed, the fusion of Islamic references and nationalistic discourse allowed this slogan to capture the imagination of a variety of social actors, well beyond the groups that participated in the Ba'athist system of governance.[7]

During the first year of the uprising the religious references mobilized by the protesters were seen as having an inclusive potential by many non-Sunnis, in part because of their similarity to the religious nationalism that developed during Bashar al-Assad's presidency. Thus, both Sunnis and members of the other religious groups, such as Christians, 'Alawis, Druze, and Ismailis, could be seen in protests that were, nevertheless, full of Islamic references. For example, in 2012 protesters in al-Qusayr, a town near Homs, started to perform body movements imitating a Sufi *dhikr*[8] while chanting anti-government slogans. Notwithstanding the obvious evocation of a Sunni Muslim ritual, there were Christians taking part in the protest as well.[9]

Even the use of mosques as spaces of protest had a multilayered symbolic dimension that went beyond the simple affirmation of Sunni Muslim identities or Islamic values. The symbolic importance acquired by the Umayyad mosques of Damascus, Aleppo,[10] and Der'a during the protests reflected not only their significance as religious spaces, but also their construction by the Assad regime as sites of memory (*lieux de mémoire*)[11] of the Syrian nation.

Despite the complexity of these symbolic references and their clear association with a religious nationalism fostered by the Assad regime itself, from the outset of the uprising the Syrian government pointed to the importance of mosques and the religious vocabulary of the protests as "proof" that the protesters were Salafi radicals or members of the Muslim Brotherhood. In a speech in January 2012 Bashar al-Assad identified the protesters with the al-Qaeda terrorists of 9/11, saying:

> What we are doing now is similar to what the West did against Islam in the wake of 9/11. ... We say that there is a great religion—Islam, and there are terrorists taking cover under Islam. ... If we go back to the 1970s and 1980s, when the devil's brothers [Muslim Brothers], who covered themselves with Islam, carried out their terrorist acts in Syria. In the beginning there were many Syrians who were misguided. ... The question is a race between the terrorism and reform.[12]

From the outset, the regime aimed to present the protesters as violent jihadists, isolating them from other groups in Syrian society and legitimizing the brutal repression of the protests through the international narrative of the American-led "War on Terror." Also, by presenting terrorism or the regime as the only possible choices, Assad's discourse made clear that the regime would in no way take the political demands of the protests into account.

My Sect is Freedom

While the geography of the protests partially overlapped with the regions where the Salafiyya[13] had a stronger presence in Syria—the Hauran, the

Euphrates valley, Idlib, and the outskirts of the big cities—this does not by itself prove that radical Muslim groups were driving the protests.[14] The Salafi milieus in Syria were heavily influenced by Nasir al-Din al-Albani (1914–1999), who preached a quietist and apolitical form of Islam,[15] and they lacked the forms of organization that could allow them to shape the dynamics of the protests. The only Islamist militant organization that had an organized presence in Syria was Hizb al-Tahrir, which is not jihadist, with a membership estimated at a thousand followers in Homs.[16]

The influence of this non-political version of Salafism could be seen in the constant denunciation by Salafi protestors themselves of jihadists or, as they were called in Syria, *takfiris* (those who accuse others of apostasy), as "foreign agents." A participant in the uprising in the region of Homs explained his rejection of the regime's accusations to a journalist as follows:

> The Muslims of the land of *Sham* [Syria] follow the path of moderation. To live well, they follow the example of the pious ancestors. … That is the original meaning of Salafist. The other meaning, the Takfirist, jihadist, terrorist version, is a creation of the Americans and Israelis. It has nothing to do with us.[17]

Despite the presence of Salafis among the protesters, when looking at the images of the demonstrations in places such as Hama and Homs until 2011, it's impossible not to notice that the carnival-like style of the protests—with *dabke* dancing and satirical songs—did not square with any pattern of radicalized Salafism, as it usually rejects such behavior.

The accusations of Sunni sectarianism and radicalism coming from the regime were refuted with irony by the protesters, who stressed the participation of non-Sunnis and non-Muslims in the demonstrations. A poster in a protest in the coastal city of Baniyas in 2011 read: "Hal al-shahid Hatim Hanna massihi salafi?" (Was the martyr Hatem Hanna a Salafi Christian?), a reference to a Christian protester killed by the security forces.[18] In the same year, a banner in a demonstration in Zabadani, near Damascus, stated: "La salafi wa la ikhwani … ana ta'ifati al-huri-yya" (Neither Salafi, nor [Muslim] Brother … My Sect is Freedom).[19] Similarly, in ethnically or religiously mixed areas such as the Kurdish regions of northern Syria or the Sunni/Christian/'Alawi cities of the coast, the chanting of "Wahid, Wahid, Wahid, al-Sh'ab al-Suri Wahid" (One, One, One, the Syrian People are One) became a common practice in the protests in 2011 and 2012.

Yet despite the efforts of the protesters to develop a counter-sectarian discourse inspired by inclusive definitions of Syrian nationalism, the regime's continuous propaganda had some success in deepening religious tensions in the society. Jonathan Littell documented several instances in 2012 of hostility toward the 'Alawi community[20]—to which the Assad family and a large part of the regime's inner core belong—among the protesters in Homs and al-Qusayr. One anti-government rebel told him: "The Army is corrupt, it's an army of thieves. ... All it does is make the Alawite community grow fatter."[21] Another one explained that Abu Musab al-Zarqawi, the Jordanian jihadist who founded al-Qaeda in Iraq, was his idol, "because he came to Iraq to confront Iran and the Shiites." However, his companion added: "But here, in Syria, it's not the same at all."[22]

These examples reflect that by 2012, while sectarian tensions were not entirely absent from the protests, many members of the opposition made considerable efforts to reject and contain these tendencies, and attempted to forge a more inclusive and open, post-Ba'athist vision of the Syrian nation. By presenting the protesters as sectarian, the regime aimed to exacerbate these tensions and delegitimize their demands, thus fracturing the opposition along sectarian lines in order to rally the country's religious minorities behind the regime. This strategy of sectarianization was hardly foreign to the regime: since Hafez al-Assad's rise to power in 1970, social divisions—sectarian, ethnic, and class—were continuously manipulated through unequal policies of cooptation and repression to shore up the regime and impose authoritarian forms of governance over Syrian society.[23]

With the repression of secular political parties, the Muslim Brotherhood became the main opposition to the Assad regime. After 1976 they engaged in an armed conflict against it.[24] By 1979 other Islamic groups had formed, and in 1980 the Islamic opposition was unified in the Islamic Front in Syria (al-Jabhat al-Islamiyya fi Suriya), under the leadership of the Muslim Brotherhood. The Brotherhood's key documents from 1980, *The Manifesto of the Islamic Revolution of Syria* and *The Programs of the Islamic Revolution*,[25] presented their project as aiming to create a political system inclusive of all Syrian citizens and respectful of the rights of individuals as well as Syria's religious and ethnic minorities.

But the documents also portrayed the Assad regime as anti-Islamic, sectarian, and 'Alawi dominated, and appealed to the 'Alawi community to stop its "attempt to force its oppressive domination over the great

SECTARIANIZATION

majority of the population."[26] The depiction of Assad's government as an "'Alawi regime," the vilification of the 'Alawis as un-Islamic, polytheistic traitors to the nation in several writings of the Islamic opposition,[27] and acts of violence committed against 'Alawis go back to the early 1980s. It was perceived as Sunni sectarianism, and thus strengthened the regime and prevented the Islamic Front from attracting support among religious minorities and secular Sunnis. The cycle of violence and radicalization culminated in a military showdown in 1982 in which the Syrian army destroyed most of Hama after the Muslim Brothers managed to take control of the city.[28]

After the bloody events in Hama, the Assad regime and the Sunni religious establishment began to seek accommodation to maintain the political status quo. The Muslim Brotherhood was banned in Syria and its leadership went into exile. Political Islam declined as an idiom for social grievances. The sectarian animosity of the period between 1979 and 1982 impacted Syrian society and politics, leading to its decline as a framework for expressing political or social discontent. However, after a long period of accommodation, sectarian tensions began to rise again under the presidency of Bashar al-Assad, as many Sunni Syrians started to express their discontent with the Shi'a appropriation of Syria's holy sites and with what they perceived as special privileges granted to Shi'a to the detriment of Sunnis.

Bashar al-Assad was building on a legacy of legitimizing Shi'a Islam in the Syrian religious landscape. The Syrian state and its Iranian counterpart joined forces to promote holy sites in Syria as destinations for Shi'a pilgrims. The establishment of a Shi'a pilgrimage route linking Iran to Syria gave a religious dimension to the geopolitical alliance between the two countries, and this new visibility of Shi'ism in Syria helped bolster the Islamic credentials of the 'Alawi community and the Assad regime.

However, the new religious and political realities created by the 2003 Anglo-American invasion and occupation of Iraq, such as the clashes between Sunni and Shi'a militias and political groups in an openly sectarian civil war between 2005 and 2008, fueled religious tensions in Syria. These reached new levels during the worst phase of the sectarian violence in Iraq between 2006 and 2008, when masses of refugees flocked into Syria. They were both Sunnis and Shi'a, but the increasing political power of the Shi'a in Iraq after 2003, together with the alliance

130

of some Shi'a political leaders with the Americans, led to a sense among Sunni Syrians that the Shi'a were some sort of "fifth column" driven by sectarian hatred against both Sunnism and Arab nationalism. Stories of the violence unleashed by Shi'a militias against Sunnis in Iraq confirmed the worst fears of many Syrians about Shi'a expansion.[29]

For Sunni Syrians the issue was to reclaim their sacred spaces and sites of memory, such as the Umayyad Mosque in Damascus, from religious actors they perceived as "foreign." The tension between Sunnis and Shi'a thus also came to be perceived as between "Syrians" and "foreigners," allowing an oblique critique of the Assad regime for privileging outsiders over its own citizens. At this point there was no explicit amalgam between the 'Alawi community and the Shi'a pilgrims who constituted the religious "other" in the discontented Sunni imaginary. Ironically, the conditions for deploying religious idioms to express grievances about the relation between the state and its citizens were created by the religious nationalism fostered by Bashar al-Assad's government.

This process led the Assad regime to change its policy from one of allowing greater visibility of Shi'ism in Syria's religious landscape to one of control and containment of public expressions of Shi'a religiosity after 2008. However, from the beginning of the protests in 2011 the regime did not hesitate to exploit religious tensions, with the aim of injecting a sectarian dimension into the uprising. Bashar al-Assad hoped to overcome his crisis of legitimacy by mobilizing the support of religious minorities in Syria and discrediting the protesters as intolerant and violent fanatics who could not be negotiated with, but had to be defeated.

Syria in Fragments: State Violence, Religious Mobilization, and Militarization in the Construction of Sectarian Strife

Five years after the beginning of the uprising, it is clear that the Assad regime has largely succeeded in inscribing a sectarian narrative into the Syrian conflict. However, it is important to understand those elements in the internal dynamics of the protests that allowed this to happen, and the social actors who contributed to this process. The continuous investment of discrete political, religious, and national imaginaries in the cultural idiom of anti-regime protests led to its saturation,[30] a process in which the capacity of the protests to provide cultural equivalence to the discrete and, sometimes, divergent meanings that were being expressed through them reached its limits.[31]

In the popular protests in Syria, the political slogan demanding the downfall of the regime was articulated with religious vocabulary and symbols, echoing the religious nationalism that had become conspicuous in the public discourse under Bashar al-Assad. While at first this religious nationalism was inclusive enough that 'Alawis, Druze, Christians, and Ismailis shared it with Sunnis in the protests, it gradually became more and more invested with exclusively Sunni meanings. This alienated the non-Sunni protesters, who became increasingly uncomfortable with the religious references mobilized in the protests, which they understood as expressions of Sunni sectarianism.

For example, the chanting of anti-Iranian and anti-Hezbollah slogans during the protests in Der'a,[32] which targeted the international allies of the Assad regime, was seen as anti-Shi'a sectarianism by many pro-regime 'Alawis. Also, the role of mosques and the use of Islamic religious vocabulary in the protests were often interpreted by some Christians as evidence of Sunni militancy. Even in all-Sunni demonstrations, the discrete religious and social imaginaries invested in the idiom of anti-regime protest took the form of incompatible social and political projects, as could be seen in the dispute over female participation in the protests in Homs.[33]

A complex web of misinformation and rumor exacerbated the precipitation of sectarian configurations in the hypersaturated universe of anti-regime protest. For example, from the beginning of the uprising, when I met Christian and 'Alawi interlocutors, they often spoke with a mix of fear and indignation about Sunni protesters in Homs and other cities, who were reportedly chanting "al-Masihiun ila Beirut wa al-'Alawiun fil-tabut" (The Christians to Beirut, and the 'Alawis in the coffin). Although none of them had actually witnessed this themselves, they were convinced it had happened. Other researchers have documented the role rumors played in collective mobilization and creating sectarian boundaries in the context of uncertainty and insecurity amidst the collapse of the Ba'athist order.[34]

The saturation of the anti-regime protests and the precipitation of divergent political visions—some of which had a sectarian character— were accentuated by the competition between discrete political and religious forces over the power to shape and control the protests. The secular opposition in Syria, the opposition in exile, and Sunni religious figures both inside Syria and in exile all vied for a leadership role in the protests. In August 2011, at the beginning of the holy month of Ramadan, the *ulama* of Damascus and Aleppo issued communiqués attributing the responsibility for the violence and deaths in Syria to the regime, urging it to end repression, start political reforms, and free political prisoners.[35]

The 'ulama' were not uniformly supportive of the uprising, however. Many high-profile religious figures, particularly those who benefited from the regime, rallied in support of Bashar al-Assad's rule. The most enthusiastic supporters of the regime were the Mufti of Syria, Ahmad Badr al-Din Hasun, and the "media shaykh," Muhammad Sa'id Ramadan al-Buti. A large part of the Sunni religious establishment in Syria, including many Sufi shaykhs in Aleppo who still remembered the repression directed against them after 1982, adopted a "wait and see" attitude in relation to the uprising. They condemned the regime's violence in their sermons but also discouraged their disciples from joining the protests. In some cases, even when a shaykh openly supported the uprising, his followers might refrain from protesting or confronting the regime.[36]

Syria's religious establishment was thus fractured along political lines, opening space for outsiders to assert themselves as moral leaders in the context of the uprising. The 'ulama' in exile began to vie for leadership of the uprising, often deploying sectarian discourses to attack the regime and its supporters. Satellite TV channels and the internet helped disseminate these discourses across Syria. A notorious case was Shaykh Adnan al-'Ar'ur, who was exiled in Saudi Arabia for having taken part in the Islamic uprising in 1982. In a TV program in June 2011, Shaykh 'Ar'ur, who was known for his anti-Shi'a positions, was commenting on the situation in Syria when he said:

> I am warning specifically the 'Alawi sect (al-ta'ifa al-'alawiyya): Those who don't take sides [in the conflict] will not be harmed. Anyone who supports us is on our side, and will be treated as any other citizen. But those who violate what is sacred, by God we will mince them in meat grinders and feed dogs with their flesh.[37]

The Sunni sectarian discourse of some of the new players in the Syrian political landscape, such as Shaykh 'Ar'ur,[38] was a gift to the regime, fueling its sectarianization narrative of the uprising as a Sunni militant revolt. The same can be said of figures who tried to reshape the uprising as *jihad*, such as Shaykh Abu Basir al-Tartusi.[39] However, some exiled Sunni shaykhs were also competing for the role of external "moral voices" of the uprising without resorting to sectarian discourses.

The Syrian Muslim Brothers, who were based in London, also tried to reestablish themselves in Syria. They became a major political force in the Syrian National Council, the umbrella political institution of the opposition, which was created in 2011 in Istanbul, and tried to recreate an internal base of support through the organization of relief aid to the protesters.[40] In preparation for a possible return to the political arena of a post-Assad Syria, the Muslim Brotherhood adopted a new charter in 2012, outlining their project of a post-Assad democratic and pluralistic political order,[41] which basically updated the main points of similar documents that the organization had issued in 1980, 2001, and 2004. All of these efforts proved ineffective in terms of creating a political base for the Brotherhood, however, in part because many Syrians still associated them with the disastrous 1982 uprising.

While the mobilization of Sunni religious authorities and organizations was expressed through a vast gamut of political and religious positions, it fed into the fears of non-Sunni communities, such as 'Alawis and Christians, who often interpreted Sunni political activism as a sign of sectarianism. With the growing Sunni assertiveness pervading the opposition, many members of non-Sunni groups ended up regarding the survival of the Assad regime as a lesser evil compared to the empowerment of Sunni sectarian figures, such as Shaykh 'Ar'ur.

The mobilization of some Sunni religious leaders inside Syria in competition over leadership of the uprising stood in contrast with the attitude of the Christian religious elite. Some Sunni shaykhs continued to support the regime, while others opposed it. Christian clerics, however, expressed their open commitment to Bashar al-Assad's rule in a much more unified way, seeing it as the sole protector of Syrian Christians. They were also instrumental in magnifying and manipulating the anxiety Christian communities felt about the prospects of the uprising turning into a Sunni "Islamic revolution." Priests of various Christian denominations expressed unconditional support for the dictator, and religious services were transformed into pro-Bashar rallies, as happened in the Sunday mass in the Church of the Cross in Damascus in 2011.[42] Some Christian clerics had free access to the media and resources, gaining national, and even international, visibility while promoting a strongly anti-Sunni sectarian discourse aimed at discrediting the opposition. The Lebanese-born Maronite nun Agnès Mariam de la Croix has toured Europe and the United States claiming that the entire opposition is composed of Islamist jihadists intent on killing Christians and 'Alawis.[43]

Dissident voices within the Christian clergy were met with silence from their churches, repressive measures from the state, and violence from sectarian groups. Interestingly, the 'Alawi shaykhs had a much less uniform reaction to the uprising, with some of them even signing a statement disavowing any connection to the 'Alawis involved with the repressive apparatus of the state.[44] However, the marginalization of the 'Alawi shaykhs, which was fostered by Hafez al-Assad's policy of religious assimilation, made their protests less effective than the sectarian discourse of the regime in mobilizing the 'Alawi community.[45]

Self-Fulfilling Prophecies and the Sectarian Distribution of Violence

Throughout 2011 and 2012, as a result of the sectarian frameworks mobilized by both the regime and the opposition, the participants in the protests became more homogeneously Sunni Muslim. Many Christians and 'Alawis refrained from participating, and identified less and less with the uprising and the political future it offered. Beyond that, the impact of massive state repression and the emergence of armed groups among the opposition created a context conducive to social and political fragmentation.[46] The hypersaturated idiom of anti-regime protest gradually precipitated along various social fault lines—sectarian, class, rural/urban, regional—into divergent social and political projects for Syria.

The dynamics of repression and the regime's strategic uses of violence were central to the sectarianization process. The repressive tactics deployed by the regime were in many ways a revival of those used in the time of the confrontation with the Islamic opposition in 1979–1982. The regime also used a selective distribution of violence in order to deepen sectarian fault lines among the protesters, dividing and isolating them. Whenever the protests occurred in mixed Sunni/'Alawi or Sunni/'Alawi/Christian cities, such as Latakiya and Baniyas, even when members from all communities took part in the protests, military and paramilitary violence was directed mainly to Sunni neighborhoods. An interlocutor who was in Latakiya in July 2011 told me: "During the day there would be protests in all neighborhoods, but at night only our [Sunni] streets were attacked by the army and the *shabiha* [ultra-violent pro-regime paramilitary gangs]."[47]

Not that the protesters from other religious communities were spared from violence, but instead of using military and paramilitary forces to deal with them, the regime used its security apparatus to mobilize internal repressive mechanisms under the threat that the entire community would be targeted if the actions of certain individuals were not suppressed. 'Alawi, Christian, and Druze protesters faced repression and violence from within their own groups, sometimes even from their own families.[48] This pattern of mobilization of community or family mechanisms of repression against non-Sunni protesters was described by the 'Alawi actress Fadwa Sulayman, who, after joining the uprising in Homs, declared in an interview in 2011 that:

> families from minority groups exert a lot of pressure on the individuals who dissent. Many splits within families are happening because of this. … People cannot voice their opposition because the government is even more brutal on dissidents belonging to minority groups than those from the majority Sunni Muslims. They threaten them and their families and children even before they decide to protest.[49]

There was thus a clear strategy of enhancing the visibility of the violence directed against Sunnis, rendering invisible the violence directed against non-Sunni groups. This fed into the regime's discourse that the uprising was led by Sunni militants and that the Assad regime was overwhelmingly supported by all the other religious groups, as their "protector" against Sunni radicalism. The resentment and suspicion created by the unequal distribution of violence between the various communities created a self-fulfilling prophecy in which the violence that the state claimed was necessary to crush sectarianism became the very mechanism through which sectarian tensions were inscribed or enhanced in the social fabric.

The regime also aimed to reinstate fear as an instrument of governance, as it had following the massacre in Hama in 1982. Paramilitary gangs known as *shabiha* (lit. "ghosts"/"shadows") were created by recruiting 'Alawi youth from impoverished areas, but also local mafias and convicts that Assad released from jail.[50] These gangs, together with regular security forces, carried out arrests, torture, mutilations, and executions in the areas that held protests against the government. The army and the *shabiha* jointly perpetrated several massacres throughout Syria. One of the largest of them happened in Hula, a village near Homs, where 108 people, including children and women, were slaughtered in May 2012 by the *shabiha*, who apparently came from nearby 'Alawi villages.[51]

This trend spread through the countryside, where religious and local identities became territorialized as villages and towns organized defense forces along sectarian lines. In religiously mixed regions, such as the

Ghab, near Hama, killings and clashes between armed groups from different villages allowed sectarian and political stereotypes, such as 'Alawi–Christian/pro-government and Sunni/anti-Ba'athist opposition, to acquire social reality by resignifying and reorganizing a variety of social conflicts that were recovered by and expressed through these categories. Arms smuggled from Lebanon fed this process of territorialization and militarization of locally produced configurations of regional, political, and sectarian identities,[52] creating a pattern of diffuse sectarian violence throughout central Syria.

Sectarianization through Militarization

Moreover, the continuous defection of soldiers and some high-ranking officials—mostly Sunnis—from the Syrian army led to the militarization of the protests. In Homs and other places, such as Idlib, defectors created brigades to defend the protesters against the army and the *shabiha*. In July 2011 a group of soldiers and officers defected from the Syrian military and created the Free Syrian Army (al-Jaysh al-Suri al-Hur, FSA). The militarization of the uprising helped inscribe a sectarian dimension in the movement as it became engulfed by the violence of civil war. The constitution of the FSA itself was overwhelmingly Sunni in all its echelons. While this fact reflected the structural disadvantages that Sunnis had to face in the Syrian armed forces as well as the fact that they were targeted by the state violence,[53] it strengthened the narrative that identified Sunnis with the opposition and non-Sunnis with the regime.

The consolidation of a sectarian understanding of the conflict happened also within the rebels groups, to the point that non-Sunni rebels were viewed with a mixture of amazement and suspicion. In 2013 an Ismaili defector went to join the FSA, and when the people who received him realized his religious affiliation, they said, "But you are not Sunni. ... So, why are you defecting?"[54] This trend was exacerbated by the selective distribution of violence through sectarian lines by the regime. By mid-2012 elements of the FSA were murdering 'Alawi villagers near Homs as a reprisal for the massacres of Sunni civilians by 'Alawi militias.[55]

While the FSA got some international support, in particular from Turkey, but also France and the USA, it did not translate into financing and access to weapons sufficient to match those of the Syrian army. Under these conditions it had problems maintaining discipline and containing the frustration of its fighters. The armed Islamist groups that proliferated after 2012 started to gain importance in this context, for they had strong support and financing from the Gulf states, in particular Qatar and Kuwait, as well as Turkey and Saudi Arabia. Many fighters in the FSA shifted their alliance to Islamic groups, fragmenting the armed opposition and boosting its Sunni character. Also, leaders of secular *katibas* (battalions) started "reinventing" themselves as Islamic *mujahidin* in order to receive funding from the Gulf states.[56]

There were many differences between the various Islamist groups that emerged in the armed opposition to Bashar. There were groups close to the Muslim Brotherhood with a "liberal" religious nationalist project; others with an "inclusive" Salafi orientation, such as Ahrar al-Sham (Freemen of Syria); and the jihadist ones, which besides fighting the regime entered into a violent competition with the other secular and Islamist groups in the opposition. Until 2013 the Islamist group that gained the most military, political, and media importance was Jabhat al-Nusra li-Ahli al-Sham (Support Front for the People of Syria), or simply Jabhat al-Nusra. It was created in 2012 as a Syrian franchise of al-Qaeda, and quickly established bases in the Euphrates region, Idlib province, and parts of Aleppo.

Besides military strength and greater resources, the rise of the Islamist groups was also due to their strong internal discipline and capacity of establishing some kind of institutional order in the territories they had conquered. Criminal activities became so widespread under the disorder created by the civil war that the inhabitants of Aleppo, which was partly occupied by the opposition in 2012, humorously fashioned a verb, *shawala* (to take away/lift/sting), to designate the systematic racketeering and pillage practiced by different militias.[57] A friend from Aleppo told me that when his father passed away in 2012, he only managed to bury the body after paying the "fees" (bribe) asked by the militia fighter who "controlled" the cemetery.[58]

While the fighters of the FSA often indulged in these practices, those of Jabhat al-Nusra were seen as more disciplined and less corrupt, to the point that in the fall of 2012 people in Aleppo sang while waiting in line for bread: "Jaysh al-Hur … harami, bidna Jaysh Islami" (Free [Syrian] Army … thieves, we want an Islamic Army).[59] Also, most of the legal institutions created in the areas controlled by the opposition claimed to follow the *shari'a* or to be inspired by it. While in most cases the *shari'a* courts were simply instances of legal mediation led by shaykhs and/or judges who had only superficial knowledge of Islamic jurisprudence,[60] they strengthened the association between the restoration of social order and Islamic rule.[61] This is one reason (among others) that Islamist militias grew in popularity.

This "normalization" of jihadist rule among populations that often did not share their interpretation of Islam or political ideals helped Jabhat al-Nusra to easily take over territories previously held by the FSA and other armed groups. It also prepared the way for the even more extreme form of jihadism of ISIS (al-Dawla al-Islamiyya fi al-'Iraq wa al-Sham; or simply al-Dawla al-Islamiyya). This group was created in 2013, and by mid-2014 had extended its presence in a vast territory in western Iraq and eastern Syria where it proclaimed the restoration of the Caliphate on June 29, 2014. This territory was conquered from Jabhat al-Nusra, the FSA, and other armed groups, rather than from the regime forces.[62]

Better armed, more tightly disciplined, and hell-bent on establishing their vision of public order, jihadist groups such as Jabhat al-Nusra and ISIS offered some semblance of stability to populations left to the mercy of unbounded state brutality, with barrel bombings and murderous incursions of the Syrian army and the *shabiha*, or the racketeering of rogue militia elements. This stability, however, came with a high price, as these groups had a strong sectarian character, accusing of disbelief (*kufr*) other Muslims with a different understanding and practice of Islam.

Thus, in the territories under its control, ISIS fined, physically punished, or killed "impious" Sunnis; executed social "deviants" (homosexuals, adulterers, prostitutes); allowed the killing and enslavement of groups considered as "apostates," such as the Yazidis; created a mass exodus of Christians after imposing on them the status of *dhimmi*; and destroyed "pagan" cultural heritage, such as the Roman temples in Palmyra, and "impious" monuments, such as the tombs of saints and Shi'a shrines in Raqqah. Jabhat al-Nusra has a less gruesome record, but also engaged in sectarian persecution of non-Sunni groups, such as the imposition of Sunni religiosity over a series of Druze villages near Idlib.[63]

The high level of sectarian violence of the jihadist groups is also related to the presence of foreign fighters among them, for they did not know or understand the cultural dynamics of Sunni Islam in Syria. While many jihadists are Syrians, there are a large number of those who crossed from Iraq or were released from jail by Assad, or came directly from Europe,

North Africa, or the Caucasus. This is particularly true in ISIS, where foreign fighters are present at all levels in the chain of command.[64]

Thus, despite its initial ease in conquering territories, ISIS faced growing resistance from the local populations to its religious policies. In June 2013 a fifteen-year-old boy who sold coffee in the streets of a well-known neighborhood in Aleppo was executed for blasphemy. He had replied to a customer, probably a fighter, who wanted free coffee with characteristic Aleppine irony, saying, "Even if Prophet Muhammad comes down from heaven, I will not give you my coffee for free." This execution caused a major uproar in Aleppo and, even if ISIS never claimed responsibility, the episode mobilized the population to help a coalition of the FSA and the Salafi group Ahrar al-Sham to expel it from Aleppo in January 2014.[65]

Furthermore, in 2013 the population of Dana, east of the city, revolted against the efforts of ISIS to impose its version of Islam on the villagers.[66] In Aleppo, Sufis organized themselves in order to protect their *zawiya*s (ritual lodges) from destruction by the jihadist/*takfiri* groups, who usually considered Sufi beliefs and practices to be un-Islamic.[67] These examples of civil resistance to the sectarian policies of the jihadist groups showed that their acceptance by the local population was due more to their capacity for restoring public order than the embracing of their worldview.

The consolidation of sectarianism via the political idiom of jihadism was not exclusive to the opposition, for Bashar al-Assad also resorted to religiously motivated paramilitary forces to reconquer lost territories. The growing number of defections from the army during 2011 and 2012 sapped the trust that the regime had in its own troops, creating a military disadvantage that was only reversed with the entrance of Hezbollah, Iraqi volunteers, and Iranian brigades into the Syrian conflict. While the constitution of these forces reflected strategic alliances among political players in the geopolitics of the Middle East, the reality on the ground was also shaped by sectarian overtones. This fed the perception among many Sunnis that the Assad regime was being propped up by a foreign/transnational web of Shi'a (and, in the case of Iran, Persian) forces.

While the Shi'a identity of Hezbollah was still blended with a pan-Arab nationalist discourse, the pro-Assad brigades created to absorb the foreign fighters who came to defend the regime had a clear Shi'a sectarian framework with references to Shi'a religious figures. Thus, the Abu al-Fadl al-'Abbas Brigade gathered Shi'a foreign fighters and has its headquarters near the Shi'a pilgrimage shrine of Sayyida Zaynab, in a suburb of

Damascus. The influx of Lebanese, Iraqi, Iranian, Yemeni, Afghan, and Pakistani Shiʻa volunteers also led to the constitution of a brigade named Dhu al-Fiqar, after the sword of Imam ʻAli, the first Shiʻa imam.[68] As they reconquered territories that were previously controlled by the opposition, these Shiʻa brigades proceeded to repress and eliminate all forms of Sunni piety that they considered reflections of Salafi tendencies.

Therefore, both sides of the conflict were territorializing religious identities and producing a more homogeneous religious landscape, inscribing their sectarian dynamic in the social reality through violence, dispossession, and expulsion of parts of the local populations. Tragically, the logic of violence and revenge is tearing apart the social fabric of the nation that all sides in the conflict claim they want to save.

Conclusion: Beyond the Sectarian Trap

After putting the contemporary situation into a broader social and historical context, we can say that the current sectarian strife in Syria is neither the inevitable result of religious antagonism nor an externally produced outcome without any base in the preexisting social reality. Sectarianism is a process of constructing political "others" along religious lines, which is unleashed and shaped by discourses and actions of specific actors who manage to mobilize religious fault lines toward political ends. It has emerged as a framework for political mobilization in a period of deep political and social crisis in the history of the Syrian nation-state, first seen in the Islamist uprising in the 1970s and 1980s, and subsequently in the aftermath of the 2011 popular uprising.

In a multi-religious and multi-ethnic society such as Syria, the failures of the state in creating a sense of equality and fairness in terms of rights and the distribution of resources can be translated into diffuse resentment and hostility against the groups that are perceived as benefiting from it. The Assad regime often exploited these tensions in order to maintain its grip over Syrian society by presenting itself as the "defender" of religious minorities and secular Muslims against the menace of a Sunni majority putatively prone to radicalization.

However, the translation of diffuse and contextual religious tensions into the systematic political antagonism that characterizes sectarianism requires intense mobilization of groups within sectarian discursive frameworks, the silencing of dissonant voices, and the drawing of boundaries through the unequal distribution of violence among the various religious communities. The cycle of violence, victimization, and revenge forces individuals and collectivities to position themselves and act according to the very sectarian categories that enable it.

While the processes of sectarianization of identities and the homogenization of local societies that resulted from the use of violence within sectarian frameworks are realities created by the civil war that probably will have long-lasting social and political effects, this does not mean that Syrian society will be forever trapped in the logic of sectarianism. There are non-sectarian forces in the conflict, and even in places controlled by sectarian groups there are many instances of resistance to and rejection of sectarianism. Therefore, if Syria survives the conflict as a unified nation-state, there are possibilities of reinventing forms of coexistence among the various religious groups within the social and political body. Nevertheless, this will not be an easy path, and will depend on the will and capacity of Syrians looking beyond the boundaries drawn by the sectarian violence and overcoming a tragic history of using religious differences to create political alterities in moments of crisis. Sectarian identities are easy to launch and activate, but, once the proverbial genie is out of the bottle, it can take on a life of its own. Putting it back in the bottle can prove much more difficult than unleashing it.

8

SECTARIANISM AS COUNTER-REVOLUTION

SAUDI RESPONSES TO THE ARAB SPRING[1]

Madawi Al-Rasheed

Saudi Arabia is a wealthy oil-producing country with a small population not exceeding 28 million, one-third of whom are foreigners. The authoritarian Al Saud ruling family has controlled the country since 1932.[2] Historically, the Saudi rentier state used economic largesse in return for loyalty to the regime.[3] Yet the literature on the rentier state does not highlight other strategies that are often deployed to gain loyalty and force the population into submission. Sectarianism as a regime strategy is often ignored in the literature on the rentier state, especially in countries where there is religious diversity.[4]

In response to the Arab Spring, sectarianism became a preemptive counter-revolutionary strategy that the Saudi regime deployed to exaggerate religious difference and hatred and prevent the development of national non-sectarian politics. Through religious discourse and practices, sectarianism in the Saudi context involves not only politicizing religious differences, but also creating a rift between the majority Sunnis and the Shi'a minority. At the political level, the rift means that Sunnis and Shi'a are unable to create joint platforms for political mobilization. Neither essentialist arguments about the resilience of sects nor historical references to seventh-century Sunni-Shi'a battles over the Caliphate can explain the persistence of antagonism and lack of common political platforms among Sunnis and Shi'a in a country like Saudi Arabia.[5] Sectarian conflict between Sunnis and Shi'a can never be understood without taking into account the role played by an agency much more powerful than the sects themselves: the authoritarian regime. In addition to massive oil rents, the Saudi regime has at its disposal a potent religious ideology, commonly known as Wahhabism, renowned for its historical rejection of the Shi'a as a legitimate Islamic community.[6]

The Saudi regime's oppression of the Shi'a minority in turn contributes to the consolidation of that minority's sectarian identity: the *sectarianization* process at work. But it is too simplistic to reduce relations between the regime and the Shi'a minority to oppression alone. The Saudi authoritarian regime deploys multiple strategies when it comes to its religious minorities and their leadership. Wholesale systematic discrimination against the Shi'a may be a characteristic of one particular historical moment, but this can be reversed. A political situation may require alternatives to repression. Sometimes repression is combined with co-optation and even promotion of minority interests and rights. Furthermore, the regime may repress the Shi'a in order to address issues relevant to the Sunni majority, for example to appease them, respond to their grievances, or simply seek their loyalty at a time when this cannot be taken for granted. Therefore, it is important to note that there is no regular and predictable strategy deployed by Saudi authoritarianism against the Shi'a. Each historical moment requires a particular response toward this community, ranging from straightforward repression to co-optation and concession. The Arab Spring and its potential impact on the country pushed the regime to reinvigorate sectarian discourse against the Shi'a in order to renew the loyalty of the Sunni majority.

In this chapter I explain how the Saudi regime used sectarian divisions to widen the gap between the two communities during the Arab Spring. The regime claimed that external agents were determined to undermine the country's stability and security. It called upon Wahhabi religious interpretations—in particular, sectarian discourse against the very politically active Shi'a minority, estimated at 2 million—in order to abort the development of "national politics" that crosses sectarian, regional, ideological, and tribal boundaries.[7] By constructing calls for demonstrations on the "Day of Rage" on March 11, 2011 as a Shi'a conspiracy against the Sunni majority with the objective of spreading Iran's influence in the Sunni homeland, the regime deepened sectarian tension and undermined efforts to mobilize the youth in various cities, including those where the Shi'a live. The Saudi regime frightened its own Sunni majority by exaggerating the Iranian expansionist project in the region and its rising influence among the Shi'a of the Arab world, including Saudi Arabia and the Gulf countries.

The regime propaganda succeeded in thwarting protest that by all expectations would not have amounted to an Egyptian-style fully fledged revolution. Instead, the very minor peaceful protests that started in 2011 in Saudi cities would merely have marked the beginning of political mobilization without amounting to a revolution. Even without the preconditions for a revolution in Saudi Arabia, an authoritarian regime was bound to take preemptive counter-revolutionary measures in anticipation of the domino effect of the Arab Spring.

Recent Saudi sectarianism must also be understood in light of events in the neighboring island of Bahrain, where a Sunni royal family rules over a Shi'a majority.[8] Sectarian discourse proved to be successful in suppressing the Bahraini pro-democracy movement. Saudi troops moved into Bahrain in February 2011 in support of the ruling Al Khalifa family against the protestors. This allowed the Saudi regime to send strong signals not only to its own politically agitated Shi'a minority, many of whom have religious, social, and kinship ties with the Bahrainis, but also more importantly to the Sunni majority inside Saudi Arabia. The regime compelled its Sunni majority, long brought up on a sectarian discourse that denounces the Shi'a as heretics, to consider their government as a protector against Shi'a conspiracies and foreign agents allegedly acting in the name of Iran, a rival regional power. The regime hoped that the Sunni majority would abandon calls for political change, at least at this critical moment of the Arab Spring. Under the pressures of a tense regional context and internal virtual and real mobilization, it seems that many Saudis have postponed their confrontation with the regime but continue to call for political reform. Moreover, the economic benefits distributed by the king in March 2011 seem to have satisfied the immediate economic and social grievances of the population, without addressing political reform.

Saudi Sectarian Politics: A Historical Overview

In Saudi Arabia, deliberate, well-documented political exclusion and systematic religious discrimination against the Shi'a pushed this community to rally around its own sectarian leadership, which provides support and resources denied in the national arena.[9] Both exclusion and discrimination contribute to the consolidation of Shi'a internal sectarian boundaries and cohesion. Moreover, while freedom of association is restricted and there is a ban on the formation of political parties and civil society, the religious sphere remains relatively open. In addition to being a place of worship, the mosque has increasingly become a platform for public mobilization around religious symbols and identities.

Since the 1970s a large Sunni and Shi'a Islamist trend has replaced earlier limited politicization, which invoked secular nationalist and leftist ideologies in Saudi Arabia. This was in line with other Arab countries, where secular leftists and nationalist movements have declined and Islamism has been on the rise. Both Saudi Sunnis and Shi'a found in Islamism inspiration for oppositional politics and mobilization.

The two communities remained divided in their political opposition, and neither was able to cross the sectarian divide and include the other group. The only exception was the brief period of the 1950s and 1960s when labor mobilization in the oil region resulted in protest not only across the Saudi sectarian, tribal, and regional divides, but also across nationalities, since the oil industry attracted laborers from all over the Arab world.[10] Following these early and short-lived labor protests, the government banned trade unions and demonstrations.

From the 1970s onward no labor mobilization was possible under the increased appeal of Sunni and Shi'a Islamism. This was a product of a combination of factors. The Iranian revolution of 1979, after which Islamism triumphed in Iran, and the Saudi regime's promotion of Islamism as a counter-ideology to nationalism and leftist political trends, led to the strengthening of political Islam not only in Saudi Arabia but also across the Arab world. National politics and mobilization across the Sunni-Shi'a divide became impossible with the rise of Islamism and the weakening of the nationalist and leftist opposition groups.

Inspired by the success of the revolution in Iran in 1979, Saudi Shi'a mobilized themselves as a repressed and discriminated-against religious minority. They were highly active in demanding religious, political, and economic rights and an end to discrimination in employment and education. For a long time they were denied religious freedom and access to a wide range of professions in education and the military. Their religious jurisprudence was not represented at the level of the judiciary. They had greater experience in staging demonstrations than the Sunni majority, as some of their activists had been involved in leftist and nationalist agitations in the Eastern Province in the 1950s and 1960s. Encouraged by the success of the Iranian revolution and the establishment of the Islamic Republic in 1979, Saudi Shi'a started an uprising that was brutally suppressed.[11] Many of their opposition leaders went into exile following a wave of repression in the Eastern Province where they lived.

In 1993 there was reconciliation with the government, followed by the return of the main exiled Shi'a opposition figures.[12] The reconciliation took place after the government promised to allow the Shi'a more religious freedom and increase their economic integration. There remained, however, a group of Shi'a activists abroad who continued to mobilize their followers inside Saudi Arabia. Inspired by the Arab Spring, the exiled Shi'a opposition, together with religious scholars and activists inside the country, called for demonstrations demanding the release of political prisoners. They also called for support for the Bahraini pro-democracy movement in its struggle against the Bahraini Sunni regime and the withdrawal of Saudi troops from Bahrain. While the Shi'a are a minority in Saudi Arabia, they are a majority in Bahrain.

The Sunni Islamist opposition in Saudi Arabia, known since the 1990s as al-Sahwa, remained grounded in Salafi discourse, especially that which demonizes the Shi'a as a heretic group, thus endorsing official religious teachings.[13] While Saudi Islamists denounce the official religious scholars for their dependence on the state and their loss of autonomy, they agree with them on the Shi'a question. They believe that the Shi'a enjoy sufficient religious freedoms and employment in the oil region. According to one Salafi scholar associated with the al-Sahwa Islamist camp, the Shi'a are not the worst off in the country. Sunnis in the marginalized southwestern area of Asir are worse off in their poor villages.[14] Some Islamists think that Shi'a political prisoners are often released as a result of internal and external pressure, while Sunni Islamists remain in jail for long periods. This Sunni resentment resurfaces whenever the regime releases Shi'a political prisoners, a step understood as a concession to a heretical minority. In this respect, the state, the official religious establishment, and the Islamists remain in agreement over the Shi'a question. While only a small minority of Islamists prefer not to discuss it openly, the majority would not hesitate to denounce the Shi'a in public.

Timid Protest

In light of the 2011 wave of Arab Spring protests, Saudi virtual activists called for a Day of Rage on March 11, 2011.[15] New youth groups appeared on the internet under names such as the National Youth Movement and the Free Youth Movement. Both called for demonstrations against the regime.[16] Their demands centered on freedom, fighting corruption, oppression, injustice, unemployment, release of political prisoners, and other grievances, all of which are non-sectarian in nature.[17] Many of these virtual forums attracted supporters without any evidence of real followers on the ground. Nobody inside Saudi Arabia could openly claim authorship of virtual anti-regime statements without risking arrest. Muhammad al-Wadani, a young activist, posted a video clip of himself denouncing the regime and announcing his intention to demonstrate on March 11, 2011. He was arrested as he prematurely participated in a minor protest after Friday prayers on March 7.[18]

Only two real Sunni opposition groups supported the Day of Rage. The Movement of Islamic Reform in Arabia (MIRA) and the newly founded Sunni Umma Party issued statements endorsing the call for demonstrations.[19] Since 2005 MIRA has occasionally called upon its supporters to stage minor protests after Friday prayers in various cities. On rare occasions, such calls have resulted in very small crowds who would emerge from the weekly prayer chanting "God is Great." MIRA and the Umma Party hoped that a spontaneous youth protest movement would spread to all Saudi cities on March 11, 2011.

Among the Shi'a, the exiled opposition abroad—mainly Khalas (Deliverance) led by personalities such as London-based Shi'a opposition veterans Hamza al-Hasan and Fuad Ibrahim—called upon their followers to respond to the call for demonstrations on March 11, 2011.[20] However, the main impetus came from Shi'a activists inside the country. Before March 11 these activists mobilized their community to demonstrate regularly after the peaceful protests in Bahrain were heavily repressed with the help of Saudi troops.

Before the Day of Rage, Saudi Sunni and Shi'a groups used YouTube, Facebook, and Twitter to spread the message that they supported the virtual protest. This was the first time for Sunni and Shiʻa opposition groups to call for demonstrations on the same day.

On March 11, 2011 the Day of Rage failed utterly, thus pointing to the limitations of so-called Facebook and Twitter revolutions in the absence of real organization and civil society willing to engage in protest.[21] Al-Sahwa, the important and much larger Sunni Islamist movement inside the country referred to earlier, as well as other recently founded political groups, distanced themselves from the call for protest. As the slogan for the demonstration was "The people want the overthrow of the regime," made famous in Cairo's Tahrir Square, no Saudi could declare his support without being arrested. In fact, many Sunni Islamist activists inside the country renewed their loyalty to the regime and denounced the chaos associated with demonstrations. They pointed to the need for reform, but not the overthrow of the regime. With the al-Sahwa Islamist movement withholding its support, the demonstrations did not materialize.

Despite the total failure of the national Day of Rage, the Shiʻa minority continued to stage their own demonstrations in the oil-rich Eastern Province, demanding equality and an end to discrimination against their community. The Shiʻa demonstrations gathered hundreds of supporters, who called for the release of their political prisoners. Women joined the protest and marched with candles over several nights to draw attention to the plight of prisoners. They called for the release of political activists held for more than sixteen years under a campaign to support the "forgotten prisoners." They also called for the withdrawal of Saudi troops sent to Bahrain to suppress the Bahraini pro-democracy uprising that had started on February 14, 2011. In Shiʻa areas repression was more obvious in response to the size of the demonstrations. The Shiʻa were able to mobilize their own people in support of their own demands, thus adopting a narrow Shiʻa agenda, and in sympathy with their co-religionists in Bahrain, only sixteen miles away from Saudi Arabia across a causeway. The security forces were swift in repressing the demonstrators.

After March 11, 2011, in Sunni-majority areas, Saudi men and women regularly gathered on special days around the Ministry of Interior demanding the release of political prisoners. Unemployed graduates assembled around relevant ministries expressing economic grievances and calling upon government officials to honor the king's promises to increase employment opportunities and speed up the placement of graduates in public-sector jobs. The king had made these promises in February when he returned to the country after receiving medical treatment in the USA. Although none of these local protests amounted to real demonstrations, they were a novelty in a country where demonstrations are totally banned. With the exception of the Sunni protest in support of political prisoners, the regime allowed these minor assemblies to take place. But between February and March it was reported that the security forces made more than 160 arrests; two of them were lone demonstrators who responded to the call for the Day of Rage, and there was one well-known political activist involved in human rights issues.[22] In July two women were held by the Ministry of Interior because of their participation in and organization of a demonstration in support of political prisoners. Demonstrations in the Shi'a Eastern Province were more brutally suppressed. The government allowed small protests around economic grievances, but was very swift to deal with demonstrators who expressed political demands or criticized the regime's repression.[23]

Sectarianism as Counter-Revolution

Although old well-known exiled Sunni Islamists such as MIRA, the new Islamist party (the Umma Party), and Shi'a activists all called for protest on March 11, 2011, the regime labeled these calls a Shi'a conspiracy and uprising backed by outside agents, mainly Iran. The state strategy aimed to achieve two objectives. First, it allowed the state security agencies to move quickly into Shi'a areas to suppress early signs of protest, which was described as a Shi'a group revolt, totally isolated from other national groups and opposition trends calling for political reform. The fact that the majority of the Shi'a live in the Eastern Province and their demonstrations have in the past taken place in predominately Shi'a cities such as al-Qatif, Seyhat, and Awamiyyah made it easy for government discourse to appear plausible. This allowed the security agencies to consider the Shi'a as the initiators of the call to demonstrate.

Second, by invoking the discourse of an Iranian-backed Shi'a regional revolt in the oil-rich province, the state rallied the Sunni majority, including those who had serious grievances and had called for political reform. The state propaganda machine described calls for protest as a foreign attempt to cause chaos, divide the country, and undermine its security. The population was led to believe that any protest would result in the fragmentation of Saudi Arabia and the resurgence of regionalism, sectarianism, and tribalism. This response was not unique to the Saudi state. During the Arab Spring, other Arab regimes resorted to the same rhetoric when they faced mass protest, as Salwa Ismail has demonstrated.[24]

Saudi official religion was the main strategy to be deployed against the possibility of protest. The regime mobilized its main religious figures to support it at the critical moment of the Arab Spring in two different ways. First, Wahhabi religious scholars used the minarets to warn against the wrath of God, which would be inflicted on the pious believers if they participated in the peaceful demonstrations planned immediately after the midday prayers of March 11, 2011. On March 7 the Council of Higher Ulama, the highest official religious authority, issued a *fatwa* (religious opinion) against demonstrations.[25] The old opinions of famous shaykhs Abdul Aziz Ibn Baz and Muhammad al-Uthaymin regarding obedience to rulers were resurrected to give impetus to recent religious opinions against demonstrations.[26] All local newspapers favorably reported on the *fatwa*, and thousands of hard copies were distributed in mosques and neighborhoods, in addition to dissemination on the internet.[27] Saudi intelligence services infiltrated internet discussion boards and posted the *fatwa* on many discussion forums with several supporting statements. My observations of several internet discussion boards during the period of the Day of Rage clearly indicated heightened official propaganda.[28] The *fatwa* against demonstrations was a political rather than a religious statement in support of the regime and against those who were calling for protest.

Second, official religious scholars warned of an Iranian–Safavid–Shi'a conspiracy directed by Saudi Shi'a and Sunni exiles in London and Washington to cause *fitna* (chaos) and divide Saudi Arabia. They relied on sectarian religious opinions against the Shi'a, historically depicted as heretics, and more recently as a fifth column acting as agents of Iran. They reminded the believers of the need for *ijma'* (consensus) around the pious rulers of the country, and warned that fragmentation, tribal warfare, civil war, and bloodbaths were to be expected if people responded to calls for demonstrations. Wahhabi scholars who are not directly associated with the official Council of Higher Ulama, and are known as the neo-Wahhabis, for example Muhammad al-Urayfi and Yusif al-Ahmad, had more freedom to denounce the Shi'a in local mosques, lectures, and sermons, recorded and publicized on YouTube. Old al-Sahwa veteran Shaykh

Nasir al-Omar joined the battle against the Shi'a, thus giving an added force to the opinions of the *'ulama'* (religious scholars) of the younger generation. While many of those scholars are critical of the king regarding new gender policies that relax the laws on mixing between the sexes in education and the workplace, they are supportive against the Shi'a, who are seen as alien, heretic, and loyal to Iran. Depicting local protest as a foreign conspiracy had already been tried during the Arab Spring.

The Saudi regime and its *'ulama'* echoed well-rehearsed rhetoric of other Arab autocrats such as Zein al-Abdin Ben Ali in Tunisia, Hosni Mubarak in Egypt, Hamad al-Khalifa in Bahrain, Muamar Qadhafi in Libya, Bashar al-Assad in Syria, and Ali Abdullah Salih in Yemen. The Saudi regime mobilized its digital intelligence services to spread rumors that the Iranians were behind the demonstrations and, if the Sunnis wanted victory, they should not respond to suspicious outside calls for protest. My observation of several internet discussion boards, such as al-Saha and the Saudi Liberal Network, clearly demonstrated unusual pro-regime postings that demonized the Shi'a and warned against foreign conspiracies. The Saudi religious strategy consisted of threatening divine wrath and invoking sectarian difference and hatred to thwart the prospect of peaceful protest to demand real political reforms. So-called independent religious scholars served the regime's interest as much as the official bureaucracy. While official *'ulama'* played a role, other preachers found an opportunity on the internet to denounce the Shi'a and boost their popularity among the youth. Facebook, YouTube, and Twitter became the new digital battlefield against the "heretical" Shi'a and their alleged Iranian backers.

While the double religious strategy of obedience to rulers and sectarianism was unfolding, the Saudi-controlled "liberal" press published articles denouncing sectarianism. Liberal authors attacked those so-called sectarian hate preachers, and many journalists and activists celebrated national unity (*wataniyya*)—that is, belonging to a nation rather than a sect or tribe. The pages of the official local press such as *al-Riyadh, al-Jazeera,* and *al-Watan,* together with pan-Arab *al-Hayat* and *al-Sharq al-Awsat,* became platforms to launch attacks on those backward forces undermining national unity.[29] This, however, does not mean that those liberal authors were in favor of close ties with the Shi'a or in support of real political protest as a means to political reform. They were simply defending the regime in another way, mainly by dividing and confusing

Saudi public opinion, an important strategy in aborting a national consensus in favor of mobilization and protest.

During the Arab Spring Saudis were exposed to two contradictory discourses, both sponsored by the state: a religious one in support of Sunni unity against Shi'a heretics; and a so-called liberal discourse denouncing religious scholars and their sectarianism. Saudis are confused and torn between those two contradictory interpretations of the crisis. The confusion can only serve regime interests by delaying the need to make political concessions. The strategy maintains divisions in society between so-called liberal intellectuals and the hate preachers, and between Sunnis and Shi'a. In this confusion, the regime confirms in the minds of people that it alone can mediate between the various camps, reining in the excesses of liberals, Islamists, Shi'a, and Sunnis. It fosters the impression that without its intervention the country will enter a Hobbesian state of nature where tribes, sects, and regions unleash their fanaticism and violence on each other and undermine the security of all Saudis, possibly inviting foreign military intervention to secure the energy sources that are so important not only to Saudis but also to the rest of the world.

In a country where there is weak nationalism and strong Islamism and sectarian tension, state strategy to depict protests as a Shi'a conspiracy was successful in pushing the Sunnis to renew their allegiance to the regime. Because Saudi Arabia does not have an organized national civil society such as trade unions, professional associations, or political parties, its opposition groups have not worked across the sectarian divide in recent times. The Shi'a opposition has worked on its own since the 1970s, while Sunni Islamism never appealed to non-Sunni groups, for example the Ismailis in the southwest and the Shi'a in the east. If Saudi Sunni Islamists had their own Islamic awakening, the Shi'a also developed their political opposition around their own religious scholars and political activists.

Saudi authoritarianism's main concern is to control both the Sunni and Shi'a populations and prevent them from pursuing political rights that would eventually lead to the overthrow of authoritarian rule. For the foreseeable future the Saudi regime will continue to frighten the majority with the Shi'a/Iranian threat to delay political reform. The real threat to Saudi authoritarianism is the development of a national opposition composed of both Sunnis and Shi'a, and Islamists and secularists. This has already begun to appear in limited forums, prompting the government to clamp down on Sunni virtual protest and the minor but real Shi'a demonstrations. If the new constitutional monarchy movement, which brings together Sunni and Shi'a liberals, develops further and becomes a force to be reckoned with, the sectarian discourse will be confined to hardline official Salafi circles, which so far have remained loyal to the regime. A national opposition that rejects sectarianism will be difficult to suppress, despite decades of sectarian discourse under the patronage of the authoritarian state.

Without a student movement, an independent women's movement, and professional associations, a Saudi revolution is unlikely to move out of the virtual world into reality. While students who are on generous government subsidies and scholarships await employment, the women's movement regards the state as its main patron and is unlikely to withdraw its support of the current king. Many Saudi women activists consider the state as the only agent capable of checking the power of the *'ulama'*. The weak professional associations, such as the Chambers of Commerce and journalist associations, remain loyal to the state, which protects them against populist politics. The economic and technocratic elite is tied in to the public sector and enjoys great rewards for its loyalty. Moreover, the main tribal groups are beneficiaries of the regime through employment in the military sector and regular subsidies and handouts. Many tribal groups are linked to the regime through marriage networks. Only drastic and prolonged economic decline would trigger mass protest. If ever there are signs of a Saudi mass protest, counter-revolutionary strategies other than sectarianism may have to be deployed to suppress a wide national movement calling for serious and real political change.

The Saudi case illustrates that sectarianism is a powerful tool at the disposal of regimes, especially during periods of turbulence. From Egypt to Iraq, similar strategies were adopted during the Arab uprisings in 2011.

How Dictatorship Feeds Sectarianism in the Middle East

Sectarianism as an eternal and primordial disposition of the societies of the Middle East fails to explain the current turmoil in the Arab world. Rather, it is the instrumentalization of religious differences, diversity, and pluralism in political struggles of regimes against their constituencies that ignite the lethal sectarianism witnessed across the region. In fact, the sectarian lens of the alleged Sunni-Shi'a divide obscures rather than illuminates complex realities on the ground. It masks the challenging political and economic changes that have swept the region, not to mention the ongoing foreign interventions and their impacts. Depicting the power struggles in the region as sectarian wars masks deep-rooted economic deprivation and inequality, resulting from decades of rural–urban migration, impoverishment of the countryside, and the appropriation of land by new elites in the cities. Added to this is the regional rivalry between Iran and Saudi Arabia, two important countries, each of which claims to support the interests of its co-religionists. The political rivalry between the two countries, and competition over spheres of influence in Lebanon, Syria, Iraq, Bahrain, and more recently, Yemen, have made sectarianism a powerful narrative concealing real political, economic, and social injustices and rivalries between groups, states, and powerful non-state actors. It is true that religious identities continue to be prominent, but sectarianism is something totally different: the deadly politicization of these religious identities.

To assess why most of the Arab world is increasingly becoming a wasteland torn apart by violence committed in the name of sectarian identity and solidarity, we must turn to hidden realities that most observers refuse to see.

One of these is the continuing ascendency of unpopular and brutal clan-type presidents and kings. Despite the election of presidents and the crowning of old kings and emirs, Middle East leaders have resisted real inclusion and continued to pursue politics by either force or bribery. They all came to realize that their narrow legitimacy can only be enhanced if they turn sections of the population into clients, benefiting from lavish economic opportunities in return for total loyalty.

Saddam Hussein, a Sunni, brought in Christians to represent him abroad, while many Shi'a dominated his Ba'ath Party, leaving security and intelligence matters in the hands of his most loyal Sunni kin. Alawite President Bashar al-Assad of Syria retains high-ranking posts in the air force and intelligence services for his loyal clan, while allowing new merchant Sunni families to benefit from neoliberal economic openings. President Hosni Mubarak of Egypt entertained the idea of speaking in the name of Sunnis before he was ousted, but in reality his concerns centered on turning his small family into a powerful clan along the lines of his contemporaries among Arab presidents and kings.

Such clan-like leadership cannot be easily considered sectarian. The rulers have no sectarian identity nor affiliation, but both their opponents—

often the excluded masses—and the outside world want to see them through a sectarian lens. These presidents worked on the assumption that to maintain control one has to classify the people as belonging to different primordial and eternal units, playing one group against another in a long and brutal political game. Ruling elites have not always been charitable toward their own co-religionists, and cannot be automatically considered loyal to their own sects. In reality, they worshiped their own clans and rewarded clients regardless of their sectarian identity.

So-called Sunni kings and emirs are even more committed to their clans than to their sects. Consider the various Saudi kings who aspired to lead the Sunni world, from King Faisal (d. 1975) to King Abdullah bin Abdulaziz (r. 2005–2015) and now King Salman, and were often accused of allowing anti-Shi'a sectarian discourse to flourish. Since the 1980s Shi'a activists have pointed to how the Saudi regime did little to control the anti-Shi'a rhetoric of Saudi religious scholars. For example, *fatwa*s against intermarriage between Sunnis and Shi'a were notorious, along with those that forbid Sunnis from eating meat slaughtered by Shi'a butchers. Shi'a activists accuse the regime of marginalizing the community in the Eastern Province, leaving their towns and villages under-developed and denying them full employment and religious freedom.[30]

But individual Saudi kings are manipulative political actors, driven by survival rather than sectarian solidarity. Take King Faisal, who in the 1960s supported the Shi'a Zaydi monarchists in Yemen against the republicans, who were backed by Gamal Abdel Nasser of Egypt.[31] Domestically, King Abdullah and his governor in the oil-rich Eastern Province manipulated various Shi'a notables and religious scholars, who were occasionally summoned to pledge allegiance to the king after the sporadic demonstrations and eruptions of violence. The king used the Shi'a and the violence in the area to frighten the majority and deter it from demanding any political changes. Every time the Shi'a demonstrated, the majority was fed the discourse of being targeted by outside forces and their local agents. When Salman replaced King Abdullah in 2015 he immediately launched a war on Yemen, dubbed Operation Decisive Storm, to absorb the domestic tension and dissatisfaction over his predecessor's policies, which appeared weak and stagnant. The Saudi narrative about this ongoing war continues to be articulated in sectarian language as it is projected as an attempt to destroy Iran's influence in the Arabian Peninsula and its surrogates, the Zaydi Houthis in

Yemen, thus demonstrating the leadership's credentials as an upholder of Sunni interests.

At the same time, the regime sees the perverse benefit of attacks on Shi'a worshipers by radical Sunni groups, which terrorize this minority. The regime then presents itself as the best protector of the Shi'a, as the alternative would be radical jihadists. After years of the Saudi press warning against Shi'a agitators allegedly backed by Iran, talk about national unity dominated the public sphere when Shi'a worshipers were attacked outside their mosque. The regime has at its disposal multiple voices, posing as intellectuals and writers, who can swing between fierce sectarian discourse and slogans of national unity, depending on the needs of the dominant ruling clan at a particular moment. Political maneuvering requires the regime to play on the fears of both the minority Shi'a and majority Sunnis rather than assume a fixed sectarian identity. The survival of the Al Saud clan, rather than the protection of an almighty Sunni world, remains the most sacred project.

Neither the professed Sunni monarchies such as Saudi Arabia and its clients nor Arab presidencies are truly embedded in eternal sectarian trenches, despite the loud rhetoric designed for mass consumption and mobilization. The same applies to the societies in which sectarianism is supposedly rife—for example, in Lebanon, Syria, Iraq, and Bahrain.[32] To consider these societies as totally immersed in sectarian identities and violence masks other political and economic cleavages, notably class differences, within each community. Sectarianism becomes an umbrella under which these cleavages are concealed to enhance illusory solidarities. Yes, the Arab region may exhibit the ugly face of sectarianism, but this should not be an excuse not to unveil more bitter realities about poverty, exclusion, marginalization, and the tyranny of both one's own sectarian community and outsiders. This is often ignored as an important dimension that stems from communitarianism in which individual interests do not always coincide with those of the community. This is important in areas such as gender equality, when the sect as a group may enforce discrimination that remains hidden, with any resistance interpreted as treason against the whole community.

If sectarianism fails to explain the political behavior of regimes and the internal diversity within sectarian groups, why does the outside world continue to see the region and its politics through a sectarian prism? The Western powers that had historically controlled the Arab world found emotionally charged primordial identities such as sects extremely useful as tools to divide and map the population. They imagined communities as solid and parallel pillars, and acted on them as historical realities that refuse to go away. The latest episode in this vision was the USA's imagining of Iraq as a country of Shi'a, Sunnis, and Kurds. The consequences of this vision proved disastrous for all citizens: as it was enshrined and institutionalized, the marginalized communities had no choice but to engage in a counter-sectarian vision.

Seeing the Arab world as a vast ocean in which sectarian sharks have the upper hand also confirms the alleged exceptionalism that is believed to be the main characteristic of the region, namely as a place where resistance to secularization, citizenship, and democracy is insurmountable. Many observers in the West still prefer such old Orientalist clichés. In *Muslim Society*, influential philosopher and anthropologist Ernest Gellner clearly stated that Muslim societies are resistant to secularization as they remain entrenched in religious and tribal identities, unable to form associations on the bases of other interests such as class, common thinking, or other non-primordial aspects of their identity.[33]

In the Arab world, and around the globe, religious identities will continue to be salient, overtly symbolized, and culturally nourished; but sectarianism is a dark hole dug by many domestic and external actors. Arab leaders may inflame sectarian imaginations, but their loyalty is above all to their clans and clients, regardless of their affiliation. Equally, Arab societies are concerned about their economic plight and marginalization, although they have recently learned how to articulate their exclusion in sectarian terms. Sectarianism is not an inherent historical quality of the Arab masses. Sectarian entrepreneurs and religious scholars continue to flourish and benefit from this narrative. Sectarianism, in other words, is a *modern* political phenomenon that is nourished by persistent dictators whose rule depends on invoking these old religious identities that become lethally politicized.

Our thinking about the Arab world and the raging wars within and between sects should move away from a historical Sunni-Shi'a divide and focus on the abysmal strategies of patron-client dictatorships and economic inequality between and within various groups. A reconsideration of the so-called eternal confessional model of the Arab world is long overdue.

9

STRATEGIC DEPTH, COUNTERINSURGENCY, AND THE LOGIC OF SECTARIANIZATION

THE ISLAMIC REPUBLIC OF IRAN'S SECURITY DOCTRINE AND ITS REGIONAL IMPLICATIONS[1]

Eskandar Sadeghi-Boroujerdi

Take heed, our capacities and capabilities are not merely those things we possess domestically, we also have important capacities outside the country; we have supporters, we have strategic depth ... in some cases because of Islam, in others because of language, and still others because of the Shi'a religion. These are the country's strategic depth (*'omq-e rahbordi*); these are part of our capabilities; we must use all of our capabilities.[2]

Ayatollah Khamene'i

The Shi'a Crescent is in the process of formation.'[3]

Major-General Mohammad Ali Ja'fari

His Eminence says that Syria is our strategic depth.[4]

Brigadier-General Hossein Hamedani (d. 2015)

We don't have a Shi'a Crescent.[5]

President Hassan Rouhani

Introduction

Following the conclusion of the preliminary agreement between the Islamic Republic of Iran and the P5+1 over the former's nuclear program, the *New York Times* published an op-ed by three fellows of the Washington Institute for New East Policy—Soner Cagaptay, James F. Jeffrey, and Mehdi Khalaji—entitled "Iran Won't Give up on its Revolution." The article argued forcefully that "Iran is a revolutionary power with hegemonic aspirations. In other words, it is a country seeking to assert its dominance in the region and it will not play by the rules."[6] Like Nazi Germany before it, they assert, Iran is a "hegemonic power," which, as if by some ontological necessity, is compelled to dominate neighboring states and reduce them to pliant, cowed vassals. Such "hegemonic aspirations" are not even regime-specific, the authors contend, but rather are deep-seated, if not indeed primordial. They go back at least half a millennium, finding their provenance in the Safavid dynasty, which conquered and ultimately unified Iran as we know it today in the sixteenth and seventeenth centuries. Iran's drive to dominate, moreover, has a distinctly, not to mention enduring, sectarian flavor. Even Nixon's "Gendarme of the Persian Gulf" was not spared. Accordingly, Shah Mohammad Reza Pahlavi "extended financial and military support to Shiite communities and its proxies around the Middle East" and was secure in power as the Syrian Alawites entered into "Iran's permanent fold." The authors do eventually acknowledge certain inconvenient facts that undermine the exclusively sectarian explanation for Iranian state behavior, among them the Islamic Republic's alliance with "belligerent Sunni actors" and Christian Armenia against Shi'a-majority Azerbaijan. But what is immutable and unchanging, they maintain, is the "imperial ambition that drives Iranian foreign policy," supplemented "by a religious or millennial worldview that rejects the principles of the classic international order."

In this chapter I will attempt to provide a very different explanation of Iranian foreign policy and the logic of sectarianization, with an assessment of Iranian counterinsurgency policy and the various constraints it has faced in Syria and Iraq following the Arab uprisings of 2011. I will argue that, rather than uniquely aggressive and sectarian, the Islamic Republic should be understood as a "regional middle power" whose foreign policy has been shaped in the context of the systemic insecurity of a regional system penetrated by hegemonic Great Powers.[7] The historical development of post-revolutionary Iran's security policies, which are intimately intertwined with its espousal of asymmetric "strategies of opposition," has often taken the form of financial and military support for politically responsive co-sectarians. These processes have dovetailed with crises of security, trust, and legitimacy in weak states, ultimately galvanizing the logic of sectarianization in local and region-wide conflicts. To frame this in terms of a putatively unyielding drive for the incorporation of Arab capitals into a Shi'a-Persian empire for the twenty-first century will be shown to be a gross oversimplification. By contrast, I will try to show through an examination of the manifold interactions between system-level and meso-level dynamics of securitization, with particular attention to the examples of Iraq and Syria, that the Islamic Republic's engagement in these conflicts varies widely and depends on a host of variables, many of which lie beyond its immediate control.

The Islamic Republic as a Regional Middle Power in a Penetrated System

Following Raymond Hinnebusch and Anoushiravan Ehteshami, I will contend that the Islamic Republic of Iran should be viewed as a "regional middle power." That is, a state that is decisive to the regional balance of power and harbors a credible deterrent capability, which, through the deployment of both hard and soft power, is able to resist coalitions of adversarial regional states against it. While regional middle powers are middle powers on a global scale, they are key actors within the regional system in which they figure.[8] Such powers assert regional leadership in the name of more general interests, but are nevertheless economically and technologically constrained by the core, which has traditionally sought to prevent any single power from organizing the regional system. Moreover, following Barry Buzan and Ole Waever, I view the regional security complex (RSC) as a key factor:[9] the security of regional states is sufficiently intertwined that they cannot be considered in isolation from one another.[10]

The Middle East's geostrategic location[11] and vast oil wealth, as well as the presence of the Israeli state, have ensured that throughout the second half of the twentieth century it has been subject to constant penetration by Great Powers.[12] Adam Hanieh has made a compelling case regarding the entwined and mutually reinforcing processes of energy flows to the core and the internationalization of capital underwriting the

American presence in the Persian Gulf since the 1970s. The "petrodollar flows from the Gulf, particularly from Saudi Arabia, played a critical role in strengthening both the financialization of the system as a whole and the specific role of the United States as the dominant power."[13]

The region's fully fledged incorporation into the world economy, and the sometimes tacit, but often explicit, *quid pro quo* between amenable regional elites and the US government, has historically entailed security guarantees, foreign aid, technology and knowledge transfers in exchange for the steady, secure flow of energy to Western markets. It is no surprise that these dynamics have proven decisive in shaping the character of regional alignments, military campaigns, and security agreements in preceding decades (the Gulf War of 1990–1991, the US-led invasion and occupation of Iraq in 2003). Such a perspective undercuts claims about unmitigated sovereignty in unalloyed Realist theory.[14]

Middle regional powers cannot completely insulate themselves from the military penetration of global powers or from entanglement in the complex web of the world capitalist system, which, following World War II, progressively forged a set of economic and security interests that bound regional and Great Power elites together. Under such circumstances, middle regional states such as Iran can merely attempt to minimize their vulnerability by diversifying their economic relations and, if possible, leveraging multi-polarity and Great Power rivalry to augment their bargaining power.[15] Another possibility is the pursuit of "internal balancing" and what Stephen Walt calls "strategies of opposition," which I will discuss in further detail below.

Bureaucratic-Institutional Rivalries and Consensus Building in Iran's National Security Policy

Following Pierre Bourdieu, one might say that in the case of Iran's national security apparatus there are overlapping political, religious, military, etc. fields, and that contestation and the accumulation and exchange of political, economic, religious, and symbolic capital crisscross these numerous fields.[16] There is plenty of movement among these bodies: former members of the Iranian Revolutionary Guard Corps (IRGC) are elected to the Majles; executive responsibilities change hands between various positions on the political chessboard.

Though by no means strictly defined along institutional lines, it is unsurprising that Iran's military and diplomatic corps, as well as disparate political factions, compete over which view of national security ought to prevail in the formulation and execution of diplomacy and national security policy.[17] For example, in numerous instances Ayatollah Khamene'i has specifically insisted, in keeping with his broad strategic oversight, on Tehran's support for Bashar al-Assad remaining in power in the face of Western demands that he step aside.[18] Meanwhile, some in the Iranian diplomatic corps have considered proposals that Assad step down in favor of a regime insider less visibly associated with the bloody repression of the last several years—above all, the deployment of chemical weapons. In keeping with their *Weltanschauungen*, skill set, capital, and the division of labor within the regime apparatus, these institutions *qua* institutions manage distinct if intimately interconnected aspects of various conflicts. In this way, Iran's Foreign Ministry can propose diplomatic initiatives calling for a political resolution to an ongoing conflict, while Revolutionary Guard commanders simultaneously proceed to supervise and train militias in hotspots across Iraq and Syria. While the president or foreign minister might forcefully denounce sectarianism, IRGC commanders managing co-sectarian assets on the ground may express geo-political rivalry in thinly veiled sectarian rhetoric—for example, by overtly attacking Wahhabism in the context of ongoing conflicts in Iraq or Syria, and indirect conflict with the Saudi kingdom and its allies.

Another rhetorical device deployed in recent years across almost all state institutions is the virtual conflation of all groups at war with allies in either Syria or Iraq as "terrorists." In this way, Iranian politicians and military personnel can eschew the severe repercussions of invoking openly sectarian language, and instead espouse the post-9/11 lingua franca of the "War on Terror," which both Western and non-Western Great Powers are less inclined to dismiss out of hand. These *modi operandi* comprise the twin elements of a fundamentally political strategy marrying persuasion and brute force, soft and hard power, domination and hegemony. In this way, the Islamic Republic can avail itself of, and adduce the norms and laws regulating, international relations, while partaking in internal balancing and irregular warfare, which I will discuss in some detail below.

Strategies of Opposition and Strategic Depth

US imperial overstretch during the presidency of George W. Bush (2001–2009), and the caution that characterized his successor,[19] have contributed to a situation in which middle regional powers can take advantage of opportunities to exercise varying degrees of autonomy and increase their power within the bounds of the regional system without fear of swift, disproportionate reprisal. The Islamic Republic has proven willing to exploit the diminished state capacity of regional states racked by civil conflicts to protect and, in certain instances, deepen what high-ranking Iranian officials, including the Supreme Leader himself, have referred to as Iran's "strategic depth" (*'omq-e rahbordi*).[20] This of course allows the Islamic Republic to keep instability and encroaching threats emanating from its antagonists at a safe distance, while ensuring that relative quiet prevails at home.[21] On the regional scale, strategic depth can also be viewed in terms of the logic of "offensive realism,"[22] "look[ing] for opportunities to alter the balance of power by acquiring additional increments of power at the expense of potential rivals," in the formulation of John Mearsheimer,[23] while in defensive fashion leveraging the cost of US regional penetration, which has been perceived by powerful individuals and institutions as a major threat to regime survival since the 1979 revolution.

Though the Islamic Republic has sought to expand trade, cultural, and religious ties in both Syria and Iraq,[24] its most potent tool for power projection is its support for a cornucopia of paramilitary organizations. As opposed to soft or economic power, its relationships with militias form the centerpiece of its manifold "strategies of opposition" vis-à-vis regional and external adversaries. Weaker states play this game of "internal balancing": mobilizing their internal resources in terms of an asymmetric strategy, shifting their competition with more powerful states to those arenas where the imbalance of power is less starkly felt.[25] Balancing of this sort is complemented by a range of strategies such as *balking*, or deliberate non-cooperation; *binding*, which entails the entanglement of self-avowed liberal states in the framework of international law and rules; *blackmail*, whereby dividends are extorted by threats or pressure; and *delegitimation*, where the legitimacy of rival regimes is persistently undermined in the international arena.[26]

The Islamic Republic's security doctrine has developed in the context of this threat posed by Great Power penetration, as further reflected in the country's official defense budget, which stands at approximately $12–14 billion (2014), including support for foreign non-state actors.[27] The Islamic Republic's conventional military forces continue to rely heavily upon arms procured under the Shah, while the US arms embargo has ensured that in the wake of the revolution the Iranian state has been severely hampered in its ability to modernize its military or acquire new state-of-the-art military technology. This of course stands in stark contrast to several of Iran's Arab Gulf neighbors. According to the Stockholm International Peace Research Institute, the military spending of the United Arab Emirates and Saudi Arabia in 2014 stood at around $22.7 billion and $80.7 billion, respectively.[28] There are discernible reasons why the sale of billions of dollars in military hardware to Iran's chief regional competitors, in tandem with the Clinton-era policy of "containment," have reinforced the Islamic Republic's calculus vis-à-vis the indispensability of support for non-state political-paramilitary actors to its security. Rather than directly engaging in conventional conflicts, since the Iran-Iraq War (1980–1988) the Revolutionary Guard has honed its conduct of asymmetrical and irregular warfare, fighting protracted wars of attrition on multiple fronts to both deter and accumulate political influence and leverage. It would not be unfair to say that Iran's utilization of such means embodies Clausewitz's famous dictum that "war is not merely an act of policy but a true political instrument, a continuation of political discourse carried on with other means."[29]

Iran's asymmetric strategies in the post-Khomeini era are best understood as emerging from its security dilemma as opposed to territorial ambitions or the intractable need to perpetually export its Islamic revolution. That being said, it is undeniable that the Supreme Leader and Commanders of the Revolutionary Guard regularly distinguish between the state (*dowlat, hokumat*) and the regime (*nezam*): the former is geographically and temporally bound, and conforms to the boundaries of the Iranian nation-state, while the *nezam* is held to be irreducible to the state, and embodies a commitment to ideological and sociopolitical revolution which is total and uncompromising in scope.[30] As should be clear by now, I hold the latter to have largely dissipated with the end of the Iran-Iraq war in 1988 and the death of Ayatollah Khomeini the following year, even while it remains an important means of framing mobilizations both at home and abroad,[31] and is on occasion deployed to undermine the legitimacy of the ruling executive on the domestic front.

Furthermore, a disproportionate emphasis on this ideological aspect of Iranian state discourse serves to obscure our understanding of the state's actual behavior, given its structural constraints, and fuels value-laden and sensationalist characterizations of the latter. The Islamic Republic's profound lack of technological edge, and the dated nature of its military hardware due to international isolation and the US arms embargo, make any notion of its ambitions to dominate manifold Arab states and incorporate them into some Persian imperial order an entirely untenable proposition. The inflammatory comments of certain politicians and military personnel—most notably those of 'Ali-Reza Zakani, a prominent conservative parliamentarian, who bombastically claimed that Iran controls four Arab capitals[32]—are best interpreted in terms of the dilemma faced by weaker regional powers trying to deter stronger ones by exaggerating their capabilities and misrepresenting their own strength.[33] It also serves to inflate Iran's role in regional conflicts, where its reach and influence are highly qualified. This is most apparent in the case of Yemen, where certain Iranian politicians cheer every Houthi victory, thereby enraging regional adversaries and embroiling Saudi armed forces ever more deeply in the conflict, to the point where "meaningful victory" becomes hard to discern. This is not to deny that certain personages in the Iranian state might aspire to such a role, but systemic pressures, hard and soft power constraints, and elite cleavages fundamentally preclude its realization.

The sectarianization of regional conflicts has been at least in part a secondary process and an outcome of Iran and other regional players engaging in balancing strategies through support for receptive co-sectarians; but sectarian identity by no means exclusively determines these political alliances. This is merely one of several processes by which civil conflicts in the Middle East have become sectarianized. Transnational solidarities and support revolving around the regional power balance have proven decisive to the construction of alliances between sub-state and foreign state actors, while the increasing salience of sectarianism, both discursively and in terms of the character of civil violence, can make such alliances across confessional lines increasingly costly to sub-state organizations, dependent as they are on foreign patronage. Hamas's effort to distance itself from Tehran in the aftermath of the Syrian uprising and the Assad regime's violent repression of it appositely illustrate this.[34] The Islamic Republic's policy of politicizing ascriptive group identities has its antecedents in the Iranian Islamist movement preceding the revolution, and Tehran's subsequent politico-ideological relationships with co-sectarian political organizations such as Hezbollah and the

Supreme Council for Islamic Revolution in Iraq (SCIRI) date back to the revolution's first decade.[35] To ascribe such resilience exclusively to the sectarian factor would be quite misleading, given that there is a complex web of political and economic interests which determine the nature and preponderance of these relationships. In a similar vein, it is not sufficient to explain why such relationships have been able to endure and in certain instances flourish.

Mass Mobilizations and Emerging Anarchy

Instead of upgrading its conventional military capabilities, for which it had only limited means as a result of the US arms embargo, the Islamic Republic has sought to harness, channel, and discursively frame the sociopolitical and armed mobilizations of politically receptive elements in weak states, which has given Tehran asymmetrical capabilities and strategic depth against both regional adversaries and perceived super-power threats. Weak states, broadly speaking, are those that for manifold reasons come to lack significant *autonomy*, i.e. the ability to perform basic tasks independently of social groups, and *capacity*, i.e. the ability of the state to execute its programs and decisions.[36] Weak states thus become staging grounds for inter-state and Great Power competition. It naturally follows that these two constraints fundamentally circumscribe the state's ability to exercise a monopoly, or even the semblance of a monopoly, on violence and coercion. Under conditions of state weakness, political receptivity and the pool from which such sociopolitical movements can effectively recruit are in turn related to people's perceptions of security and insecurity, or what Barry Posen calls "emerging anarchy."[37] The Islamic Republic's own Revolutionary Guards and Basij Forces—whose very name means "mobilization"—were born at the juncture of a major social revolution and inter-state (Iran-Iraq) war, just as Lebanon's Hezbollah emerged from the battleground of the Lebanese Civil War (1975–1990) and the Israeli invasion and occupation of Beirut in 1982. It was in the course of this process that the Islamic Republic was able to forge a model of political, social, and armed mobilization that proved remarkably durable, and which it has turned to, time and again, over the course of some three decades.

Most recently, these resources and know-how have been deployed in the internecine conflicts of post-2003 Iraq and the post-2011 Syrian civil war, in both cases to support regional allies experiencing challenges to their legitimacy from armed political opponents. The nature of Iranian engagement, however, is intimately bound up with several interrelated factors, the most important of which are state weakness and highly dysfunctional state institutions. From these, several corollaries arguably follow:

- the presence of ascriptive identity groups sceptical of state neutrality
- poor or absent welfare provision[38]
- a pool of political entrepreneurs and violence specialists ready to ally themselves with strong external states to further their immediate political and material goals
- a political economy riddled with politicized patronage networks and afflicted by deep-seated inequality and structural unemployment

State weakness in the case of Iraq, however, did not simply appear in a vacuum. American imperialism not only destroyed the Baʿathist state and the last vestiges of Iraqi associational life, but also played a decisive role in the new state's reconstitution and the effective institutionalization of the ethno-sectarian constitutional order. While it would be disingenuous to claim that sectarianism in Iraq began with the American invasion and occupation, there are strong grounds to contend that the new political-constitutional order, often euphemistically referred to as "consociational democracy," generated unprecedented modes of sectarian identification and competition—novel in Iraq's history—and incentivized political actors' recourse to sectarian-laden (or sect-centric, in Fanar Haddad's phrase) discourses and forms of mobilization. Thus, as Anne Alexander has commented, "sectarian 'balance'—and therefore its corollary, sectarian competition—was enshrined in America's Iraq from the start. The practice of *muhasasa*, or the use of a sectarian quota system for appointments, was implemented by political parties whose survival was bound up with entrenching sectarianism."[39]

The sectarianization of civil and inter-state conflicts is the outcome of highly contentious civil and militarized mobilizations and counter-mobilizations stemming from a combination of domestic and inter-state security dilemmas. Thus at the domestic level, where the central state is perceived as lacking both autonomy and capacity, and is unable to provide security for its population—especially when it is perceived to be confessional in its provision of security and welfare services[40]—the likelihood of a security dilemma emerging along confessional lines increases, as does the prominence of those forces that take up the role of providing security and presenting themselves as defenders of the ascriptive identity group in question.[41]

This analytical framework seeks to provide an account of the driving forces behind the efficacy of the Islamic Republic's balancing strategies as deployed in its patronage of and alliances with various actors in Iraq and Syria and its efforts to preserve strategic depth through recourse to armed political organizations. In this way, following Rogers Brubaker, we can dispense with groupist assumptions, and instead regard sectarian identity as a variable rather than a constant.[42] Sinisa Malesevic's conceptualization of ethnicity is also relevant to the framing of the Islamic Republic's relationships with political organizations bearing ascriptive confessional identities. He frames such identities as politicized social action, where "cultural differences are politicized in the context of intensive group interaction."[43]

"Militias" have been a key vehicle for the extension of Iranian influence. Militias can be thought of as armed and politicized social action—or, in Charles Tilly's formulation, a form of contentious politics.[44] But a genuine problem associated with the use of the term "militia" is that it often obscures the social-embeddedness of certain armed sub-state organizations and the fact that they are ultimately political organizations pursuing political aims. It is, however, necessary to concede that not all, or even the majority, of the organizations patronized by the Islamic Republic in Iraq and Syria emanated from broad-based social movements. In fact, it often seems to be quite the opposite, insofar as a number of political actors with close-knit relations to Tehran were first founded as politico-military organizations only to begin the process of establishing social, cultural, and welfare networks later down the line. This is observable in the case of Syria, but certain militias in Iraq (such as Kata'ib Hizbullah and Saraya al-Khorasani) present a similar problem. That being said, those organizations that Iranian state operatives have had a direct hand in establishing are only a fraction of the multitude of groups currently embroiled in these conflicts.

Without becoming preoccupied with this issue, which is beyond the scope of this chapter, it is essential to acknowledge, following Melani Cammett, that "where public welfare functions are underdeveloped and religious or ethnic organizations provide social protection, the provision of social services both constitute and reproduces the politics of sectarianism."[45]

Social and welfare protections are thus important counterparts to the physical security that militias often claim to provide. One recent notable example is that of 'Asa'ib Ahl al-Haqq, which seceded from the Sadrist movement in 2006 and was initially best known for its January 2007 raid against US Army headquarters in Karbala, killing one soldier and kidnapping four more. Since this time, as its relationships with former Iraqi prime minister Nuri al-Maliki, his allies in so-called *Malikyun*, and the Islamic Republic have developed, so has its media, educational, and sociocultural outreach.[46] Nonetheless, it should be noted that in the cases of both Iraq and Syria, militarized political groups that have received arms and training from the Islamic Republic, despite intermittent recourse to sectarian language and symbols, have often embedded their claims in more comprehensive ones, in the name of a contested vision of the nation and issues of social justice.[47] They have thus been able to advance sectional interests and mobilize subaltern and marginalized classes in the agonistic struggle for political power and resources.

Balance of Power and the Origins of the "Axis of Resistance"

An important factor in Iran's security doctrine in the cases of Iraq and Syria has been said to reside in a combination of defensive and offensive realism, depending on whether it is the international or regional scale. According to John Mearsheimer, offensive realism maintains that states strive to become the hegemon of the anarchic system of which they form a part,[48] and this ultimately stems from the drive to increase their chances of survival. Defensive realism, as initially theorized by Kenneth Waltz, instead focused on how states under conditions of anarchy are primarily occupied with deterring threats and balancing against those threats to their security. Defensive realism contends that states achieve this by acting defensively and maintaining the extant balance of power, rather than seeking to overturn it.[49] Thus, while defensive realism argues that states tend to reinforce the status quo, offensive realism holds that anarchy leads states to "seek more power to maximize the odds of survival," making for more "aggressive" and robust security competition.[50]

But a combination of these two models, namely a defensive realism taken up with respect to extra-regional hegemonic powers (say, the United States) and offensive realism vis-à-vis fellow regional powers, will not suffice as an explanation, since it merely affords insight into the broader structural factors and dynamics that shape Iran's behavior. Moreover, it should be acknowledged that offensive realism was originally developed by Mearsheimer for analyzing the behavior of "Great Powers" on a global scale. The framework of my analysis is a complex of regional states in which security is highly interdependent[51]—a regional security complex—in this case, one that is overdetermined by Great Power penetration, a fact that has an obvious impact on the calculations of powerful states in the region, such as Iran, Saudi Arabia, and Turkey.

One way of integrating Great Power rivalry into the regional security complex is by including the USA in the RSC, as Gregory Gause does in his delineation of the Persian Gulf Regional Security Complex.[52] But since the Levant is peripheral to this approach and the profoundly interdependent and strategic character of the so-called Axis of Resistance (Iran, Syria, Hezbollah) understated, it seems more accurate to retain a broader view of regional security, one that simultaneously acknowledges that Great Power competition still has a formidable role to play. Russia's aerial bombing campaign in Syria beginning in October 2015 is a stark reminder of just this fact. Another possible way to frame this problem is to regard the Persian Gulf RSC as one of multiple sub-complexes within the wider Middle East.[53] Nevertheless, the simple application of the defensive and offensive realist paradigms to the case of the Islamic Republic's security doctrine proves problematic, since these paradigms fail to account for the historical genealogy and evolution of this doctrine, with its specific characteristics and *modus operandi*. In the following pages I will attempt to qualify and further complicate the application of such models to the Iranian case.

The Tehran-Damascus Alliance

Iran's relationship with Syria dates to the Iranian revolution of 1978–1979. It was initially based on balancing against the rival Ba'athist regime in Iraq—a mutual foe of Iran and Syria—and its efforts to cast itself in the role of aspiring regional hegemon following the collapse of the Shah's regime.[54] But this argument, which Ehteshami and Hinnebusch have also advanced,[55] could not envisage how enduring the Tehran-Damascus alliance would prove, despite the overthrow of Saddam Hussein and the subsequent emergence of a Tehran-friendly regime in Baghdad, which has provoked a seismic shift in the region's political landscape. The overthrow of the Ba'athist regime in Iraq induced a regional shift from multipolarity to bipolarity, where Iran and Saudi Arabia remain the only two formidable powers in the Gulf[56]— which in turn has ushered in a watershed transformation in the dynamics of securitization.

The Tehran-Damascus alliance has generally been seen to rest upon geostrategic considerations, such as opposition to US and Israeli policies in the region and the pivotal role played by Hezbollah in bulwarking the influence of both countries in Lebanon. But as the Syrian uprising escalated into full-blown civil war, besides the aforementioned geostrategic considerations, the issue of omnibalancing had become especially acute: the Syrian regime had to assess whether the greatest threat emanated from foreign or domestic sources.[57] The existential threat to the Assad regime itself in light of the challenge posed by the armed opposition galvanized the Tehran-Damascus alliance and compelled the Assad regime to accept a host of encroachments,[58] many of which it would not have previously countenanced.

By contrast, Tehran's present-day alliance with Baghdad originates in the US invasion and occupation of Iraq and the effective liquidation of many of the erstwhile institutions of the former regime. The neoconservative architects of that war had convinced themselves it would result in a democratic, pro-Western polity that would stand as an exemplar to the region and tilt the regional balance against Tehran and Damascus. As we know today, the exact opposite occurred. Indeed, it was the burgeoning alliance between Iran and several powerful political forces within Iraq's new ruling elite that led Jordan's King Abdullah II to resort to the ideologically loaded image of a "Shi'a Crescent."

It is worth recalling that in the months immediately following the invasion of Iraq, Sadeq Kharazi, Iran's former ambassador to France and a relative-by-marriage of the Supreme Leader, sent a proposal to Washington via the Swiss embassy. It pledged that there would be "no Iranian endeavours to develop or possess WMD" and "full cooperation with IAEA," but also to demobilize Lebanese Hezbollah, transforming it into a strictly political party.[59] Whether such an offer would ever have come to fruition had the Bush administration chosen to indulge its Iranian counterparts at that critical juncture is open to debate. But what subsequently happened during the catastrophic viceroyship of Paul Bremer and the now infamous policy of de-Ba'athification undertaken by the Coalition Provisional Authority guaranteed that it would remain a counterfactual left to the judgment of posterity.

The fierce Iraqi insurgency against the occupation, which cut across sectarian lines, provided the conditions under which the Islamic Republic and the Syrian regime could employ a slew of strategies of opposition to increase the cost of the American occupation, and thus help instigate the circumstances of its eventual withdrawal. The Assad regime's intentional neglect of Syria's shared border facilitated a mass influx of Sunni jihadists into Iraq to fight US occupying forces,[60] while the Islamic Republic supported and trained groups with a shared stake in vanquishing the Americans, and cultivated clients such as the Badr Organization, which progressively took over elements of the state apparatus itself.[61] These strategies can be interpreted as classic cases of "internal balancing" undertaken by asymmetric powers. In the years that followed, the Islamic Republic cultivated its relationships with numerous Shi'a factions, and in several cases set itself up as patron and arbiter, as was seen in the intra-Shi'a conflicts in Karbala in 2007[62] and Basra in March 2008.[63]

Political Entrepreneurs, Proxies, and Sectarianization

The composition of the myriad militias in Syria and Iraq (especially the latter), in view of their confessional makeup, has often been taken as evidence of the incontrovertibly sectarian character of the current civil conflicts cum proxy wars overrunning these countries. Some analysts depict the relationships in simple dyadic terms,[64] a vertical patron-client relationship in which the client straightforwardly obeys the patron's demands. A more sophisticated approach, however, acknowledges that there is a clear typology of militias. A more attentive sociological analysis of the composition, geographical location, and socio-economic profiles of the militias in question is necessary. In short, we need a typology of the kinds of militias that operate in these arenas, as well as a nuanced understanding of the nature of "dependence" and "control" that various forms of patronage might afford.

Given the sheer number of militias operating in Iraq and Syria, it is also necessary to examine the levels at which they operate, since many of them function on a merely local rather than national basis. My chief concern is those with ties to Iranian armed forces and operatives, and the nature of those ties, which in numerous cases vary qualitatively. Armed groups range in nature across a wide spectrum, and can be distinguished in several ways, with militias in Iraq and Syria either approximating or amounting to an amalgam of the idealized types below, the two extremes ranging from independent social movement to dependent client:

1) an armed group embedded within a broader social movement and series of local networks, which possesses an independent political agenda, and enjoys a self-sustaining stream of revenue extracted from its social base
2) an armed group with access to domestic state funds through co-opted state institutions and/or leveraged by means of intra-elite bargaining, but receiving military training and political support from an external power
3) an armed client group funded, organized, and trained exclusively by an external patron and serving the latter's goals

Apart from the question of a militia's fiscal base, it is also necessary to consider confessional and ideological factors, which impact the nature of cooperation and how the relationship changes in accordance with shifting geopolitical circumstances. This yields a further typology, which would overlay that enumerated above:

1) ideologically committed and co-sectarian
2) ideologically committed but non-Twelver Shi'a
3) instrumental political commitment and co-sectarian
4) instrumental political commitment but non-Twelver Shi'a

To reiterate, these are generalized types, which serve a heuristic purpose in the effort to shed light on the nature of the Islamic Republic's sponsorship and support for armed paramilitary organizations, which, as should by now be clear, vary widely on several counts, as do the roles they play in the plural dynamics of civil conflicts and their "sectarianization."

My initial contention was that the Islamic Republic's security dilemma at the regional and international levels has pushed it to pursue strategic depth through support for co-sectarian paramilitary organizations such as Lebanon's Hezbollah and the Badr Organization in Iraq. The relationship between Syria's National Defense Force (Quwat ad-Defa' al-Watani, NDF) and the Islamic Republic has its own unique dynamics, which I will attempt to clarify. Each one of these organizations has traversed specific paths of development, but at bottom—and especially in their initial stages—they were composed of what Tilly has termed "political entrepreneurs" and "violence specialists." These individuals respond to the security dilemmas experienced by members of confessional communities in societies gripped by civil conflict and highly diminished state autonomy and capacity. They agitate, organize, and present themselves as the defenders of their respective communities. They often resort to emotive language, crafting narratives that resonate with people and soliciting their emotional investment in them.[65]

According to this model, interpersonal networks are central to such mobilizations.[66] Relationships with foreign states—in this instance, the Islamic Republic—can prove mutually beneficial in both material and political terms, and are not necessarily the simple outcome of transnational sectarian affinities. One guiding hypothesis, which would require a separate study to vindicate empirically, is that the "cost" of acquiring and retaining the political loyalty of such political entrepreneurs is diminished in relation to the extent of ideological and sectarian overlap between sponsors and sponsored.[67] Such costs, however, are multi-faceted: far from being exclusively monetary in nature, they morph with circumstances and depend on levels of insecurity as gauged by political entrepreneurs and the populace at large. Moreover, while patronage does have the capacity to draw an organization—especially one devoid of an independent social constituency—ever closer into the ideological orbit of its patron, this is by no means automatic or a foregone conclusion.

The more paramilitary organizations are able to successfully fulfill the capacities of war-making and extraction through the likes of foreign funding, donations, protection rents, and bureaucratized taxation,[68] the more they are able to assume the basic functions of a state,[69] and even domestically legitimize their militarized social network vis-à-vis the *de jure* government. This has been precisely the case with Hezbollah in Lebanon. The Population Mobilization Units of Iraq remain in a state of flux, as various political factions and the Iranian state endeavor to influence the process of their institutionalization.[70] The more a militarized political organization assuming certain responsibilities of the state is able to generate or underwrite the conditions for capital accumulation, so the logic goes, the more it should be able to exercise autonomy vis-à-vis its one-time state sponsor. And given that the leaders of several Shi'a militias in Iraq, including those whose detractors accuse them of being beholden to Tehran, have been able to assume national office and

175

thereby attain access to the largess of one of the world's largest oil-producing nations (Iraq itself), questions remain as to how the relationship will evolve if/when the threat posed by organizations such as ISIS is eventually neutralized.[71]

As previously mentioned, political entrepreneurs engage in forms of brokerage and create connections between various sites and groups. More importantly, they specialize in representation and advocate on behalf of highly politicized identities.[72] In this way they are also able to activate us–them boundaries and contribute to the polarization of communities that had coexisted peacefully for generations, as they emphasize merely one dimension—the confessional—of people's plural, overlapping identities (Iraqi, Shi'a, Basrawi, female, middle class, etc.). They build networks of supporters upon which they can draw, and thereby sustain and augment their own power.[73] Violence specialists, very simply, possess expertise in the use and deployment of inflicting, organizing, and dispensing violence.

These figures are hardly unique to the Middle East, as Eric Hobsbawm's classic *Bandits*,[74] and the more recent scholarship of Janice Thompson on early modern Europe, attest.[75] Both works describe in great detail the variety of actors—pirates, mercenaries, rebels, and private armies—that exercised violence in pursuit of their aims alongside one another and harbored the capacity to both agitate against and cooperate with the ascendant power of the day. It is worth noting that the supposedly impervious "monopoly on violence" that we automatically associate with the modern state only came to exist in Western Europe in recent memory, and has never been experienced by a great many countries in the global South.

As Tilly makes clear, the roles of political entrepreneurs and violence specialists can overlap considerably. In the case of Iraq, former prime minister Nuri al-Maliki, 'Asa'ib's Qays al-Khaz'ali, the Badr Organization's Hadi al-'Ameri and the Sadrist movement's Muqtada al-Sadr, are all fitting examples of individuals who have been able to fulfill the roles of both political entrepreneur and violence specialist, even if they might approximate one more than the other. But most importantly, it is through these actors' claims to represent the nation and/or the faithful, and the framing processes which accompany such claims—and the real and virtual prominence of such advocates in public life—that conflicts of this nature become "sectarianized," while their origins in the state weakness and insecurity are elided.

Realpolitik and the Pluralization of Violence: Militias and Counterinsurgency in Iraq and Syria

The Shi'a paramilitary organizations that have developed over the course of the last several years in Iraq, and the predominantly (though by no means exclusively) Alawite/Christian NDF in Syria, have been the subject of considerable debate and controversy.[76] In certain instances (especially in Iraq) these irregular armed groups have been commended for fighting in the name of the homeland (the *watan*), particularly in the aftermath of Mosul's fall to ISIS in June 2014, an event that was widely depicted as an existential threat to the Iraqi polity itself. Indeed, the overwhelmingly Shi'a Popular Mobilization Units (Hashd al-Sha'bi), which were formed in the aftermath of Grand Ayatollah Sistani's *fatwa* (*wajib al-kifa'i*) calling on Iraqis to defend "their country and their people and their holy places," have now received formal legal recognition and have in principle been made accountable to, and are funded by, the prime minister's office, in an effort to diminish the downward spiral into what one commentator has described as a "militia state."[77]

In the face of the Iraqi army's rapid disintegration, the opportunity structure was such that a significant swathe of the Shi'a community mobilized in reaction to the perceived threat not only to their holy places but to their lives on an individual and communal basis.[78] The emergence of ISIS has introduced a new dynamic into regional power calculations and the valencies of sectarianism. The signifier *takfiri*,[79] largely used by the Islamic Republic and allies such as Hezbollah, eschews outright sectarian denunciation, whereas jihadi Salafists openly espouse the excommunication of Shi'a as *rawafidh* ("rejectionists"). The negation of the other is integral to their identity in a way that it clearly is not in the case of Iranian Islamism and its radical Shi'a counterparts in Iraq, Lebanon, and elsewhere. The Islamic Republic's pan-Islamist commitments and post-colonial imbrications—and the minority status of Shi'a in the broader region—mitigate its overt resort to and exploitation of sectarian rhetoric and symbols. There is, nonetheless, a relational and co-constitutive discursive process at work: when Iran deploys sectarianism at the discursive level, it is not other-centered in the way one finds in the language of ISIS and its cognates. That is, a negation of Sunni Islam is not integral to Iran's self-image and ideological projection. Rather, the Islamic Republic assertively brandishes markers of Shi'a identity in ways that have been abjured not only by Sunni Islamists but also by pan-Arabists and secularists in the Middle East.[80]

Apart from Sistani's *fatwa* and his office's role in encouraging and religiously legitimizing the mobilization, the financing, training, and operational coordination was a joint effort of the Iraqi government, the Shi'a tribes (though it should be noted that many tribes cut across sect), local governments and shrines, established militias (the most powerful of which have strong ties with the Islamic Republic of Iran), and other members of the Shi'a religious establishment.[81] This was a juncture at which the Iraqi central government struggled to exercise control and in certain respects engendered a scenario in which foreign states such as Iran could further enmesh their allies and clients within the fabric of the putatively national security apparatus. This is what had already effectively taken place during the peak of sectarian violence in 2006–2007, when the Badr Organization—which was at the time still the armed wing of the Islamic Supreme Council of Iraq (ISCI)—had infiltrated the Interior Ministry and its police forces and relied on the veneer of officialdom to partake in retaliatory attacks against sectarian and co-sectarian adversaries and even assassinate former Iraqi pilots allegedly responsible for bombing Iranian cities in the Iran-Iraq war.[82]

Nonetheless, it is now difficult to deny that the Popular Mobilization Units—as the interior minister, Mohammed al-Ghabban (himself a member of the Badr Organization), has contended—is "an inseparable element of Iraq's fabric," with a differentiated set of social bases and revenue streams.[83] Neither can one ignore the fact that many of the men heading its polycephalous paramilitary organizations—figures such as al-'Ameri, Abu Mahdi al-Muhandis, Qays al-Khaz'ali, and Muqtada al-Sadr—comprise part of Iraq's political elite and acquire their ability to act as power-brokers by virtue of their social constituencies and/or the armed men they command. These factors—their own domestic resources and constituencies—temper their relationship with the Iranian state, whose support they regard as a mixed blessing. While they are grateful in view of the common threat they face, suspicion looms over Iranian penetration, given the prominence of individuals such al-'Ameri and al-Muhandis, who were formerly based in and solely reliant on Tehran. Domestic pressures to "Iraqicize" have been particularly pronounced in the case of the ISCI. According to one account, it was the Badr Organization's "Iran-orientation" that led to its break with the council in